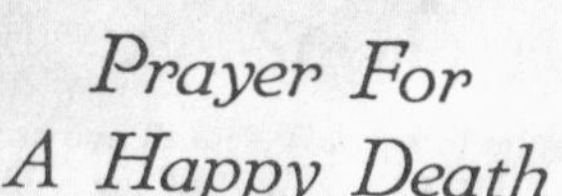

Prayer For A Happy Death

My Lord and my Saviour, support me in that hour in the strong arms of Thy Sacraments, and by the fresh fragrance of Thy consolations. Let the absolving words be said over me, and the holy oil sign and seal me, and Thy Own Body be my food, and Thy Blood my sprinkling; and let my sweet Mother Mary, breathe on me, and my Angel whisper peace to me, and my glorious Saints . . . smile upon me; that in them all, and through them all, I may receive the gift of perseverence; and die, as I desire to live, in Thy faith, in Thy Church, in Thy service, and in Thy love. Amen.

—Cardinal Newman

Joe Kotcka

Gerffert 147 Litho in Italy

CONVERSATION WITH THE BIBLE

MARKUS BARTH

CONVERSATION WITH THE BIBLE

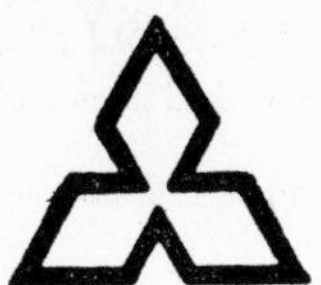

HOLT, RINEHART AND WINSTON • NEW YORK CHICAGO SAN FRANCISCO

Published simultaneously in Canada
by Holt, Rinehart and Winston of Canada, Limited.

Library of Congress Catalog Card Number: 64–14366

Designer: Ernst Reichl

80839–0214

Printed in the United States of America

First Edition

ACKNOWLEDGMENTS

I would like to express my gratitude to the following institutions for inviting me to deliver the lectures which provided the basis for the present work:

Knox College, Toronto (the Laidlaw Lectures, October, 1961); Bethel Biblical Seminary, Chicago (the Hoff Lectures, October, 1962); the Graduate Biblical Seminary, Enid, Oklahoma (the Oreon E. Scott Lectures, November, 1963); and the McMaster Divinity School, Hamilton, Ontario (the Ker Lectures, December, 1963).

The scripture quotations in this publication are from the *Revised Standard Version of the Bible,* copyrighted 1946 and 1952 by the Division of Christian Education, National Council of Churches and used by permission.

FOREWORD

The Bible is a charter of liberty. It treats of the free God who grants and protects the freedom of his children. There is little reason to organize a defense of this powerful voice and record of liberation, and even less reason to pretend that its authority may be forced upon anyone. For the manifold biblical voices are speaking for themselves, and the best possible interpretation can do no more than cry out with excitement, "Listen to what is said!—and give your reply!"

It is in such hearkening and responding that I wish to be engaged and to engage others. *Conversation with the Bible* is to be understood in its widest possible meaning. I am not an admirer of those who tend to make conversation, as such, a sacrament, whatever they may mean by this term. But I pay my respects to the geology professor Hans Cloos, of Bonn, who wrote a wonderful and scientific book under the title *Gespräch mit der Erde* (Munich, 1947), and to the physicist Hellmut Fritzsche, in Chicago, who showed in discussions why the traditional clerical talk about the authority of the Bible should give way to a more humble approach to the subject.

I owe much more than I am able to show to thinkers and scholars who—with much better equipment—have plowed the same ground on which I am working. Among them my father, Karl Barth, is to be mentioned specifically. When the final manuscript was nearing completion, he gave me much encouragement by calling, on American soil, for a theology of freedom.

I am indebted to Miss Ruth Nanda Anshen, in New York, for challenging me to write a book for the cultured among the non-Jewish and non-Christian students of sacred books and to explain to them what, if anything, is special about the Bible.

Finally, I am grateful for the encouragement and co-operation of Arthur A. Cohen, of Holt, Rinehart and Winston. Mr. Cohen is one of those distinguished thinkers who, during the past few years, has deepened and strengthened my awareness of the intimate and indissoluble brotherhood of Christians and Jews.

I am also grateful to the many institutions of higher learning, and to the many ministerial and congregational assemblies which have invited me, during the past seven years, to present, in a less formal way, some of the material out of which the present work has grown. I have been most kindly received wherever I went, and more often than not it appeared that the present stalemate between rigorous conservative and pathetically humanist views of the Bible was in the process of yielding to an openness to new questions and to a fresh approach to the problems of authority, freedom, and responsibility. Through discussions with non-Christians and with church members, with colleagues, troubled ministers, eager seminarians, and critical college students, I was stimulated again and again to rethink and rewrite preliminary drafts of this book and to broaden its basis. The present form of *Conversation with the Bible* is different from any of the lecture series I gave on this theme, but it should not seem entirely strange to anyone who has heard them.

After the manuscript of this book was completed, the Second Vatican Council began to assemble. During the first session, the representatives of the Roman Catholic Church showed their readiness to modify—or at least to make more specific—some of the traditional Roman statements on the relationship between Revelation, Scripture, and Tradition. In the second session, and since, some signs of increased concern for affirming Christian solidarity with Israel have become visible. In both cases, more than a mere breath of fresh air entered stuffy chambers. Since strong forces inside the Roman walls are now working for manifold renewal, it seems less urgent than before to engage in polemics against what has appeared to be, ever since the Reformation, a typically Roman usage of the Bible. We Protestants, together with all Jews and Christians, have all the more reason to rethink our position and to recover an open, listening attitude to the Bible. Many Protestants, in harmony with some medieval scholars and the Reformers, have not become tired of affirming the supreme authority of Scripture. Indeed, among Christians the confession, *sola Scriptura!*—through the Bible alone!—is inseparably linked with the affirmations: Christ alone! By grace alone! But is it necessary to underline and buttress these confessional statements by claiming the infallibility of the Bible? On the other hand, is it appropriate to take refuge in an ultimate skepticism because the historical origin and character of the Bible is more obvious to modern readers than to the generations of the past? Is it impossible for us to say: The Bible is the Word of God; have we not reasons similar to those of our fathers, who, in fear and trembling, full of amazement and joy, made precisely this confession?

I hope that the reading of this book, and the corrective responses it may provoke, will help Jews, Catholics, Protestants, and many others, to seek and find new ways to enjoy, and to impart to others, a sincere enjoyment of the unique message and dignity of the Bible.

MARKUS BARTH

Pittsburgh Theological Seminary
December 17, 1963

CONTENTS

INTRODUCTION

A DIALOGUE OF LOVERS

When two people are absorbed in a conversation and a third man happens to pass by and hear their words, surprising things can occur. Whether they talk in a whisper or shout at each other, whether the third man understands all or only a part of what they say, if they happen to be talking about him, his interest is excited as by no other kind of conversation. Imagine that the two men are doctors discussing his chances to live, a prosecutor and a defense attorney discussing a case in which he is vitally involved, or only gossips, pretending to know all. In any case, the third man, arrested inadvertently by the specific personal relevance of the conversation, will be touched in a unique way by references to his father, his mother, or his children, and may be cut to the quick by their evaluation of his past conduct, his strengths and weaknesses, his public self, his hidden secrets, and his future.

What if the two speakers were to say, "His father was a loafer;

his mother was picked up in the street; his own children are illegitimate; he is himself in debt beyond his knowledge or imagination —and yet he has been chosen for a responsible appointment and has been established heir to an immense fortune. If only he knew and appreciated it!" The two speakers may not be equal in wisdom, or rank, or power. They may be more different than a king and a beggar, a great judge and a hardened criminal, an expert and an idiot. They may not mind being overheard and may invite the third man to participate in their conversation; they may even urge him to base his actions on what they have said.

This is our position before the open Bible.[1] For the Bible is a dialogue: God and man are the partners in a conversation which is meant to be overheard. The Bible is often called the "Word of God," for many generations have found in it more than they themselves could say. In it they have heard the mighty and inescapable voice of a father and lord who is better and stronger than human authorities. But the reader of the Bible does not always, or only, hear God speaking. There are many words which—if he is honest —he must admit he does not understand, and which he cannot, or cannot yet, respect as the word of God. There are also sections in the Bible which are spoken by men to God, or about God, but they are not spoken by God himself or in his name. There are texts in which men speak at their own risk and in terms of their own insight and charity, and there are even some in which they speak out flatly against God. Because the Bible professes to be a book in which we hear what both God and man are saying, it is primarily a record of conversation.

The ample place which is given to men's responses, wise or unwise, and even to their murmurs and outbursts, distinguishes the Bible from mere collections of divine laws or revelations. Compared with other holy books, the Bible seems to be far less divine; it is certainly extremely human. At times, human voices sounding from the Old and New Testaments fill our ears with a more penetrating clamor than God's voice.

> Wicked and deceitful mouths are opened against me. . . . When he is tried, let him come forth guilty; let his prayer be counted as sin! . . . My God, my God, why hast thou forsaken me? . . . O daughter of Babylon, you devastator! Happy shall he be who requites you with what you have done to us! Happy shall he be who takes your little ones and dashes them against the rock! . . . They shouted out, "Crucify, crucify him!" . . . And their voices prevailed. . . . For about two hours they all with one voice cried out, "Great is Artemis of the Ephesians!" . . . (Ps 109:2, 7; 22:1; 137:8–9; Lk 23:21, 23; Acts 19:34)

An attempt can be made to offset the impact of such human shrieks and groans with lofty quotations from Isaiah 40–55 or Christ's discourse at the Last Supper (Jn 13–17). Apologetics for the Bible are usually built upon its exemplary theistic, religious, and ethical elements; the human voices are then treated as a slightly embarrassing background noise. When this happens, the distinctive character of the Bible, its openness to all that man has to say when he is addressed by God, is negated.

But there are obviously some things which God alone can say. "Let there be light. . . . I am who I am. . . . I am the Lord your God. . . . Be holy, for I am holy. . . . Have I not commanded you? Be strong and of good courage. . . . I will put my law within them, and I will write it upon their hearts. . . . I will forgive their iniquity. . . . I create new heavens and a new earth" (Gen. 1:3; Ex 3:14; 20:2; Lev 11:44; Josh 1:9; Jer 31:33–34; Is 65:17). That man errs who claims for himself, "I am a god" (Ezek 28:2, 9). That voice is wicked that suggests, "You will be like God" (Gen 3:5). He is called a fool who says in his heart, "There is no God" (Ps 14:1). It would be better for man to keep silent and listen to what God says. "Be still, and know that I am God. . . . If one wished to contend with him, one could not answer him once in a thousand times. . . . Behold, you will be silent and unable to speak" (Ps 46:10; Job 9:3; Lk 1:20).

But man is not destined only to listen and never to reply or question. It is God himself who provokes answers, entreaties, and proclamations. The Bible contains men's widely different responses: "Here am I. . . . In thee I trust. . . . I have done according to all that thou hast commanded me. . . . I am not ashamed of the gospel. . . . I tremble with fear. . . . Thou hast deceived me, and I was deceived. . . . Depart from me. . . . The wise man dies just like the fool. . . . Have mercy upon me, O Lord. . . . To die is gain. . . . I shall not die, but I shall live, and recount the deeds of the Lord" (Ex 3:4; Ps 25:2; Deut 26:14; Rom 1:16; Heb 12:21; Jer 20:7; Lk 5:8; Eccles 2:16; Mt 15:22; Phil 1:21; Ps 118:17). Not all words directed to God are equally acceptable, even when there is no lack of religious feeling and good intention. The man who begs, "God, be merciful to me a sinner," is more "justified" than his more respected partner who thanks God "that I am not like other men" (Lk 18:10–15).

As may happen in any dialogue, one partner may quote or question the words of the other. So we find God's words on the lips of his creatures and man's words coming from the mouth of God. "Thou hast said, 'Seek ye my face!' . . . What do you mean . . . 'The fathers have eaten sour grapes, and the children's teeth are set on edge'? . . . You have said, 'It is vain to serve God'" (Ps 27:8; Ezek 18:2; Mal 3:14).

Finally, we also hear each partner talking to himself. "God said, 'Let us make man in our image, after our likeness' . . . The land of a rich man brought forth plentifully; and he said to himself . . . 'You have ample goods laid up for many years; take your ease, eat, drink, be merry'" (Gen 1:26; Lk 12:16–17, 19). Both God and man may rethink what they have said earlier. "God repented of the evil which he had said he would do. . . . [the younger son] came to himself" (Jn 3:10; Lk 15:17). The partner in the dialogue who is expected to speak in the tones of thunder and earthquake sometimes chooses "a still small voice." On the other hand, when the man Jesus is about to die on the cross, he cries out "with a loud voice" (1 Kings 19:12; Mk 15:34).

The Bible is the record of such conversation; commandment and supplication, promise and trust, oath and blessing, curse and doubt, are found close together. This book does not tell only of God; it tells of God *and* man. If, in its totality, it is called "holy" (as Paul calls Old Testament writings in Rom 1:2; 2 Tim 3:15), its holiness must include those passages in which the weakest features of humanity are heard crying to heaven. There is nothing human that is alien to Scripture. The intimate whisper of lovers (Song of Solomon), the gurgling sounds of the reeling drunkard (Is 28:7–10), the competitive voices of religious enthusiasts (1 Sam 10:5, 10; 1 Cor 14), possible errors and obvious contradictions in the recording of names, figures, places, dates, quotations (Lk 2:1–2; Mt 13:35), and worst of all, pretension, boasting, lying, cheating, betrayal—all this is registered in the Bible.

Not all that man has to say during his conversation with God is of this character! The Bible tells of men and of human words that were sometimes profound, memorable, faithful replies to God. It seems, however, that believers need to be reminded not to use the same tongue for blessing and for cursing (Jas 2:6–12).

But how can a book containing so many human words possess any sort of authority? One key to its special authority may be found in that part of the Bible which seems strangest, most embarrassing, and most beautiful—the Song of Solomon. This collection of love songs shows a use of words that is an excellent illustration of a unique authority. We note, first, that the words exchanged between the lovers are obviously a means of uniting the king and his love and giving expression to their union. They serve as a bond between person and person; they are not final judgments on geography, botany, or cosmology. In addition, the spoken words concern the seeking and finding in which the lover and the beloved are engaged. They are not mere words, therefore, but they flow from, accompany, or produce action. Finally, the words of this song reflect the longing and seeking of love; they are not cheap words, but are paid for with much suffering. Nevertheless, love's anguish is finally swallowed up in jubilation: What joy it is for both partners not only to speak to and of each other, but to belong to one another!

We do not need to decide here whether the topic treated in the Song of Solomon was understood allegorically long before these love songs were composed or collected (as in Is 5:1–7; Hos 1–3; Ezek 16 and 23; perhaps also Ps 45), or whether the Song of Solomon was the text of a drama written for wedding pageantry, or whether it was ritually enacted and applauded as a celebration of a king's *hieros gamos*. It is enough to say that it has not only won applause in the taverns of Rabbi Akiba's time (*ca.* A.D. 130), and the acclaim of people who are open to love and beauty in every generation, but that it has also found passionate defendants in both synagogue and church. The very mystery of God's relation to Israel and the church was found expressed in this song. Was this interpretation the minstrel's or that of the many authors of the love songs? Whatever the answer, many of the song's hearers and readers were happy to find its contents a lovely and transparent parable of the words exchanged and the deeds performed by God and man.

When the words which God exchanged with Israel and the church are at least as intimate, suggestive, and enjoyable as the whispers or cries of two lovers, then no formal authority, no external verification, and no rational proof of validity are required to make hearers listen and respond. Love speaks for itself.

The Bible as a whole deals with a subject, and uses a language that has much to do with the lovers' song. It treats of the covenant between God and man, and of the love of its two partners. To listen to the Bible means to listen to the call, the jealousy, the intensity of God's love, and also to hear the manifold reply which God receives from man.

I will betroth you to me for ever; I will betroth you to me in righteousness and in justice, in steadfast love, and in mercy. I will betroth you to me in faithfulness; and you shall know the Lord. . . . I will make a new covenant . . . not like the covenant which I made with their fathers when I took them by the hand to bring them out of the land of Egypt, my covenant which they broke, though I was their husband. . . . I will put my law within them, and I will write it upon their hearts; and I will be their God, and they shall be my people. . . . They shall all know me. . . . A man shall leave his father and mother and be joined to his wife, and the two shall become one. . . . This is a great mystery, and I take it to mean Christ and the church. . . . Hallelujah! . . . The marriage of the lamb has come, and his bride has made herself ready. . . . God so loved the world. . . . God is love (Hos 2:19–20; Jer 31:31–34; Heb 8:8–12; Gen 2:24; Eph 5:31–32; Rev 19:6–7; Jn 3:16; 1 Jn 4:7–8).

The unique power of the Bible flows from the fact that the biblical words are words of love between God and man—a love that comes from God as his free gift; that is repudiated, betrayed, and forsaken by man; and that is nonetheless invincible and succeeds in making men respond with love to God. "God's love has been poured into our hearts through the Holy Spirit" (Rom 5:5). The Bible is the good news of this love.

The reading of the Bible, therefore, should be compared to the reading of love letters, rather than to the study and use of a law book. There is no need and no way to prove the authority of letters written by lovers to each other or to third parties, for they will speak for themselves. And there is no key with which to open and to understand them, unless the reader is drawn into the communion to which they bear witness, and unless he participates in it with the response of a similar love. Augustine[2] asserted that the love of God and the love of the neighbor are the sum of the Bible; that full understanding is identified with love; and that there is no other way to interpret the Bible than by loving. For a long time[3] he may have paid too little attention to the history told in the Bible and to the literal meaning of its texts. But the Bible itself gave him sufficient reason to recognize the centrality of love. The Bible is an invitation to learn of God's love, to enjoy it, and to respond to it.

If it could be shown that God's love for man is manifested in the Bible more clearly than in any other book (though it may be referred to, explained, and applied in other works), then it would make sense to speak of the uniqueness of the Bible. The Bible does affirm that it treats of a God who is unlike any other god, and of a people of God whose ways differ from those of other nations or religions. In the next part we will attempt to let the Bible's utterances about God, about man, and about their covenant relationship speak for themselves.

PART ONE

THE CONTENTS OF THE BIBLE

CHAPTER I

THE COVENANT OF THE FREE

The One Holy God

From the first to the last page, the Bible talks about God. In only one among its sixty-six books is God not explicitly mentioned. The Book of Esther speaks of "another side" from which help will come. But all the various books of the Bible, including Esther, owe their inclusion in the biblical canon to the fact that, in different ages and places, worshipers of God recognized these writings as "profitable" (2 Tim 3:16) tools with which to learn of God's nature and his deeds, and of faith in God and obedience to him.

The Bible speaks of God in different ways. He is introduced as speaking for himself in sentences beginning, "*I,* the Lord, your God"; he is addressed in the form of prayer directed to him saying, "*Thou* art . . ."; and public confession is made to him when his nature and mighty acts are proclaimed in statements beginning with the words, "*He* is," "*He* has done," "*He* will do." What these modes of speaking of God have in common is their confessional character. He alone can speak of God who first listens to him in order, then, to pray to him, or to proclaim him. In each case the speaker is fully committed and knows himself entitled to convince others; a detached, neutral, onlooker-like attitude is neither sought nor found. In the natural sciences or philosophy the subject matter treated may be described, defined, or analyzed. The God of whom the Bible speaks cannot be defined; he is not subsumed among beings of the same genus.

Who is this God, and what is said of him? Though it is preposterous to describe someone who, according to the Bible, is beyond the grasp of man's limited faculties, the reader of the Bible, unlike the faithful Hindu, is not finally left with nothing to say but "*Neti, neti*" ("not this, not that"). Only on rare occasions, and in the later books (for example, 1 Tim 1:17; 6:16), is God described negatively as, for instance, "immortal" or "invisible." Positive—as it were, pragmatic—statements are preferred to all those that might be considered abstract, purely reflective, or rationalistic. Even though man does not possess an innate capacity to know and to speak of God, it is stated over and over again in stories, sermons, and prayers, that God is willing and strong enough to make himself known to man. God introduces himself, and is introduced to the people of the Bible and all those who read it as one who opens the ears and eyes and minds of men so that they may perceive him. God can and will so direct human life and thought that men are enabled to speak to him and of him.

But what is known of him? Who is he who in this book is called God?

1 *God's Name*

Whereas in many religions, oracles, revelations, or signs serve to reveal to certain men some specific present fact or future fate,

it is a distinctive feature of the God of the Bible that in his revelation he always finally reveals himself for the ultimate benefit of all men. "You shall know that I am the Lord your God"—so Israel is promised, and this the Pharaoh will learn to respect (Ex. 6:7). "They shall all know me, from the least of them to the greatest. . . . My people shall know my name. . . . The earth shall be full of knowledge of the Lord as the waters cover the sea" (Jer 31:34; Is 52:6; 11:9; Hab 2:14). "This is eternal life, that they know thee the only true God" (Jn 17:3).

When it pleased God to reveal himself he let it be known that his name is "I am who I am," or shorter, "I, I" (Ex 3:14; Deut 32:39; Is 43:11–25; 46:4; 48:12; Jn 8:58; Rev 1:8, etc.). Many different interpretations of this name appear to be possible, and the Bible itself gives more than one. Common to all of them is the affirmation that God is not a thing or an idea, but a person; he is *I,* and not it. He is not a changeling; in both eternity and time, in being and action, he is always identical with himself. He is not subject to anybody or anything, but submits all things to himself. He is the Lord; as such he cannot be a captive of laws and concepts, but is free to will and to do what is good in his own judgment. The name of God, "I am who I am," is usually not spelled out in the Bible; the exclamation, "Lord," is used as a fitting substitute.

The Bible does not suggest that there is a God beyond that God who introduces himself by saying "I," who is addressed with the intimate "Thou," and who is proclaimed in using the word "He." The reader of the Bible cannot help but acknowledge that the God of whom this book speaks is eminently personal, consistent, creative, and free. He is warned not to measure God according to preconceived categories of what may constitute human personality, identity, causality, or free will. "He is not a man" (1 Sam 15:29). God is God, the first and the last, the same in time and eternity, true to himself in his many manifestations, always, and in glorious fashion, He, Himself!

II *God Is One*

Both the revelation of this God and the confession to this God affirm that he is one. "Hear, O Israel: The Lord our God is one. . . . We know that 'an idol has no real existence,' and that 'there is no God but one'. . . . For us there is one God, the Father . . . and one Lord, Jesus Christ" (Deut 6:4;[4] 1 Cor 8:4, 6). Such statements are sometimes quoted to prove that Hebrews and Christians advance a religion that belongs among mankind's many monotheistic systems of belief. But the first impression may be wrong. Even if monotheistic religions are considered the highest, and Jews and Christians, therefore, part of the noblest tradition, the Bible does not guarantee the validity of that association. The serene tolerance that is characteristic of great monotheistic religions is missing from the Bible. The one God of whom the Bible speaks is jealous; he is jealous of all other powers that are also called gods. His claim on the hearts and inclinations of his servants is exclusive. As a spokesman for many humanists, Arnold Toynbee[5] may resent this jealousy; it is still there. "The Lord your God is a devouring fire; a jealous God" (Deut 4:24; Josh 24:19–20; Nahum 1:2). Even in the New Testament, a lie against the Holy Spirit is punished by death (Acts 5:1–11). The Bible speaks frequently of God's wrath. It is a holy wrath; for it is the temperature of God's love for those he has chosen to be his people. It is manifested before all men, in that moment when God reveals his will, and provides the mediator to make right the wrong done by all, Jews and Gentiles alike (Rom 1:16–18; 3:24–30; 11:32). The oneness of God is not, therefore, the content of a monotheistic theory, but the fitting description of God's unique way of revealing himself and of showing mercy to all mankind.

On the other hand, the Old and the New Testaments contain passages in which it is freely admitted that there are other gods and lords besides the Lord, our God. "Who is like thee, O Lord, among the gods. . . . In the midst of the gods he holds judgment. . . . Indeed there are many 'gods' and many 'lords' " (Ex 15:11; Ps 82:1; 1 Cor 8:5). The Bible does not proffer a general view of the world; it does not say that, among all things, unique or paired or multiple, the world contains but one God. But this is said in the first of the Ten Commandments given to Israel, and this is what Israel is given to learn in her long history: Beside the One who revealed himself by mighty acts as Israel's creator, judge, and redeemer, Israel need not and must not serve any other God. "Monolatry" may be a more appropriate term than monotheism to express the relationship of the people of the Old and New Testaments to their God.

When, therefore, in Israel or in the church the one God is proclaimed and believed, "one" has a much deeper meaning than is proper to a numeral. When God calls himself one or is hailed as one God, the God of the Fathers (Abraham, Isaac, Jacob) is being identified with the God manifested in the liberation from Egypt, or in the covenant made on Mount Sinai. It is an acknowledgment of the power and sufficiency of that God to give possession of the promised land, to grant his blessing on houses, fields, and stables, to bestow victory in war and rest under the vine and the fig tree. Creator, lord, and judge of both heaven and earth, this God alone can make Israel resist the lure of other gods—gods of war, of nature, or of fertility. He is calling, maintaining, and judging Israel, but, if need be, he can choose and overcome, together with Israel, the many nations of the world. His will is to show grace to all Jews and Gentiles, and he stands ever faithful to his promises. He rightly asks for obedience from the whole man—spirit, soul, and body; he claims the whole heart and the offering of all created things for his service; he wishes to be praised in the midst of a community composed of citizens, immigrant laborers, and foreigners. He is the power to call nonbeing into being; he is not confronted with a second god or an antideity capable of resisting him. "Thou didst crush Rahab like a carcass" (Ps 89:10). Even chaos, darkness, sin, and hatred cannot ultimately question his sovereignty.

Therefore, the interpretation and proclamation of God's oneness is made in the announcement and praise of God's faithfulness to himself; in the revelation of God's adequacy to rule under any given circumstances; in the identity of the creator, redeemer, and final judge; in a series of chosen men, from Adam to the coming Son of Man; in the formation of a worshiping and obeying people who witness his uniqueness by being *one* people among and for all nations.

To say it in other words, the God of the Bible does not first prove *that he is* in order eventually to fill a vague or empty concept of God with some details. Rather, by showing *who and what* he is, wills, can do, and completes, he reveals that he is. Evidence of his holiness and righteousness is the only proof he gives of his existence. "The Holy God shows himself holy in righteousness" (Is 5:16). Except as holy and righteous, as "the Lord [who is] the Lord, a God merciful and gracious . . . slow to anger, and abounding in steadfast love and faithfulness" (Ex 34:6), he does not exist. Therefore, there is but one demonstration of God's existence—the evidence which God himself gives of himself in his mighty and gracious dealing with mankind. Those who know of him cannot help but assert that this God who deigned to be called God of Abraham, Refuge of David, Father of Jesus Christ, is a God unlike other gods. Of him they say: He is our God, he is the Lord. He is one and the same! He is who he is! According to one biblical author, his uniqueness is best described by the statement, "God is one; and he will justify" both Jews and Gentiles, through faith alone (Rom 3:29–30).

But equally amazing things as are said about his oneness, are said about the holiness of God.

III *God Is Holy*

In both secular and religious books holiness is sometimes understood as the transcendence, absoluteness, or otherness of a divine being, or the uncontrollable, mystical character of a religious experience that overcomes, confronts, and limits man. In this case the Holy is identical with the mystery that is experienced whenever an absolute principle makes itself felt—whether it is a power that lies outside man's rational or emotional control, or a will strong enough to break or inspire the reasoning, planning, and volition of man. Holiness has also been defined as the sum total of what distinguishes more or less primitive and sophisticated religious ceremonies, traditions, institutions, or books. Though these meanings of the term are not absent from the Old and the New Testaments, the distinctively biblical concept of God's holiness lies elsewhere.

In the Bible, holiness is not first of all the quality of an It, but holy is what He is, God the Lord. "I the Lord your God am holy. . . . Holy, holy, holy is the Lord of hosts. . . . I am the Lord your God, the Holy One of Israel, your Savior. . . . For the sake of my holy name . . . I will vindicate the holiness of my great name . . . through you I vindicate my holiness before [the eyes of the nations]. . . . Hallowed be thy name" (Lev 11:44; 19:2; 21:8; Is 6:3; 43:3; Ezek 36:22–23; Mt 6:9). Priests and prophets may, at different periods of Israel's history, put conflicting emphasis on ceremonial laws, or ethical demands. The restoration of the Aaronitic forms of worship, or of the Davidic dynasty's political power may be their prevailing message or hope. Emphasis may fall on the renewal of the heart by forgiveness, or the assembly and reconciliation of those dispersed or hostile; on the intimate bond between God and his chosen one, or the world-wide refraction of God's glory. But common to all these statements about holiness is the recognition that from God himself much more is derived than instruction concerning the character of holiness. God in person is called the Holy One; he alone can make holy. Only by acknowledgment of Him is the holy known. The sanctification of everything depends on Him and can be conveyed by, and derived from him alone. Obviously God is identical with holiness, and this identity excludes the assumption that he is a participant in something greater than himself, or in something attributed to him. The holiness of God means that he is gloriously, radiantly, powerfully nothing but Himself.

His holiness is therefore not only of *its* own kind, but it is and remains of *his* kind. What is the difference between his holiness and other sorts of holiness that may exist? "Consecrate yourselves . . . and be holy, for I am holy. . . . You . . . shall be perfect, as your heavenly Father is perfect. . . . He is kind to the ungrateful and the selfish. Be merciful, even as your Father is merciful" (Lev 11:44–45; 19:2; Mt 5:48; Lk 6:35–36). The holiness of the biblical God is such that he makes holy. Far from being afraid of contact with unholy places, things, and sinners, he will make them holy. "The place on which you are standing is holy ground" (Ex 3:5). Zechariah (14:20) predicts that the horse's bells shall be inscribed "Holy to the Lord." Paul greets people who live in the wicked city of ancient Corinth by calling them "sanctified" (1 Cor 1:2). According to the Fourth Gospel Jesus said, "For their sake I sanctify [consecrate] myself, that they also may be sanctified [consecrated] in truth. . . . I am glorified in them" (Jn 17:19, 10).

God's eternity and majesty are contained in his holiness. God is so eternal that he creates time, and can use time to manifest himself in man's realm of spatial and temporal limitations and conditions. God is so high and so great that he does not lose the slightest trace of his dignity when he is also low and humble among those having a contrite heart, when he is afflicted with their afflictions, when he takes upon himself the consequences of a curse they could not bear (Is 57:15; 63:9; Ps 22:24; Gal 3:13; 2 Cor 5:21). Zeus lost dignity through his visits to the daughters of men. While the Duke of Windsor was still king of Britain, his surprise visits to the blighted huts of Welsh miners were paid for with a loss of respect among the throne's guardians. But God revealed his glory by dwelling in the midst of men, and by participating in the history and quality of their flesh and blood (Jn 1:14; Heb 2:14). God can change his decisions, to the glory of his name and to the good of man, without changing his eternal plan. He suffers under the rebellion and foolishness of his chosen men without becoming weak. He is not immutable, but he is living. It is in these terms that we should understand his holiness.

In his mighty acts God is not playing a strange role; he is not hiding himself in a masquerade. Rather, through different acts of revelation, he discloses what was formerly hidden and obscure to men; but what was hidden to men was never strange to God. There is no duality or tension between what God is in himself and what he reveals by his acts. If there seems to be such tension, then God is boldly challenged for hiding his face and cheating man. When he acts like an enemy, the bitter complaint is made, "Thou hast wrapped thyself with a cloud so that no prayer can pass through" (cf. Job 13:24; Jer 20:7; Ps 22:1; Mk 15:34; Lam 3:44).

According to the Bible, God does not become holy in the process of the history of his revelation. When he revealed his name, he also revealed his holiness. God's attribute, "holy," appears in the Exodus and Sinai traditions; in the accounts and prophetic oracles of the periods when the monarchy was established, and when Israel's tribes split into two groups and were led into exile in Mesopotamia; in exilic and post-exilic literature; and finally in the records of the time of Jesus Christ. It is always the holy God who proves himself holy (or who sanctifies himself, his name) in acts of judgment. If human concepts of God and forms of worship change, it is yet the same God who makes himself known and whose deeds are celebrated.

So the holiness of God is God's joy and freedom to be himself and to be true to himself in his revelation and in the creation of a holy people. His holiness is not a static attribute that might fit a dead thing or an abstraction. For it is the power eradiated in God's acts of creation, redemption, glorification; and it is triumphantly mirrored in the life, the deeds, the sufferings of people who are chosen to be a living reflection of God's own essence.

Like several other Hebrew theological key terms (such as righteous, faithful), the concept "holy" describes essence *and* action *and* success at the same time. In the narrowest and most sublime sense it refers to the nature of God and to his creative and effective relation to chosen men. When the term "holy" is applied to things, as when the Old Testament speaks of holy places and times, or when Paul speaks of the holy law and holy scriptures (Rom. 7:12; 1:2), it describes instruments that are set apart by God for the sanctification of his people. Holiness of things, unlike God's holiness, is functional and not essential; unholy use or contact may destroy its holiness. If a chosen instrument, location, or time is manipulated as if it possessed a holiness and a sanctifying power of its own, then prophetic voices call God's people to order. Even the holy mountain of God's revelation, the holy city, the holy sacrifice offered in the holy temple, or the holy law cannot substitute for the eradiating, burning, and healing essence and power of God's own holiness.

In sum, God alone is holy; he is the holy One. Such is his holiness that he wants to reveal it by making men rejoice and share in it. God's holiness is his very life.

IV *God Is Living*

In biblical narratives ranging from the creation of the first man to the description of the new heaven and new earth, in oaths sworn by God or by men knowing of God, and in hymns of praise raised to God, it is again and again stated that God lives. Our concept of life, derived from the characteristics of atoms or cells, from the evolution of species or the development of individuals, from the rise, fall, and interaction of nations, cultures, or ideas, is radically inadequate to describe God's life. God does not share in this or that life or life-giving spirit, and he does not receive it from anyone, from anything, or from any composition of elements and forces. In his essence he is life (or spirit), and he is the giver of life and existence to all that is created. "In him was life. . . . God is spirit. . . . With thee is the fountain of life. . . . When thou sendest forth thy Spirit, they are created. . . . It is the spirit that gives life . . . the words I have spoken to you are spirit and life. . . . Man lives by everything that proceeds out of the mouth of the Lord" (Jn 1:4; 4:24; Ps 36:9; 104:30; Jn 6:63; Deut 8:3). The distinction between God's life and imparted, finite, creaturely life is sometimes made plain by reference to God's "eternal life" (Deut 32:40, etc.). In the Bible, eternity is not an unlimited number of successive aeons; it is God's own way of being, which is independent of the passing eras. On the other hand, God's eternity is not timelessness, but, as we have already seen, includes the creation, control, and limitation of time. God is "from age to age"; he is the Lord of time, without restriction, existing outside the limits by which creaturely life is bound.

What, then, is the distinctive character of God's life? Its nature can only be pointed out when we take our start from the climax of God's self-manifestation, the witness of the New Covenant. The life of God is that he is Father, Son, and Spirit, one in three and three in one. Though the Old Testament, if read without regard to events recorded in the New Testament, would hardly lead to the recognition of God's "Trinity," the two Testaments combined point to this mystery of God's identity and life. It was said before that the numerical meaning of the digit one does not suffice to denote the qualitative uniqueness of God. It has to be added now that the quality of God's uniqueness among the gods of monotheistic, henotheistic, theistic, and polytheistic systems is most incisively revealed when (as in Mk 1:9–11; Mt 28:19; Rom 1:1–4; 2 Cor 1:21–22; 13:14; 1 Pet 1:2; Rev 1:4–6), in narrative, didactic, or hymnic form, God the Father, God the Son, and God the Spirit are mentioned simultaneously.

What the Old Testament texts, as well as parts of the New Testament, say about the Angel, the Word, the Spirit, the Wisdom, the Son, the Court of God, has sometimes been explained in terms of remnants of a primitive polytheism, or a hypostatization of divine powers that was supposedly indicative of the original monotheism's dilution into a polytheistic pattern. But the New Testament insists as much as the Old that God is and remains one in his essence and existence (Lk 18:19; 1 Tim 2:5).

He is manifested and praised as Father and Creator because, in relation to his creatures, he is and remains the one who is above, prior, and free. He is manifested and praised as God the Son, or the Son of Man, because he chose to be among men, in time, called to obedience, and afflicted by suffering and death as man is. He is manifested and praised as God the Spirit because he has proved and is proving free and willing to be not only above and among men but also in the heart, the community, and the action of men. Most gods are majestic and rule from afar; some gods make appearances among mankind that humiliate themselves or are humiliating for those visited; a divine element in man's soul, or in the life of a given tribe or caste, is hailed among all peoples, whether or not they possess a highly developed form of religion. But that the same God is, at the same time and without any loss of glory, above, with, in, and through man—this is disclosed only in the Bible. God is as truly in heaven as on the cross or in the heart and community and witness of his servants. He is, at the same time, authority *and* obedience *and* love. He is not a shut-in, in the prison of loneliness; for he converses with himself. He is not tied to the throne of majesty, to the sanctuary of worshipers, or to the seclusion of individual sufferers. For he is manifold and one at the same time; he is on high and he chooses to dwell here or there; he suffers and he lifts up! He is creator-spirit, mighty, and willing to work in and through his creatures and to be inseparably associated with the historic names of Abraham, Moses, Paul, and the historic communities of Israel and the church. Above all, he has identified himself with man's condition, affliction, and salvation through Jesus Christ who was born and lived and was killed and raised from the dead at a specific time in the land given to the Jews.

God's life is the communion, splendor, and power of God the Father, the Son, and the Spirit. No other reason exists to speak or write or sing of the God whose life is so distinctly and uniquely his own than God's self-disclosure to chosen men! And no other way is found to show and to communicate knowledge of the triune God than by a confession of faith in him who is one in three, and three in one.

Still, it may be asked whether the dependence of all statements concerning God's trinity upon revelation and faith implies that, behind the God who manifested himself and who is believed, there may be another, perhaps even a higher, solitary God? Indeed, if God were not more than some priests or zealots, some outstanding teachers or amorphous communities confess him to be, how could he be God of his own right? But the dependence of all men upon this or that manifestation of God, and the dimness and obliqueness of their keenest confession does not prevent biblical authors from stating that God is who he is; that is, he is in himself what he shows himself to be in his acts of self-disclosure. It is not a view or image of God which Israel and the church have made and chosen to worship; it is God himself. The God who manifests himself as One who *makes* righteous, *is* righteous (Rom 3:26). The God who gives just wages to his servants does not play an actor's role, but "he is" (Heb 11:6). From age to age, he was and is and will be always the same. God does not become Father by creating the world and by making men his children; he is father of all men because, from eternity, he is in himself Father, even Father of Jesus Christ. Jesus Christ does not introduce obedience into the Trinity or into the world as though it were something strange to God. He is, in eternity, the obedient Son. The Spirit's gift to many does not mean the loss of original power or the gain of new power; it is the manifestation of the powerful love and life that are eternally proper to God. The Trinity, therefore, is the very essence and character of God's life.

And all that is called life, or that is given essence and existence, is called into being, limited, and supported by the living God. His life and trinity are the very ground of all being. Before ontological, existential, ethical questions were raised, He Who Is, "I, I," was the answer. "Because I live, you will live also. . . . Before the mountains were brought forth . . . thou art God. . . . Your Father knows what you need before you ask him" (Jn 14:19; Ps 90:2; Mt 6:8).

The manifestation and the acknowledgment of the triune God make superfluous any sort of Hebrew or Christian philosophy or world view and replace the function of ontology in a comprehensive philosophy. While philosophical systems or comprehensive world views tend to imagine or depict an order of being in which life of different sorts may have some place, the Bible affirms that God's glorious life is source and standard and destiny of all things and all life.

His life is the life of the community of Father, Son, and Spirit, and it is life that in eternity elects, and in God's own time calls to life children of God, brothers of Christ, inspired servants, a holy assembly.

The survey of biblical statements about God has to be concluded with a critical question and a final affirmation.

v *God's Engagement*

A serious objection often raised by both devoted and skeptical Bible readers is this: What if the highest and finest things confessed about the Name, the Oneness, the Holiness, the Life of God were nothing more than expressions of human imagination? Some biblical scholars speak rather defensively of the Bible's anthropomorphisms. Other Bible readers employ a more or less concealed attack by saying that even if some profound utterances of God and about God seem to indicate that there is a noble intention to speak of the "totally Other," there are yet statements in the Bible that seem to reveal a God-idea fabricated after man's image. For God is called "a man of war"; he is seen "sitting on his throne," or in "a likeness as it were of a human form"; the *man* Jesus of Nazareth asserts that he is one with the Father; "He who has seen me, has seen the Father" (Ex 15:3; 1 Kings 22:19; Ezek 1:26; Jn 10:30; 14:9).

Not only in the oldest and most primitive stages of Israel's history, but throughout the Bible, God's person and limbs, his movements and emotions, his deeds and commandments, are so described that he resembles a mighty and passionate personality—tribal, imperial, or paternal—who comes to claim or exert his rights (see Is 30:27–28; Deut 33:2–3; Hos; Lk 18:1–8). The seventy inspired men who, according to the legend, translated the Old Testament from Hebrew into Greek sometime after 300 B.C., attempted to replace blatant anthropomorphisms with more respectable descriptions of God (e.g., Ex 4:24; 15:3; 19:3; 24:11;

32:12; Job 42:7). Did they engage in a noble and necessary operation when they pointed to a purely spiritual and metaphysical idea of God? The New Testament's assertion that God in Jesus Christ was walking on earth and reconciling the world certainly did much to sabotage this effort. In addition, even the biblical utterances about God the Spirit or the Spirit of God do not contribute to a holy war against anthropomorphism. Both Testaments are describing the Spirit's essence, work, and effects in a manner that is all too obviously derived from human experience. A definition of a pure and absolute spirit might be found by philosophers one day, but the Bible does not attempt to equate God with such a spirit. When they speak of God, the authors of the Bible use human language and imagery, parables, metaphors, and analogies derived from the experience of man in the world of space and time.

Does this mean that prophets and apostles are exponents of nothing better than anthropomorphic ideas of God? Are their statements equivalent to mythical notions that depict the gods as admirable or vicious supermen, or that bring wishful or fearful projections of the human quest into the metaphysical realm? Four observations may help to answer this burning question.

First, the biblical authors themselves are aware of the problem and meet the challenge by affirming passionately that God is not man. Jesus Christ is neither a Moses, nor an Elijah, nor a John the Baptist, but God's only Son; the Spirit is holy and, though he may be compared, he cannot be identified with the wind in the trees, or man's mind, or the breath, or the forms of intoxication man indulges in (Num 23:19; 1 Sam 15:29; Is 31:3; Ezek 28:9; Hos 11:9; Job 32:13; Mk 6:14–15; 8:27–29; Jn 1:1, 14, 18; 20:28; Heb 1:1–4; Rom 8:16; 1 Cor 2:11; Acts 2:15 ff.; Eph 5:18). But we must concede that this God might be no more distinct from man than one supreme idea is different from others; the witnesses' intention to speak of God as of One who is not man does not prove that they avoid presenting a God according to man's image and imagination.

Second, the Bible throws special light on the so-called anthropomorphic statements about God when it states that there is a true and a false image of God.

> Jesus Christ is the image of the invisible God. . . . He reflects the glory of God and bears the very stamp of his nature. . . . The Word was God. . . . God said, "Let us make man in our image, after our likeness." . . . So God created man in his own image. . . . You shall make for yourself no molten gods. . . . You shall not make yourself a graven image, or any likeness of anything that is in heaven above, or that is in the earth beneath, or that is in the water under the earth; you shall not bow down to them or serve them. . . . They exchanged the glory of the immortal God for images resembling mortal man or birds or animals or reptiles (Col 1:15; Heb 1:3; Jn 1:1; Gen 1:26–27; Ex 34:17; 20:4, 5; Rom 1:23).

Such biblical statements are in opposition to the anthropomorphic or theriomorphic images and symbols of God used in the cultus of the Canaanite, Egyptian, and Mesopotamian neighbors of Israel—and also, at times, in the sanctuaries of the God of Israel. Except in a few passages (for example, Judg 17:3; Ps 17:15, or when Jesus or man is called God's image), the image or symbol is identified with a foreign god; its liturgical use is prohibited and it is called an idol.[6]

The biblical injunction against material images of the divine also applies to the making of images with thoughts and words. We should not assume that biblical writers found carved or cast images of God unsuitable, and then proceeded to replace them with verbal imagery depicting God in human fashion.

When the Bible affirms that God lives, plans, decides, hears, sees, speaks, comes, acts, or repents, it is implying that man is created in God's image or that Jesus Christ has revealed God's nature and will (Gen 1:26–27; Col 1:16; Jn 1:1, 18). The statement that man is created in God's image has both a positive and a negative meaning. While it excludes the notion that God is (or is to be) created anthropomorphically, it affirms that man is created theomorphically![7] Indications of man's theomorphic structure are not restricted to his mind or to his dominion over other creatures; they include the gifts of hearing, speaking, moving, standing upright, feeling, suffering, and deciding. Man cannot define the nature of God's own hearing and speaking and moving, but he does nothing that is foreign to God when he uses and enjoys his senses, his mind, or his power. The God of glory crowns man with glory and honor! (Ps 8:1–3, 9, 4–8)

Third, the Bible does not make only lofty statements about the grandeur and strength of God; seemingly degrading, if not preposterous things are also ascribed to him and done in his name. With equal emphasis it is said that God's love is that of a father, and that he is jealous and punishes vigorously. God, or the spirit of God, is praised for many great deeds, but is also held responsible for the destruction of almost all mankind, of flourishing cities, and proud members of his people. Devastating acts of judgment are seen not only in past events that might better be forgotten, but also in predictions about the future of both church and world (Gen 6:13, 17; Num 16; 1 Sam 6:19; 2 Sam 24:15; 2 Kings 1:9–14; Amos; Acts 5:1–11; Rom 1:18 ff.; Rev 6:8–9; 16–18). In his name dreadful deeds are committed. People who are devoted worshipers, or who consider themselves God's children, often do terrible things. The Levites slaughter their own brothers, not in disobedience to God, but in order to glorify his name. The judge Samuel enforces the execution of a defeated and captive enemy, including wives and children. The prophet Elijah kills hundreds of Baal's clergymen. Ezra, the scribe, keeps fellow Israelites standing in the rain for three days while the law is read to them. Nehemiah, the administrator, drives foreign-born wives and their children into misery. Jesus Christ mentions hatred of one's father, mother, wife, and children—and even of one's own soul—among the costs of discipleship. He calls all messiahs or saviors that came before him thieves and murderers. The apostle Paul delivers his own kin to the wrath of God, and he wishes the enemies of the Gospel of grace would castrate themselves. Slain martyrs can hardly wait to see God's revenge meted out to their enemies (Ex 32:26–29; Num 25:7–9; 1 Sam 15:3, 32–33; 1 Kings 18:40; Ezra 10:9–19, 44; Neh 13:23–29; Lk 14:26; 1 Cor 5:3–5; 1 Thess 2:14–16; Gal 5:12; Rev 6:9–11). What God is this who is thus described, and who is served by such actions?

It is impossible at this point to deal with the great problems raised by these passages. Obviously the God of the Bible does not introduce himself, nor is he described as a paragon, exemplifying the sublimest human standards. We have shown earlier that the holiness of God cannot simply be equated with the highest human ethical principles and moral performance. The God of the Bible is revealed and praised as one who is free to be God in his own right; to set, change, and fulfill standards according to his own pleasure; to create, to accept, to do, and to suffer what no man would judge acceptable. We have also shown that this freedom does not make God's rule a sequence of arbitrary measures. God is true to himself in his manifestations; but these reveal that he is a living God rather than a set of principles, a projection of virtues, or the sum total of what man might consider humanistic, religious, or social values. At different periods he chooses different ways to disclose his reign and presence. The culmination of his revelation is the appearance, death, and resurrection of Jesus Christ; it is not to be identified with the final stage of an evolutionary process to which God himself might be submitted. For at all stages of his history with man, under all cultural, political, psychological, or sociological circumstances, God is one and the same God. The biblical statements that the God of Abraham, of Moses, of David, of the prophets, of Jesus Christ, and of the Jerusalem and Corinthian churches is the same God destroy any anthropomorphic explanation of his origin and character. If he had been man's creation, either a more consistent and higher God idea, or horrible and changing images would have been the natural result. The freedom in which God chooses to be God, revealing himself in many surprising ways, and yet in faithfulness to himself, has its roots beyond the confines of anthropomorphism. The authors and readers of the Bible cannot suppress their surprise at the identity of the living God who introduces himself to them.

Fourth, in considering biblical anthropomorphism, it is to be emphasized that all the amazing biblical statements about God and his sovereign freedom culminate in summary sentences like these:

> Yea, he loved his people. . . . The Lord your God has chosen you . . . because the Lord loves you. . . . The Lord set his heart in love upon your fathers. . . . I will betroth you to me for ever. . . . God so loved the world that he gave his only Son. . . . God is love. . . . God's love has been poured into our hearts. . . . The goodness and loving kindness of God our Savior appeared. . . . Pray then like this: Our Father. . . . Because you are sons, God has sent the Spirit of his Son into our hearts crying, "Abba! Father!" (Deut 33:3; 7:6–8; 10:15; Hos 2:19–20; Jn 3:16; 1 Jn 4:8; Rom 5:5; Tit 3:4; Mt 6:9; Gal 4:6)

According to such statements, God is a friend and benefactor of man, not by accident, but in essence. What God is and has, he does not desire to retain without making man a participant in wonder, joy, and bliss.

It is characteristic of the God of the Bible that he so continually links himself with man that nobody can really speak of him without also mentioning a man's name. "God of Abraham! God of Israel! Father of Jesus Christ! My God! I am the Lord your God!"

If such names or descriptions of God referred only to religious formulas fostered by a particular patriarch, prophet, or cultic community during a given period of Israel's life, or to an individual man in misery, and if this material was merely compiled later by clever collectors of folklore, legend, and liturgy, the God of the Bible might be no more than a collection of religious ideas. Man would be the measure of individual and collected God-ideas alike.

What the Bible actually attempts to emphasize is just the opposite. It is God who makes one covenant after another with men chosen out of Israel until he fulfills his eternal plan in a covenant made with both Israel and the Gentiles. It is he who gathers worshipers to himself at all times. It is he who "rejoices in doing them good," and whose wisdom "delights in the sons of men," who "delights" even in him who is inclined to call himself "a worm and no man" (Jer 32:41; Prov 8:31; Ps 22:6–8). The God of the Bible, therefore, is one who voluntarily chooses to be associated with sinful men, to have men seek and find him, to make them revere him and bear witness to him.

Is God anthropomorphic, therefore, or is he not? We recall that in the Pauline Epistles (Phil 2:6–8; cf. Phil 3:21) what is called the form (*morphe* or *schema*) of God or Christ is not thought of as opposed to his real essence or nature; on the contrary, the form of God is the very mode and character of his essence.[8] Interpreting the term anthropomorph in its deepest possible sense, we may say that if anthropomorphism is discovered in an abundance of biblical statements about God, they may be understood to describe God's very nature, rather than as a pitiful accommodation to human ideas and language. These statements are saying that by nature, in eternity, and in reality, God is for man—even if this seems to put God into a shameful association. The God of the Bible is he who is "not ashamed to call them brethren. . . . [He] is not ashamed to be called their God" (Heb. 2:11; 11:16). Although men may be ashamed of man, *God* cares for him. We may have difficulty in believing in God, but God believes in man, he is faithful to him. For this reason it is impossible to talk of God without talking of Adam and Christ, of Jews and Christians, of good men and bad. If he were too spiritual to be engaged in covenants of love with sinful men, too eternal to manifest himself in dealings with specific men in time, ashamed to be called upon and proclaimed abroad in human language and human concepts, he would not be the God of the Bible.

After this astonishing testimony which the Bible bears to God, let us turn to its testimony concerning man.

The Man Chosen for Freedom

I *Theology and Anthropology*

If the Bible conveyed nothing but an astonishing record of God's self-manifestation and of man's confession of faith, it would probably be less disturbing a book than it actually is. But even if a man could succeed in summing up all the Bible says about God, he would not have encountered the breadth and depth of its contents. For the Bible points not only to the revelation of God, but also to the revelation of man. It makes men aware of words and events, and a history through which the nature and destiny of man is manifested. The reader of the Bible finds himself exposed to unsettling statements about his ancestors, his brothers, his children—and about himself, too. It is probably more difficult to accept what is said about man than what is said about God.

For man presumes to know about himself; at the very least, he believes that he can ask the decisive questions and eventually formulate satisfactory answers. The investigations of natural science have helped to explain the operation and order of the universe and man's relation to those laws which seem to govern the world.

Man has found that in such areas as medicine, technology, or meteorology, he can attain some understanding of the forces working in the world around him; and he can submit some of them to his control. As regards man's historical, social, and psychological constitution, contemporary anthropological studies are constantly seeking more penetrating and all-embracing answers. Whatever the theoretical position from which he starts, man seems to succeed in understanding not only what controls him but also to what extent he can control himself and the world around him. Finally, man accepts the task of testing the validity, practicality, and acceptability of his own experiences. In creating and admiring art, in the judicial, ethical, and philosophical quest for the right, the good, and the true, and finally in religious traditions and reformations, he both seeks and finds value in his existence.

Because man is so able or willing to take care of himself, the most surprising parts of the Bible are those that bring in, as if from outside, a revelation and determination of his nature and destiny. According to Genesis 3, God asks man, "Where are you?" before man asks for God. In Psalm 8, the question, "What is man?" is answered by a reference to humiliating and elevating deeds of God. Wisdom literature displays not only great wisdom, but also skepticism, in regard to man; both are marked by what is called "fear of the Lord." The Gospel according to John not only describes God, his Son, and his Spirit, but also the essence of man. Jesus Christ is called the Son of God, and also "a man," or "the man" (1:18, 30; 8:40; 19:5). In Paul's teaching, especially in Romans 1–3, the whole of mankind comes under judgment: "None is righteous. . . . There is no distinction, since all have sinned" (3:10, 23); but in the same context it is stated that God justifies the godless without distinction between Jew and Gentile (1:16, 17; 3:29–30).

In these examples of biblical anthropology a verdict is passed on man that is so radical that heroic or skeptic pessimism becomes pale in its burning light. And yet a confidence and hope are expressed in regard to man the sinner that go beyond all optimism. The miracle of the sinner's justification (Rom 4:5) is so enormous that no man can feel left out. Wherever a man may turn in his flight, the Bible asserts that God is already there and finds him; for it is God who knows man (cf. Ps 139:1–12), and it is from God that man has to learn about himself (Ps 8:3–8): "God is greater than our hearts, and he knows everything" (1 Jn 3:20).

It is obvious that God sees man from a different perspective than is available to his creature. "The Lord sees not as man sees; man looks on the outward appearance, but the Lord looks on the heart. . . . O Lord, do not thy eyes look for truth?" (1 Sam 16:7; Jer 5:3) Man may at best be an onlooker; blind to essentials, he cannot see as clearly as God does. God, however, is not only an unbiased observer; he can and will *look* to it that all things go his way. His is a creative, dynamic, governing "providence." "God saw everything that he had made, and behold, it was very good" (Gen. 1:31).

How does this omnipotent providence affect man's position before God? We read that God "establishes" that all men are represented by the disobedient first man, Adam. Yet by the same God's judgment, the obedient and righteous Jesus Christ is established and made the new and final representative for those convicted of sin. Through him they are "constituted" as righteous (Rom 5:12–21, especially verse 19). If God's view of man is more critical than man's sharpest judgment or deepest despair, his judgment is also more gracious than man's most indulgent hope for himself would allow.

Only incidentally, and in rather conflicting ways, does the Bible provide analytic statements about man, describing him as soul and body, or spirit and flesh; only occasionally does it make statements about his individual or communal characteristics. The Bible's anthropological method has its basis in the many stories of the men chosen by God; stories which become one long story of the position of the Jews and the Gentiles in the light of God's election, his covenant of love, and his judgments. If one is to understand biblical anthropology, he must study the dynamic history of man before God, rather than the static elements that constitute *homo sapiens.* God's judgments on man are decisive; that the Bible, when it speaks of man, refers to God as the only judge shows its distinctiveness from other books dealing with the human condition. Characteristically, the equation, "man is flesh" (flesh being understood in a pejorative sense), is used in the Old Testament only when reporting God's verdict on man, or when flesh is contrasted with the Spirit (Gen 6:3; cf. 12–13; Is 31:3; 40:6). And the New Testament apostle, Paul, sums up the biblical attitude on this point when he teaches that men are sinners because they have sinned against *God* and are found guilty before *God,* and that only the final judgment of *God* can establish them as righteous.

Naturally, the biblical writers also give ample evidence of man's understanding of himself and his inclination to play the judge. Nevertheless, they feel constrained, above all, to record God's judgment on man. They do not merely quote God's statements about himself but try to convey knowledge of his will and of his decisions regarding man.

Of course, what the Bible says of man need not always be in conflict with what man believes he knows about himself. It does, however, concern a dimension of humanity whose presence and relevance cannot possibly be tested by modern science. Biblical anthropology can enjoy its freedom from the yoke of the natural and anthropological sciences only when it is inseparably tied to biblical theology. Anthropology does not exist without theology, nor can there be theology without anthropology—not if we are looking for the God and the man revealed in the Bible.

This does not mean that theology and anthropology should be identified.[9] A doctrine of man is not a doctrine of God. But the Bible can teach us that faith *in God* is inseparable from a faithful acceptance of God's election *of man.* By ignoring what God does and says to man concerning man's own being and calling, we would ignore both his will and his work—and thereby himself! According to his own words and deeds—and therefore in essence and by definition—the God of the Bible is the God of men, from Abraham to Paul. We cannot accept God and then divest him of the company he has chosen. He who murmurs against Moses' commission murmurs against the Lord; rebellion against Aaron's priesthood and Samuel's ministry is rejection of God; disobedience against Paul's commandments is disobedience of God's word. "He who rejects you rejects me" (Ex 16:8; Num 16:11; 1 Sam 8:7; 1 Thess 2:13; 2 Thess 3:4, 10, 12; Rom 6:17; Lk 10:16). The opposite is proclaimed with even greater insistence: "If you believed Moses, you would believe me. . . . Believe in the Lord your God, and you will be established; believe his prophets, and you will succeed. . . . They believed in the Lord and in his servant Moses. . . . He who receives you receives me" (Jn 5:46; 2 Chron 20:20; Ex 14:31; Mt 10:40).

Belief in Moses and the reception of God's other messengers must not lead to the fabrication of any abstract or ideal image of man. Unlike a physiology, psychology, or sociology textbook, the Bible does not offer a general image of man. Its stories are of distinct men or peoples who were called and judged at specific times. Biblical anthropology proceeds from the specific to the universal, from Abraham's or Paul's relationship with God to the meaning of that relationship for Israel and the Gentiles, for the human race, and hence for each of us. Biblical utterances are based, not on man's relationship with himself or with society in general, but always on a specific man's relationship with God.

We will try to find the core of man's history before God by listening to the biblical utterances concerning Jesus Christ. In the Fourth Gospel it is recorded that when Jesus Christ stood in court, indicted, probably, for being a messianic pretender, the Roman procurator Pontius Pilate said, "*Ecce homo*" ("Here is the man!") (Jn 19:5) The evangelist obviously understood this statement to mean more than just, "That's him!" What does it mean that in this place John—as on other occasions Paul and Luke, Mark and James—introduces Jesus as the Man (or Son of Man) par excellence? What is man, if Jesus Christ—rather than another individual, or a composite image—is *The Man?*

II *God's Man*

Before his Jewish and Gentile judges, Jesus Christ stands in dreadful loneliness and helplessness. But it would be a mistake to draw the conclusion that man is basically alone and without assistance. The opposite is proclaimed on every page of the Bible. Man is created by God; man is given a human partner by God; man is created as the last of all creatures, so that he may find dry ground to stand upon, light to see by and stars to measure time, fruit to eat, rest to enjoy, and land to cultivate (Gen 1–2). Obviously, man is treated as God's favorite among his creatures. To be man means to be related, first of all, to the gracious creator; then, to fellow men; and finally, to the world of animals, plants, and other living things. Man is a partner of God—a lower, mortal, fallible partner, indeed, but still a living proof of God's philanthropy and the outstanding example of the goodness of creation.

To be man means to be given royal privileges; therefore, the position of man, or the "son of man," is described in terms that may have been derived from, or may have led up to, the description of a king (Ps 8; 89; Dan 7; Ezek 28). Before God, the royal man deserves to be and is humiliated. But the same God who abases man also extols him. Man is told both to be humble and to walk upright before God. He may feel threatened or overawed by the animals; but he is to exert dominion over them. It is God's pleasure to make man the witness of glory despite suffering, of righteousness despite failure, and of honor despite shame.

But is the man standing accused and beaten before Pontius Pilate really a royal person? His actual history and fate seem to contradict the proposition that he represents every man's election to royal dignity and responsibility.

What is hidden to Jews and Greeks can only become manifest and recognized when God himself reveals it. In the Bible, man owes his existence to creation and his preeminence among creatures to God's favor; he is responsible to his fellow men because they are made in God's image. But man's humanity also depends upon the gracious event by which God makes manifest what is to be the relationship between God and man, and the true interrelationship among men. Jesus Christ's kingship was announced in words of promise spoken by the Old Testament prophets in God's name; it was made apparent, to those given eyes to see and ears to hear, during Jesus' ministry; and it was finally established by his resurrection from the dead. That Abraham is God's friend, that Moses is God's faithful servant, and that Israel and David are each, in his own way, God's "son" was demonstrated by God's revelations to them and to others. According to the Bible, man's existence differs from that of plants or animals because he is chosen to be God's partner in an eternal covenant in which God's faithfulness and righteousness find a response in man's faith and obedience. "This is eternal life, that they know thee" (Jn 17:3). To be estranged from God, to be without his help, our prayer unanswered—this is equal to death (Is 38:10–20; Ps 88). "Stupid, ignorant, like a beast before Thee"—these are the words of self-criticism spoken by one who denies that man lives by knowing the Lord and obeying him (Ps 73).

The conviction that no one can be truly man, unless God steps to his side as revealer, redeemer, vindicator, is grounded upon resurrection. This faith is formulated in only a few passages of the later Old Testament (see Is 24; Dan 12); it becomes more and more explicit in Jewish intertestamental and rabbinical literature; in the New Testament it receives its final expression. He who believes in "God . . . who gives life to the dead" (Rom 4:17) acknowledges that it is God alone who will show what man is before Him. No man can give himself or others that life which is given by a judge who has the power and the will to raise the dead.

Man belongs to God in still another way. He is given the opportunity and the means to act and speak as God's witness. Jesus Christ makes "a good confession before Pontius Pilate." Unless he had lived as one who revealed what he knew of the Father, he would not have been called the Son of God (1 Tim 6:13; Mt 11:25–27; Jn 1:18). The salvation and enlightenment that are given to a man are given to him in order that he may let his light shine before others (1 Tim 1:15–16; Mt 5:16; Eph 5:7–8). According to the Bible, the true Man cannot remain hidden; when he appears, what all men are shall be revealed before God (1 Jn 3:1–2). What is said and done to the man whom God has chosen is also announced as a blessing for coming generations, and is to be heard even to the ends of the earth (Gen 12:3; Jer 22:29; Acts 1:8). "I will send you to Pharaoh that you may bring forth my people. . . . What I tell you in the dark, utter in the light; and what you hear whispered, proclaim upon the housetops" (Ex 3:10; Mt 10:27). The man is called, equipped, and sent out for the benefit of many. If, in an epiphany, God reveals that he has chosen a man to be his servant, God also commits him to a service among many. "The righteous one, my servant, [shall] make many to be accounted righteous" (Is 53:11). The privilege granted by God to his chosen servant is too great to be hidden or to perish with him. Even if the man chosen behaves as recalcitrantly as Moses, Jeremiah, Jonah, or Paul, others must benefit; God's man is one who stands for many fellow men because God has decided to be gracious to him.

How does the Bible unfold the confession that man is God's man?

III *Man by the Word*

The concentration of recent philosophy on the thorough study of language and logic should be welcomed by everyone who knows what importance the Bible attributes to the word. Language is more than one among many means of human communication; it may well be the one element that makes human communication truly human. As long as philosophers are "friends of wisdom," they will have to devote their energies to seeking those words by which man's quest for truth may find appropriate expression.

But unlike language analysts, the biblical writers are not passionately concerned with language for its own sake. They concentrate instead on *whose* speech is decisive for man. Their experience and insight are concentrated in one statement: "Man does not live by bread alone, but . . . by everything [every word] that proceeds out of the mouth of the Lord." In neither of the two contexts in which it is found (Deut 8:3 and Mt 4:4) does this statement indicate that man needs two different things—nourishment for the body, and nourishment for the soul. It says that, by the word of God, *all* the requirements and conditions of man's life are met. Rising and hoping, working and plowing, harvesting and celebrating, taking and giving—all things vital to man's essence and existence come from God alone.

To be specific, man owes his life to God's gracious will; by a word, he calls nonbeing into being. He addresses himself to man with words of care, direction, and warning; he establishes a covenant with man, binding himself by holy oaths and making a claim on man's devotion; he gives laws whose fulfillment means continuous blessing and whose neglect incurs wrath; he watches over kings and prophets and priests, that they may keep, apply, and teach his commandments; finally, he passes judgment, humiliating the proud and extolling the needy. The word of God does not return empty but always effects what it says. It is recognized as his word because it is a creative, useful, and sufficient tool of salvation and its message comes to pass (Is 55:11; Ps 33:9; Deut 18:22; Rom 1:16; Mt 8:8, 13). If it is essentially divine to speak this word, then it is substantially human to live by it. Winds and seas, mountains and fig trees are also under its dominion; this is seen frequently in the Old Testament, and also in the New Testament (Mk 4:39; 11:23; Mt 21:19). God upholds the universe by "his word of power," since all things are made by the word (Heb 1:3; Jn 1:3). But it is the specific privilege of man to hear and to understand that word. He is to rejoice in the fact that everybody and everything lives by the word of God alone.

Luther, and leading German Lutheran theologians, have attempted to make a sharp distinction between two sorts of words that God has addressed to man. The word of the constraining and killing Law was contrasted with the word of the forgiving and life-giving Gospel. Sometimes the whole Old Testament was classified as Law, and the New as Gospel; or both Law and Gospel were found side by side in both Testaments. In either case, it was emphasized that God confronts man with his Law and the demand for a righteousness which man does not and cannot fulfill. If he should attempt to do so, he is said to incur God's wrath because of his implied zeal for self-justification. According to the same teaching, it is only later that God meets man as a loving father, who forgives the transgression, and who transforms the Law's slave into a free child. If 2 Corinthians 3:6 is quoted, "The written code kills, but the Spirit gives life" (cf. Rom 7:9–10, "When the commandment came . . . I died"; Rom 1:16, "The Gospel . . . is the power of God for salvation"), this understanding appears to be confirmed. In Galatians 3:19 to 4:7, a similar, though hardly just the Lutheran doctrine is unfolded by Paul. The distinction between Law and Gospel certainly enhances the dramatic and existential character of God's speech to man. It shows that the life given through the word of God is not simply the maintenance or extension of biological or psychic life, but a life snatched from death, a life that had passed through the eye of the needle, a life saved from the burning fire of well-deserved condemnation.

Nevertheless, Paul's polemic against the Law—or rather, against a "Judaizing" group of legalists (Gal 2:14)—is not the only key to the understanding of certain features and functions of God's word. More justice is rendered to the whole Bible when it is stated that both Law and Gospel are the one word of God. In its legal form this word shows who God is (one, the bearer of the holy name, a sanctifier and giver of rest, a faithful covenant partner, true to himself), and who man is (one who obviously must be warned against idolatry, murder, and covetousness, because he is prone to them). This revelation is given in the categorical form of commandment in order to make clear, even to the most rebellious or desperate man, that he shall be as holy and perfect as God. In the Old Testament, God revealed that he will provide Israel with a covenant, a leader, and a new heart by which his will is to be completely fulfilled; the New Testament goes on to assert that now, through the coming of Jesus, all is accomplished. "Think not that I have come to abolish the law and the prophets; I have come not to abolish them but to fulfill them. . . . Christ is the end [i.e., the purpose and fulfillment] of the law" (Mt. 5:17; Rom 10:4). The Gospel is based upon the fact that all words of God are not "words only," but that God's word has become flesh, is realized and proven true even in the world of rebellion, darkness, and death (Jn 1:1–18).

However, man's condition and history would be incompletely described if reference were made solely to the word that is spoken by God. Man indeed lives by the word of God; but this word is pronounced in order to be heard and answered. It is essentially human not only to be addressed by God but also to be able to listen, to understand, and to respond. If God's word were not heard, obeyed, and glorified in words and deeds that reflect its content, it would prove empty and futile. But God does not fail in his communication with man. "Speak, Lord, for thy servant hears. . . . Thy words were found, and I ate them, and thy words became to me a joy and the delight of my heart. . . . Blessed are . . . your ears, for they hear" (1 Sam 3:9; Jer 15:16; Mt 13:16). To live as a man means to respond joyfully to God's word, to answer his promise with hope, his commandment with obedience, his judgment with humility; it means to respond to all he says and does with faith.

The biblical authors are fully aware that not every man listens to God and obeys. The Israelites, the disciples of Jesus, and the Christians—God's own people—are scolded more than outsiders for ignoring God, for behaving like animals, for being hard of hearing and far from ready to teach others (e.g., Is 1:3; Mk 9:16–20; Heb 5:11–14). But even though they have failed to respond to their commission with obedience and faith, God still does not give them up. He judges them harshly for neglecting both him and those entrusted to their care. The responsiveness for which they were created assumes the dreadful character of responsibility for rebellion and injustice (see Deut 26:5 to 27:26; Rom 1:18 to 3:20). Instead of behaving in a human way, they have become like animals, or worse than animals (Dan 4:13–33; Rom 3:13–15). But God still remembers them, and they are made to admit that their behavior is not human (Ps 73:22).

As he stands before Pontius Pilate, Jesus Christ, he who is to be delivered up for crucifixion because he accepts the condemnation deserved by all men, epitomizes both the word of God sent to man and the response expected from man (Jn 1:1, 14; 17:1–6; Mt 6:9–13; Acts 10:36; 1 Tim 6:12–13). "All the promises of God find their Yes in him. That is why we utter the Amen through him, to the glory of God" (2 Cor 1:20). Precisely he who wears the painful mockery of a crown of thorns and a soldier's purple cape is called "the Man." This name makes evident what other biblical authors more or less explicitly indicate, that it is essential to man's constitution thus to live *by* the word of God; that man's whole life is an appropriate response to it. Both the word addressed to man and the reply given by true man are a gift of God. Jesus Christ is in himself that double gift.

IV *Man Under Judgment*

We can begin to understand man's condition before God only when we look more closely at Christ, after his disciples have fled, standing alone before accusers who believe they are safeguarding the law, and at the tribunal of Pilate, who does not care for any Jew's life. The words of Isaiah, spoken more than five hundred years before, fit exactly. "Many were astonished at him—his appearance was so marred, beyond human semblance. . . . He had no form or comeliness that we should look at him, and no beauty that we should desire him. He was despised and rejected by men; a man of sorrows, and acquainted with grief . . . and we esteemed him not" (Is 52:14; 53:2–3; cf. the similar description found in the apocryphal Wisdom of Solomon 2:10–20). It is not just Nietzsche or a power-hungry superman that is disgusted by the image of man presented here; every man feels entitled to turn way from such a representation of the human species! Rejection will be even more intense when this same Jesus is said to be the image *of God,* and when it is stated that all men, since they are created in God's image, are "predestined to be conformed to the image of [Christ]" (Col 1:15; Gen 1:26–27; Rom 8:29). It is not only that there have been times when Jews and Gentiles alike repudiated and condemned the servants established by God in their midst; at all times, including the present, the human reaction to those chosen by God, above all against the man who is called Son of God, is negative. The biblical authors themselves say that to be a man of God means to be a man under judgment.

This condition of the man of God is ascribed neither to accident nor simply to human misjudgment. Life under judgment is the very will of God. The writers of the first three Gospels tirelessly repeat statements of Jesus according to which "the Son of man must suffer many things" at the hands of those with the right and the power to judge (Mk 8:31; 9:12, 31; 10:33–34; Lk 22:15, 22; 24:26–27, 44–46). The authenticity of these statements has been questioned by some recent interpreters; the predictions seem to them too accurate to be free of suspicion. Nevertheless, the evangelists were convinced that the whole of the Old Testament was summed up by Jesus in such statements.

Moses, for example, who was considered the archetype of a prophet of the Lord (Deut 18:15, 18; Num 12:6–8), is described as a man "very meek, more than all men that were on the face of the earth" (Num 12:3). The reason given is that he bore a heavy burden while he served as a leader and interceded for the people entrusted to him (Ex 18:18; Num 11:11–15; Ex 32:30–32; Deut 1:37; 3:26; 4:21; 9:17–20, 25–29). On the pattern of this Moses, the high priest, a prophet like Ezekiel, or the faithful servant "bears" the judgment of Israel (Ex 28:12, 29, 30, 38; Ezek 4:4–8; Is 53:5–12). As a mighty prophet and man of God, Jesus could not expect an easier ministry.

David was a successful king who greatly increased Israel's political power. He was described as the ideal shepherd-ruler of his people. His submission to God and his care for the poor and needy are praised in the dramatic accounts of the Books of Samuel and are reflected in many psalms. The establishment or renewal of a genuine kingship is seen in terms of David's appointment by God and his way of dealing with social and political issues. A "son of David"—that is, a man like David, of the same origin and spirit—is fervently expected. But the Books of Samuel, as well as the Psalms, depict David as a man who underwent persecution, dishonor, and suffering. Again and again, out of deepest distress, David had to cry for God's help. He cried out—and he was helped.

Clearly, pious men in David's time, and in later periods in Israel, were glad to have a king who was both "victorious and humble" (cf. Zech 9:9). Because he was himself a man of grief, he would understand the grievances of the poor and give them justice. It is instructive to realize that about half of the 150 canonical psalms bear his name—especially since the contents of the "David psalms" indicates that most of them were composed long after his death. This is no paradox if it is kept in mind that those praying, composing, and singing these psalms felt represented by their beloved king in his encounters with himself, with fellow men, with life—and with God. In his name they found the courage to utter their own prayer and to trust that God would rescue them from any sort of misery. Jesus knew these psalms. If he was the "Son of David" (as Matthew emphasizes; cf. also Rom 1:3; Heb 7:14), he could not expect to be spared suffering; he anticipated it, and he accepted it when the hour came.

To the Son of David, God promised to be father; that son was to be called God's son. What does it mean to be Son of God? An ancient oracle, versions of which are also quoted in psalms treating of Israel's king (see Ps 2; 89; 132), gives the following answer: "I will be his father, and he shall be my son. When he commits iniquity, I will chasten him with the rod of men, with the stripes of the son of men; but I will not take my steadfast love from him" (2 Sam 7:14–15). When David disobeyed God and exploited his subjects (2 Sam 11), he had to experience such punishment. But in Isaiah 53 it is made unmistakably clear that stripes have also fallen, or are to fall, upon a man who has *not* committed any misdeed of his own. His association with sinners and his intercession for them is reason enough for the punishment of the servant described by Isaiah. If the title "Son of God" has anything to do with the Old Testament and later Jewish use of this term for Israel (the slave people in Egypt), for the king of the Davidic dynasty, or for a devout worshiper (Ex 4:22; Ps 2:7; cf. Sirach 4:10; Wisdom of Solomon 2:10 ff.), then suffering at the hands of both God and man would never be simply accidental for Jesus. Although for a long time his disciples did not realize what it meant to hail him as the Son of God, the Gospels make it clear that he knew and accepted it (see especially Mt 16:16, 21–23).

He who accepts God's chastisement, however, is not to be chastised indefinitely. David's punishment only lasted for a time. Those singing the "David psalms" hope or give thanks for salvation from the dangers to which they are exposed. Jesus emphasizes repeatedly that the Son of Man is not simply to suffer, but will be raised again after his humiliation. No more than the proverbial "three days" (cf. Hos 6:2) will be required; the destructive aspect of God's judgment will be overcome by the miracle of new life given even to the man subject to death (Mk 8:31; 9:31; 10:34; Jn 2:19–22; 3:13; 10:18).

It is essential, therefore, to biblical anthropology that he alone is called the Man, the Son of Man, or the Son of God who accepts God's judgment. All men, whether they know it or not, are under God's creative and directive word; what is specifically characteristic of God's man, however, is that God's will and the execution of his judgment are accepted. What distinguishes Jesus the man from many of those who attempt to live righteously and to overcome evil by being or doing good, is that he enters the ranks of the guilty to associate with them; he confesses guilt without having committed a crime; he prays for his enemies and takes upon himself what they deserve; he gives himself completely to fulfill the ministry of atonement, i.e., to reconcile men to God (Mt 3:13–15; Lk 23:34; Heb 5:7–10; 7:25; Mk 10:45; Rom 3:24–25; 2 Cor 5:21).

If this Jesus is the Man par excellence, we can understand why so many of the outstanding figures described in the Bible as his forerunners or followers do not convey the impression of being heroes before either God or men. Adam, Abraham, Moses, David, Elijah, Jeremiah, Job, the Psalmists, Peter, and Paul all failed to be great men according to current human standards. They play a role in the Bible not because they are flawless, but because they were led to accept God's judgment. They accepted it in terms of their own sin, or as mediators for others. According to the Bible, the man whose life story should be retold, whose name is to be remembered is a man willing to bow his head before the heavenly judge and receive the blows inflicted by earthly judges.

This image of man finds its test and reflection in biblical historiography and biography. While it is common experience that a nation's historiographer extols the merits of his chosen hero and suppresses his faults, the Bible tells of Israel's, and the early church's history in an almost scandalous fashion. The sins of the fathers are not covered up by the sons. The chosen people is depicted as an ungrateful band of murmurers and rebels. The holy community of the New Testament exposes to the public the name of the traitor Judas, the hypocrisy of thieves like Ananias and Sapphira, the passionate disputes between Paul and his adversaries in Galatia and Corinth. The beloved David is a murderer and adulterer (2 Sam 11); Peter denies the Lord on the very night of the Last Supper, and his feelings are hurt when he is asked whether he loves his master (Jn 6:68–69; 21:15 ff.).

We are faced with an alternative: Either the historical and biographical parts of the Bible exhibit an unhealthy and immoral masochism, or they correspond to its didactic and hymnic sections. The latter is more plausible. Those who are describing God's judgments in the history of man accept his judgment as valid. In Luke's Gospel, the acceptance of baptism—which includes a confession of sin, the plea for forgiveness, and the prayer for the gift of the Spirit—is called an act by which God is "praised as righteous." Paul and the Book of Revelation attest that one day all men shall recognize and acknowledge the justice of God's verdict (Lk 7:29; Rom 3:4; Rev 1:7; 15:3; 19:2).

The content of God's verdict is recapitulated by Paul, who described his whole message as a disclosure of "God's righteousness." By this the apostle means, first of all, that God is faithful to himself, true to the covenant, and impartial as a judge. He is also thinking of the judicial act by which God makes right what is wrong, and of the miraculous result of God's judgment, that sinners now stand in grace before God (Rom. 1:16–17; 3:25–26; 5:1; 2 Cor 5:21). How is it that for Paul the Gospel is nothing but the good news of God's righteousness? Because he has become aware that the final verdict of God has already been passed, by means of Christ's death and resurrection. The judgment, which will be revealed to all on the last day, is proclaimed by Paul, as by the court's messenger; it has already been executed: "There is no distinction; since all have sinned and fall short of the glory of God, they are justified by his grace as a gift, through the redemption which is in Christ Jesus" (Rom 3:23–24).

The first half of this verdict is unfolded by Paul in Romans 1:18 to 3:20. This passage (especially if read together with Rom 7:7–24) appears to give expression to a pessimistic view of man, or to a negative, possibly traumatic, reaction to the law. "None is righteous, no, not one.... Whatever the law says it speaks to those who are under the law, so that every mouth may be stopped, and the whole world may be held accountable to God. For no human being will be justified in his sight by works of the law, since through the law comes knowledge of sin.... If it had not been for the law, I should not have known sin.... The very commandment which promised life proved to be death to me.... Wretched man that I am! Who will deliver me from this body of death?" (Rom 3:10, 19–20; 7:7, 10, 24) Nevertheless, the primary purpose of this section is not the unfolding of an antinomian or despairingly existentialist philosophy. Rather than present the Romans with a world view, the Apostle wants to remind them that God alone is just and that no one can escape *his* judgment (3:4, 19).

One can easily follow the various stages in which Paul explains this point. He first explains (Rom 1:18–32) that religion—i.e., the making of idols and the pretense of being wise—is the real sin against which God's wrath is kindled. What is usually called "moral sin" is not equated with "ungodliness and unrighteousness." Such things as impure desires, shameful conduct, murder, and lies are described, not as the essence of sin but as the consequences into which God "has delivered" the idolators (1:24, 26, 28–32). They are inexcusable because they disregard God's many acts of election and judgment (1:19–20, 32).

Paul then goes on to say (2:1–16) that whoever tries to escape from God's judgment by making himself a judge over his fellow man will not be safe before the throne of the one true and righteous judge (cf. Mt 7:1–5; Jas 4:11–12). The judgment of man can only condemn; it cannot also save. God, however, can and will save even Gentiles—provided he finds them doing what the law prescribes (2:14–16). The Old Testament and the Gospels give examples of such Gentiles. The Ninevites described in the Book of Jonah (and apostrophized in Lk 11:32–33; Mt 12:41) repented of their sin when they were faced with the message of God's judgment. According to Romans 2:16, God passes a gracious judgment on people like them because he accepts "things hidden to man" as grounds for acquittal, i.e., the effect of Christ's intercession, and man's regeneration by the Spirit.

Paul shows next (2:17–29) that the Jew who is prone to boast of his name (Judah means "he who praises God"; Gen 29:35), or the possession of the law, or of being circumcised, is in no way exempt from God's judgment. He would not have received the commandments unless he needed them. Nor can circumcision protect the transgressor. Only the fulfillment of the law and the circumcision of the heart are truly profitable.

In the next section (3:1–20), a series of possible objections is answered by the statement that God alone is the righteous, universal, inescapable judge; then the preceding section (1:18 ff.) is summed up in the conclusion that before him all men are nothing but total sinners. The proposition that man is evil and in hopeless condition is never advanced, but it is stated that *before the righteous God* all man's attempts at self-justification are futile.

The concluding statement of God's judgment, and its exposition, are even more surprising. The Romans are informed that the same men who were convicted of sin are "justified by his grace" (Rom 3:24; cf. 5:19; 11:32). How can God pass such a seemingly contradictory judgment? The mystery is beyond reason; interpreters of Paul may never be able to grasp more than a small part of the Apostle's argument.[10] Here we can only point out that, after Paul has said that the judgment under which man stands is not man's but God's own and exclusive judgment, he affirms that, because it is God's, it is a judgment of *grace*. He alone is a gracious judge who, by his pardon, neither repudiates righteousness nor sows inquity. To have God for a judge is to have a gracious judge; hence, to be man is to be under the judgment of grace!

The law courts of Jews and Gentiles in which Jesus Christ is tried are characterized by everything but the presence of grace; yet in his acceptance of judgment, this Man is a recipient and an example of grace. For while some men submit him to shameful mistrials, a great trial involving God and all mankind is going on. It is a lawsuit for the salvation of the guilty. Genesis 22 records a trial of Abraham's faith; he had to obey by offering his son, and God proved faithful to him. 1 Kings 18 describes another trial in which God proved faithful; he did not forsake his servant Elijah and his people. In the trial of Jesus Christ,[11] God himself sacrifices his only Son for the benefit of enemies, and the Son obeys by interceding for sinful mankind, even to the end (Jn 17; Heb 4:14 ff.; 7–10; Lk 23:34; Rom 3:25). Jesus accepts both God's and man's judgment in order that God's grace to man shall triumph. "By one man's obedience . . . where sin increased, grace abounded all the more, so that, as sin reigned in death, grace also might reign through righteousness to eternal life through Jesus Christ our Lord" (Rom 5:19–21).

To be human, therefore, is to live under the judgment of grace. But such a conviction is quite different from the view of an optimistic secular humanism. The triumph of grace is proclaimed exclusively on the basis of one specific historic event—Christ's death and resurrection (Rom 4:25; 8:29). This grace is not cheaply won, nor is it at man's disposal, for it is given by God alone. In addition, to be judged by grace is both far more humiliating and more effective than to be judged by a legal standard or an abstract principle. Man finds a way to feel secure and proud even when confronted with the demands of law, but "God's kindness is meant to lead you to repentance" (Rom 2:4). A father's arms, open wide to receive his erring child, help us to see our confidence in our abilities or our claims of good intentions for what they are; we can no longer boast of our good works (Lk 15:11–32). In both prophetic and Pauline teaching (Is 63:7–16; Rom 8), God's righteousness is displayed, repentance bears fruit, and man's condition is most truly described when God is honored as man's *Father*. To live under God's judgment is to live under the chastisement of a father whose love never fades (cf. 2 Sam 7:14–15).

Is such an existence under the judgment of grace preached only in the Bible? Modern existentialist writers[12] know that to exist is to be under judgment and to accept suffering. Socrates, as Plato remembered—and the Stoics imitated him—accepted his judges and their verdict without seeking escape by suicide, bribe, or subterfuge. Mahayana Buddhism proclaims Buddha the compassionate, and teaches man to yield to grace that bears all things and abundantly fills the needs of suffering humanity. The Oriental Wisdom tradition was drawn upon in the writing of the Old

Testament Wisdom literature, and quotations from Greek writers are incorporated in Paul's dicta (Acts 17:28; Tit 1:12).

It is obvious, therefore, that the biblical statements about man are not original and unique. After all, they speak of the God who brings peace to those near and far, who is the God not only of the Jews but also of the Gentiles (Eph 2:13–22; Mt 5:45; Rom 3:30). And the man whom Christ represented and prayed for is not only he who already confesses his faith in the triune God. "One has died for all; therefore all have died. . . . God . . . desires all men to be saved and to come to the knowledge of the truth. . . . At the name of Jesus every knee should bow . . . and every tongue confess" (2 Cor 5:14; 1 Tim 2:4; Phil 2:10–11). The Old Testament is ready to acknowledge the wisdom of the Midianite Jethro (Moses' father-in-law), the search for righteousness of Cyrus, the Persian, the patience of the stranger Job. And Paul commands his brethren in Philippi to ponder *all* that is true, honorable, just, virtuous, and laudable—not merely his own words or those of other Jews and Christians (Ex 18; Is 45; Ezek 14:14, 20; Phil 4:8–9).

Nevertheless, the difference between the Bible's anthropological statements and those of nonbiblical wisdom cannot be overlooked. The Bible deals only marginally with the general problem of suffering or of existence. Ideas of the good or the true are neither sought nor discussed. When, for Jeremiah or Paul, or for the whole congregation, the pain of existence becomes a problem, suffering is presented as a participation in God's suffering by and for man (Jer 12:7–12; Is 53:9; Col 1:24; 1 Pet 4:12 ff.), or as suffering borne in solidarity by a people that has deserved punishment (Ex 32:30–32; Lam; Is 53; Mt 3:15; Rom 9:3; 1 Pet 3:18; Rev 6:9–11). In either case, suffering is a ministerial function and necessity rather than a problem of individual existence whose solution might be derived from an ontological principle, or a psychological, intellectual, or emotional adjustment. Biblical man is bound to specific manifestations of God in history; he finds himself confronted by a God who acts faithfully and effectively. Man's life and death through God's judgment are not a fate to be borne in solitude and for an unknown purpose; they are an appointment, a suffering, a dying, and a rising with Jesus Christ (Rom 6:5–11; 14:7–9; 2 Cor 5:14; Col 3:1–4).

v *The Jew*

It is also important to understand that participation in Christ's life and death implies participation in the specific history that shaped and was shaped by Israel. The man of whom Pontius Pilate said, "Here is the man," is a Jew. Whether in mockery or in earnest, he is executed as "King of the Jews"; he is made to pay dearly for belonging to the Jewish people and representing all that distinguishes them from the nations of the world. Biblical writers are aware that non-Jews feel the distinctiveness of the Jewish people living in their midst (Ex 1:10; Num 23:9; Esther 3:8; Dan 3:10). In most cases this sensitivity is born of, or leads to, hatred, persecution, or so-called anti-Semitism. The reasons given include Israel's service to a God unlike the Gentile gods, and their alien laws.

But not only Gentiles feel the difference. The Bible also describes the high destiny and the pride of the chosen people. Jews and Christians consider it a privilege to be God's elected men, to be given covenant, commandments, and promises. "You are a chosen race, a royal priesthood, a holy nation, God's own people, that you may declare the wonderful deeds of him who called you. . . . Aliens shall stand and feed your flocks, foreigners shall be your plowmen and vinedressers . . . you shall eat the wealth of the nations. . . . What advantage has the Jew? . . . Much in every way" (1 Pet 2:9; Is 61:5–9; Rom 3:1–2; 9:4). The Bible also provides evidence that Jews themselves resented being different. At times they would prefer to be "like all the nations"; even some of their kings condone or instigate worship of foreign gods. As for Christians, though they may be called the "Israel of God," they, too, have to be warned not to do as the world does. All this is true not only of the common people, but of distinguished leaders as well. The prophet Elijah complains bitterly about his lonely mission, Jeremiah is near despair, and Jonah tries to obstruct the ministry entrusted to him. The chosen people and the special messengers of God are victims of their election, and struggle against it. The second Isaiah describes how everyone resents the Lord's servant; and Paul, the Jew, joins ranks with Jesus and with the Hellenist Stephen when he describes the Jews as a people who murder God's prophets and incur God's wrath (1 Sam 8:5, 7, 19–20; both Books of Kings; Amos; Hos; Gal 6:16; Rom 12:2; 1 Kings 19:3–4, 10; Jer 20:7–18; Jon; Is 52:13–53:12; Mt 21:33–41; 22:1–7; 23:37–38; Acts 7; 1 Thess 2:14–16). No pagan anti-Semitic outbursts can be as lacerating as what Jew inflicts upon Jew.

Now Jesus, the Man, is a Jew. And the Bible invites all men to recognize that every man, whether Jew or Gentile, is represented by this Jew, Jesus. What does this mean? According to the Bible, the essence of a Jew (as the etymology of this name, and the repeated statements of Moses, the prophets, Jesus, and the apostles indicate) is to be elected for the "praise of God" among the Gentiles. What does this "praise" look like in real life?

The Bible answers that to be man in the image of the Jew is to be chosen to have one's sin uncovered and to praise God, the loving father, even when he shows his love by chastisement (Prov 13:1, 24; Heb 12:6–7). This seems a dire election; natural man will not like it, but God's man experiences it. A morally enlightened man might well accept the necessity that sin deserves to be unmasked, and that such punishment is to the advantage of the evildoer that he may turn to religion and learn from it. But the man whom God has elected cannot even take flight into religion! The passionate Mosaic and prophetic outbursts against Israel's idolatry go far beyond the invective hurled at Gentile religions. Not only Jerusalem but even God's Temple is repeatedly destroyed. Jesus and Paul, the Fourth Gospel and Stephen, and finally, the Letter to the Hebrews are indicting the very laws and traditional ceremonies of Israel.

In such utterances we see the real weight of man's sin. Where he presumed to find refuge in religion, his sin is shown to be the worst rebellion, a deliberate deafness to God's word. To be man in the image of the Jew means to be exposed as a *religious* criminal against God. "Against thee, thee only, have I sinned. . . . Behold, I was brought forth in iniquity, and in sin did my mother conceive me. . . . Let us lie down in our shame, and let our dishonor cover us; for we have sinned against the Lord our God, we and our fathers, from our youth even to this day. . . . Alas, this people have sinned a great sin" (Ps 51:4, 5; Jer 3:25; Ex 32:31). A Jew has to "praise God" by such confessions! If the Jew Jesus cannot be convicted of any sin (Mt 26:59–60; Jn 8:46; 18:38; 19:4, 6; 2 Cor 5:21), nevertheless, he is sent by God and he is willing to take the place of, and to receive the treatment of a sinner. Hence the Jew stands as a sinner before God and his fellow man. Even if he is relatively innocent, as is asserted of Noah, Daniel, and Job (Ezek 14:14, 20), even if he is fully obedient as only Jesus Christ is, his character and function are to represent sinners.

In addition, the Jew is the man who, before, during, and after his sinning, is destined to be a witness to God's reign and his goodness to all men. "You are my witnesses. . . . I have given you as a covenant to the people, a light to the nations, to open the eyes that are blind . . . that my salvation shall reach to the end of the earth" (Is 43:12; 42:6; 49:6; Acts 1:8). God has not only granted his people a covenant, but since Abraham's days they have been blessed in order that through them "all the families of the earth shall bless themselves" (Gen 12:1–3). Israel is redeemed from Egypt, and again from Babylonian captivity, in order that all neighboring nations may see what God is able to perform (Ex 1 ff.; Is 40 ff.). In Daniel 1–6 and Jonah we see that the privilege of Israel, whether represented by obedient or disobedient servants of God, is to lead Gentiles to repentance. The calling of Jesus' disciples and the conversion of Paul are events by which these men were equipped for their ministry as witnesses to others.

Neither Israel nor Christianity has always been aware that the election, justification, and salvation of a sinner means an immediate commitment to a ministry. Between the sinful original state and the later act of obedience there is no room for "individual experience" or "personal salvation." Just as grace and apostolate are one and the same for Paul (Acts 9:15; 22:14–15; 26:16–18; Rom 1:5; Phil 1:12), so to be a Jew is to be made a public singer of God's grace. There is no election except for service.

This is what Paul calls God's "justification of the sinner": He sets apart, he convicts, he acquits, he commissions, he makes a sinful man ready to be, despite his sins, a herald of overflowing grace to all men. Paul explains how sinners of Gentile origin were joined to the commonwealth of sinful Israel for the purpose of showing "to [in] the coming ages" the "immeasurable riches of [God's] grace" (Eph 2:7). He applies this to himself: "Necessity is laid upon me. Woe to me, if I do not preach the gospel!" (1 Cor 9:16)

While all Jews are given this ministry, the Jew Jesus is the only man who truly fulfills it. He does not seek his own benefit; he gives himself totally to others. By sending his obedient Son, God calls all men to recognize that the service of God is the only true human existence. God will not leave unrewarded those who follow Jesus' footsteps, giving up life and security in order to give witness to others.

To be a Jew, and therefore to be represented by Jesus, means to be a type, or example, of God's will for man. It means to serve unselfishly in the historical place assigned by God, as a model for other men.

Jewish history is earthly history; it is not a mythical ideal. The Jew's commission concerns men on earth. It does not reach out into a realm beyond history. Jewish historiography and prophetic speech (in both Old and New Testaments) describe events of the past and recall them to a new generation. This is not done out of antiquarian concern, but to demonstrate that what God has done and said to men of the past, and what, in turn, men have experienced or performed, is still valid. The past is treated as a precedent.

However, the exemplary character of the past is not exploited in a narrow, legalistic sense. Not every author refers to every past event! Only as the Spirit—or necessity, or intuition—moves them do the biblical writers appeal to particulars of the past and state: This happened "typically." That man is "a type." When they speak of the present, they are also aware that they themselves and their history may serve as "types." This is stated explicitly by Paul (1 Cor 10:11; Rom 5:14; 6:17; Phil 3:17; 1 Tim 1:16), and it is implicitly found not only in the typological interpretations of the Old Testament which occur in the New Testament but also in the Old Testament itself—for example, when the former covenant, or the appointment of a king or prophet, is made a means to announce a new covenant or a coming savior.

In his historic existence and experience, the Jew has been an exemplar to people near and far. Instead of finding meaning in the transhistorical existence of an absolute spirit or a set of abstract principles, the Jew is what his history is. This history includes God's revelation to the forefathers, God's action among and through the Gentiles in the present, and God's promise to Jews and Gentiles, which is to be fulfilled in the future. That God makes, shapes, judges, and uses his history, that God is with him ("Immanuel," Is 7:14) even in the darkness and ambiguity of events, is enough for the Jew. Upon this he lives. Because of this he cannot be destroyed. Similarly, it was enough for Jesus Christ to be incarnate once, at Christmas, for good and all. He did not have to deny the limitations and relativity of history in order to be God's man for the benefit of all. "I thank thee, Father . . . yea, Father, for such was thy gracious will. . . . I glorified thee on earth. . . . It is finished" (Mt 11:25–26; Jn 17:4; 19:30).

This acceptance of history by the Jew permanently upsets many mythical notions concerning man's nature and destiny. Men have held, for example, that the original, or real man (e.g., the King, Ezek 28; or Adam, Gen 3:4), is equal to God or is God himself; that man is ultimately alone and should be left alone, or at least spared the temptations he likes to ascribe to his carnal female partner;[13] and that man is left to make his own choices, like Hercules at the crossroads, or is left with his own pride and punishment, like Daedalus, Prometheus, or Sisyphus. Related mythical ideas present man as a composite of the ideal and the material, who should save his soul from the tomb of the body; or as hopelessly exposed to principalities and powers, to *Zeitgeist* and tradition, to his libido or environment, to causality, evolution, or fatal destiny—without any effective help at the right time. If this attitude is accepted, it follows that man has to live as an enemy to other men and that his heroic or catastrophic fate is nothing but a constant sense of dread and a tragic death.

Each of these mythical notions has repeatedly found new representations in religious, cultic actions, and in corresponding secular cultural patterns. The Jew's call, however, is to be a man who lives in the conviction that God is with him, that God has sent him, that God does not forsake him. The Jew Jesus Christ, who lives in and from the reality of "God with us," is the supreme realist. The Bible makes it clear that Pontius Pilate, the Jewish officials, and Jesus' disciples did not like his sort of humanity. Biblical anthropology does not claim that it has been, is, or will be popular with Jews or Gentiles; it affirms that through Jesus the true image of God and type of man is established, revealed, and realized.

At all times the Jew had to go—and is going—the way on which God has sent him. He stumbles, but is given power to rise again. He suffers, but not for himself only, for he bears his suffering with God and for others. He seems to belong to the past, but God's Spirit keeps him alive and distinguishes him as a Jew throughout the centuries. God's promises point out his future. To be human means to be aware of the existence and history of the Jews; it means to be called—and to call others—through ridicule and persecution, to the glory of God. Anti-Semitism in forgetting the words of Jesus, that for all men "salvation is from the Jews" (Jn 4:22), denies that humanity which is set forth by the biblical testimony of man.

VI *The Free Man*

We have seen that man's commission is to live without resentment in the limited time given to him, to learn from earlier history about the present and future history of God and man, and to be a proof of its continuity. The election for this ministry is an election to freedom and joy. If God calls man by name and claims him for himself, then all bondages that have held man captive to powers other than God are like feathers and burnt strings.

But there is another vital and amazing characteristic of biblical man. He is free to be different from God and his fellow man! He need not fit into any kind of uniform. Even when he is urged to "put on Christ," or "the new man," or "the whole armor of God" (Gal 3:27; Eph 4:24; 6:10 ff.), he is not asked to accept a yoke of conformity; rather he is invited to enjoy the freedom to live, to struggle, and to suffer as a child of God under the conditions in which he finds himself. He is delivered from the slavery of Egypt and of sin and death in order that he may exercise his freedom (Gal 4–6; Rom 6:12 ff.; 1 Cor 7:21–23). If he is still called a servant and admonished to serve with enthusiasm (Rom 1:1; Eph 6:5–8), this is because it is a privilege and a joy to serve that Lord who is the supreme liberator under any historic condition.

The freedom for which man is liberated (Gal 5:1; Rom 6:18) has nothing in common with a libertinism which would by-pass the commandments given by God to his redeemed people. But which commandments will the redeemed man keep? How will he keep them?

Rabbinical interpreters of the Old Testament have enumerated 613 commandments to be kept. This may look like a heavy burden —but they considered it a privilege to know God's will. The Old Testament books of the Law contain, among other ancient materials, the ten cultic and moral commandments (Ex 20; 34:11 ff.; Deut 5). The radical, apodictic commandments, beginning with the words, "Thou shalt not . . .," are augmented by a collection of casuistic statements or precedential judgments that begins with the words, "When a man . . ." (as found in Ex 21–23). In the later half of the eighth century before Christ, the prophet Micah fought ceremonialism and promoted ethical teaching by recapitulating the will of God under three headings. "He has showed you, O man, what is good; and what does the Lord require of you but to do justice, and to love kindness, and to walk humbly with your God?" (Mic 6:8) Habakkuk (after 586 B.C.) reduces the description of the righteous man's life to one feature only: "The righteous shall live by his [Greek text: by God's] faith" (Hab 2:4). Jesus speaks of the love of God and the love of neighbor; he states that these two commandments are the hinges or pegs on which "hang" the whole Law and the Prophets (Mt 22:34–40). The Gospel and First Letter of John concur with this summary. Paul quotes Habakkuk to show that all depends on faith; but he also feels free to mention faith, hope, and love together and to give love the supreme place (Rom 1:17; 13:10; 1 Cor 13). To give witness to the word of God and the testimony of Christ, even at the expense of suffering martyrdom, is, according to both the Revelation to John and 1 Peter (cf. Mt 10:39; 24:9), the sign of true life.

The narrative material of the Bible shows that, despite different experiences, settings, and temperaments, throughout the history of Israel there lived men who accepted their election by God. Despite their natural inclination to hate God and their fellow man, Abraham and Moses, Jeremiah and Jonah, Peter, Paul, and many others were freed, and therefore were free to love their enemies, to treat brothers and foreigners with equal justice, to pray and work and hope for the conversion of the evildoer. The freedom of those chosen becomes apparent when a forfeited life is saved; when help is given to the helpless; when reconciliation begins to prevail among those formerly estranged; when intercession is made for rulers and those ruled; when obedience flows from the heart rather than from slavish fear; when devotion and faith are maintained even at the cost of great suffering.

Biblical descriptions of the conduct of a child of God are quite different from what is found in pious biographies or moral handbooks. They are too specific, and apparently contradictory, to be literally and legalistically applicable to the solution of the moral problems of later times. If ethical decisions could be justified merely by reference to a specific text (see Ps 137:9; Jer 38:2; Lk 14:25), murder, treason, and hatred of parents might seem permissible! On the other hand, the Bible's exhortations are too general and open-ended to permit a casuistic exploitation. "All are yours. . . . All things are lawful. . . . I am free from all men. . . . I have become all things to all men" (1 Cor 3:22–23; 6:12; 9:19–22). Not even a magician can make such glorious words serve moral conformism and ritual punctiliousness. They preclude the construction of a code of either Hebrew or Christian ideal behavior, or a set of Hebrew-Christian principles, middle axioms, or values from which, on each given occasion, the right decision for a man of God might be derived. The faith and obedience of a free man cannot be legislated; it is a new miracle each time a man is prepared by his conduct to become a witness of God's good will toward all men. The Bible affirms that to be human means to be chosen for the experience of this miracle of freedom.

Jesus Christ is the man who fulfills the Law and the Prophets by a free choice. He knows that it is "fitting for us to fulfill all righteousness"; and God immediately shows his approval of him: "This is my beloved Son" (Mt 3:13–17; 5:17; 17:5). Whether Jesus turns to God the Father in prayer and in the sacrifice of his life, or whether he gives himself in word and deed to his fellow men, he is the bringer and the inspiring proof of freedom. "If the Son makes you free, you will be free indeed. . . . For freedom Christ has set us free" (Jn 8:36; Gal 5:1).

The life he leads, and to which he calls us, is eternal. This must be understood as a qualitative description of life, rather than as a promise of quantitative extension. Eternal life is a life that participates in God's own life. When asked by a rich man what men must do to inherit eternal life, Jesus first affirms God's commandments, and then points to the one thing that is missing: readiness to give up all his possessions and follow Him. Such conduct may look impracticable to a man rich in heritage and success—or in works of obedience; it may also look too extreme to those disciples of Jesus who are not rich. But Jesus proclaims that God is strong enough to bring it to pass (Mk 10:17–27).

This story of the rich young ruler shows that the most exact obedience is not enough to make a man free. It is in the intimate attachment to Jesus Christ, and his willingness to follow Him, not in a submission to principles or high purposes, that man accomplishes God's will. On another occasion people asked, "What must we do, to be doing the works of God?" Jesus answered them, "This is the work of God, that you believe in him whom he has sent" (Jn 6:28–29). He who has God for a father, Jesus Christ for his brother, and the Spirit in his heart, "perceives" the "perfect law, the law of liberty, and perseveres" (Jas 1:25; 2:8, 12; cf. Rom 8:2). There is no knowledge of God which is separate from awareness of his will or from the commission he gives his servants and children, here and now. To know God means to know what to do. When a man ignores God, his blundering steps will lead him into the abyss, as is seen in the lives of King Saul and the disciple Judas (1 Sam 28:31; Mt 26–27; Acts 1:16–19). For the man of God, the bond of faith by which he is tied to God in heaven is also the rein that lets him find, step by step, the right path on earth. Jesus Christ calls his yoke easy, and his burden light (Mt 11:29–30).

God created man for freedom; he had no use for an impeccable machine, since he wanted a partner who would respond with voluntary love and show cordial affection for his fellow men. This involved the risk of man's disobedience, and God endured man's sin until the time of redemption. God's continued preference for trust rather than mechanical obedience gave such long reins to man that the freedom brought by Jesus Christ was misused by some and transformed into libertinism. "The dog turns back to his own vomit, and the sow is washed only to wallow in the mire" (2 Pet 2:22). The Letters to the Corinthians and Galatians, the Letter of Jude, and the letters found in Revelation 2 and 3 give disgusting pictures of the worship and conduct of lascivious Christians. But *abusus non tollit usum*. According to the biblical teaching on man, God would rather grant forgiveness than refuse to let man make his own decisions. The Father even allows his Son to endure estrangement and misery in order to receive him again in grace (Lk 15:11–32). "The Lord is the Spirit, and where the Spirit of the Lord is, there is freedom. . . . Beholding the glory of the Lord [we] are being changed into his likeness from one degree of glory to another; for this comes from the Lord who is the Spirit" (2 Cor 3:17–18). The freedom for which Christ has liberated man is found only in grateful response to God and faithful witness before men. It is freedom to reflect God's own freedom.

It is obvious that each of the elements of biblical anthropology was and is dependent upon theology. It is equally clear that all that is said about man is actually an elucidation of statements made in the Bible about God. Despite his sin, man is no obstacle to God. Unlike some Greek gods, the God of Abraham, the Father of Jesus Christ, is not jealous of man's bliss or success. He cares for man. To be man is to be cared for by God himself; "For his glory and our salvation," man was created.

CHAPTER II

THE EVIDENCE OF FREEDOM

The Manifold Testimony

1 *The Scandal of Contradictions*

The biblical testimony to God is borne by means of different human witnesses. Their variety is perplexing. But since the Bible is written in a wide range of literary styles covering a long period of time, the variety is natural. This book has not fallen from heaven. Even within the same author's works, different steps of development are recognizable. Indeed, contradictions may be found in different authors and parts of the Bible in regard to narrative, exhortatory, and doctrinal elements. For example, Genesis 1 tells of the simultaneous creation of man and woman; Genesis 2 of their successive creation. After the exile it is ridiculous to build a temple, says one prophet (Is 66). Another prophet, perhaps during the same period, scolds Israel for not building a temple (Hag 1). In John 2:13–16, Jesus cleansed the temple of those selling sacrificial animals at the beginning of his public career, but according to Mark 11:15–18, he took the same revolutionary step only shortly before his trial and execution. The apostle Paul refers to Abraham as an illustration of justification by faith alone (Rom 4; Gal 3:6–9), but James teaches that Abraham was justified by works and that all Christians have to do the works of Abraham (Jas 2:14–26). In John 8:37–59, a still different interpretation of the Abraham stories is found. Although some of the sayings of Jesus found in the Gospels indicate that his second coming will occur in the days of this generation (Mk 9:1; Mt 10:23; 26:29; cf. 1 Thess 4:13–14), there are parables in the same Gospels, and didactic utterances in the Epistles, in which a lengthy delay of this parousia is anticipated (Mt 25:5; Mk 13:33–37; Acts 1:7; 2 Pet 3:8–10; Phil 1:19–23).

Such contradictions are so numerous and significant that they are embarrassing to the reader of the Bible. They concern not only names and dates, but the very substance of God's saving action. Should they simply be ignored? A careful student of the Bible will be unwilling to disregard them. Could the contradictions be ascribed to the errors of negligent scribes or copyists? Of course, errors may have been made—though pains were taken to avoid them—but the contradictions are not the product of single words and sentences alone; they are supported by whole chapters and books. Should the contradictions be ascribed to interpolations made by individuals or sectarian groups? Even if redactors substantially altered the text of the Bible, their revisions obviously enjoyed the approbation of either the people as a whole or their religious leaders. The texts containing contradictions were obviously considered canonical by the orthodox majority! Finally, should the variations found in the treatment of the same topic, and their mutual exclusiveness be regarded simply as evidence of the *human* element in the Bible? Should only those statements that are uncontradicted be considered the infallible word of God?

Indeed, there are passages in which biblical writers explicitly state that they "speak in a human way," give their own "opinion," or display their learning (Rom 3:5; 6:19; 1 Cor 7:6, 25, 40; Lk 1:1–4). But no one can be blind to the fact that on all pages of the Bible, and not only on some, the message of God to man, the prayer of man to God, and the preaching in God's name are presented in a human way. It might even be said that it is precisely in their human way of speaking that the biblical writers are consistent, and that the humanity of the Bible does not necessarily involve contradiction. On the other hand, when biblical authors refer to oracles of God and speak in his name, we become aware of tensions and contrasts found in God's own words and actions!

Consider some Old Testament statements concerning God's ability or willingness to repent. In Numbers 23:19; 1 Samuel 15:29; Psalm 110:4; Jeremiah 4:28; 20:16; Zechariah 8:14 (cf. Heb 7:21; Rom 11:29); and Ezekiel 24:14, it is stated that God cannot repent—since he is not man—or will not repent. Either a specific decision or an oath which he made is given as the reason for his faithfulness to his decision and word. But if God will not repent in specific circumstances, other circumstances may move him to change his decision. According to Exodus 32:14; 2 Samuel 24:16; 1 Chronicles 21:15; Psalm 106:45; Jeremiah 18:8; 26:3, 13, 19; 42:10; Joel 2:13; Amos 7:3, 6; and Jonah 3:10, God actually repents of the punishment he threatened to send his people. The stubborn prophet Jonah is deeply dissatisfied with this. He feels that if a man serves a God who repents, he is bound to be cheated and ridiculed (Jn 4:2–4, 9). It is even more disconcerting when the Bible states that God sometimes also repents of the good he has done or promised (Gen 6:6–7; 1 Sam 15:11, 35; Jer 18:10).

Therefore, the tensions and contradictions found in the Bible need not be due simply to human error. The Bible tells the deeds of the living God, not of an immutable highest principle. Consequently, the writers of the Bible present reports that are as different from—and as contradictory to—one another, as are the various acts and words of God. If the records had been streamlined to eliminate contradiction, they would not be faithful to the *living* God!

To acknowledge the unsystematic and manifold character of the Bible means to admit that no one single theology or anthropology can be derived from the Bible. What is called "doctrine" in the Bible (as in Jer 18:18; Rom 6:17; 2 Jn 9; Heb 6:1–2; 1 Tim 1:10; 4:6) is never a closed system. The New Testament brands such systems as heretical or pagan (Heb 13:9; Rev 2:14–15; Col 2; 1 Tim 6:20–21). According to the Bible, "doctrine" is what Halakah is in rabbinical instruction: the act of pointing men toward the way of the Lord, and practical help in walking in that direction.

The announcement of the good news of God's presence and help,[14] biblical preaching, is always practical advice about "the way" or "the ways of the Lord" (Gen 18:19; Ex 13:21; Deut 5:30; Ps 51:13; Is 2:3; 40:3; Jer 5:4–5; Mal 3:1; Lk 3:3 ff.; Mt 21:32; Acts 2:28; 16:17; 18:26, etc.). The Bible renders its readers a service "profitable for teaching" (2 Tim 3:16) by recording the many ways (Heb 1:1) in which God, by word and deed, has acted upon man, and in which men have found God, or have deviated from him. No doubt God's ways with man have cause and purpose, order and meaning. However, unless the length, the variety, even the steepness, narrowness, and cumbersomeness of that way is seen and accepted, it cannot be followed (Mt 7:13–14).

The existence of biblical variations and contradictions has to be accepted as a fact, even if it looks like a scandalous fact. But the question we now have to ask is how such widely different books as the sixty-six books that form the Bible, and such obviously distinct affirmations as are found in them, could be understood as a unit and still be respected as the source of doctrine and the norm of conduct?

II *The Character of a Witness*

There are many signposts indicating directions for the man who wants to find the way to the city, but signposts vary as to height, readability, and state of preservation. One sign may be worm-eaten while another has golden letters engraved in Carrara marble. Travelers will read them with different emotions, and people will never agree on which is the most useful or beautiful. They stand at their assigned places, pointing out the right way; they were made to be read and followed, and many find them useful. But they would be contradictory and purposeless if they were turned in a different direction, or if they were uprooted, piled up at random, and stored in a barn or museum.

The purpose and usefulness of the various parts of the Bible resemble the role of signposts.[15] When we take note of them, just where they stand, despite their variable state of repair, they encourage us to proceed to the next sign, and finally to the journey's end. Their number and distribution allows people coming from different directions to meet at the same place. Thus the variety in age, place, clarity, and direction of the biblical books need *not* be the expression of a hopeless confusion. The divergent statements they make need not be senseless contradictions. When they are read with due regard for their historical, geographical, and functional origin; when their proven effectiveness is tested—and perhaps also trusted—they may still perform their service.

The New Testament states the conviction that the words of the Old Testament could fulfill their function in the time after Jesus Christ's coming just as well as, if not better than among past generations. "For good news came to us just as to them; but the message which they heard did not benefit them, because it did not meet with faith in the hearers. . . . The word of God is living. . . . Today, when you hear his voice, do not harden your hearts" (Heb 4:2, 7, 12). The context (Heb 3:7 to 4:13) of these statements offers a beautiful illustration of how an unknown Christian teacher of the second half of the first century A.D. reads seemingly contradictory biblical texts and discovers their underlying unity. He understands them as different pointers on the path where God's people finds itself. Paul emphasizes that the words written about Abraham "were not written for his sake alone, but for ours also" (Rom 4:23–24). Since the events to which he refers concern Abraham and his posterity—the extension of Abraham's blessing over "many Gentiles"—Paul assumes that the Christian Gentiles whom he addresses in Rome (together with their Jewish-Christian brethren) are addressed by the biblical text. Since the Bible treats of their blessing, they can only profit by heeding its words. Paul states: "Whatever was written in former days was written for our instruction, that by steadfastness and by the encouragement of the scriptures we might have hope. . . . For it is written in the law of Moses. . . . These things [i.e., the ancient events narrated in the Bible] happened to them as a warning, but they were written down for our instruction, upon whom the end of the ages has come" (Rom 15:4; 1 Cor 9:9–10; 10:6, 11). A counsel given to the Bishop of Ephesus is also relevant here: "The sacred writings . . . are able to instruct you for salvation through faith in Christ Jesus. All Scripture is inspired by God and profitable for teaching, for reproof, for correction, and for training in righteousness, that the man of God may be complete, equipped for every good work" (2 Tim 3:15–16). This helps us recall the utilitarian character of the Bible; it is considered "useful" in equipping its hearers and readers with examples and directions that can keep them on the right path.

The simile of the signposts brings us close to the meaning of the Hebrew term *torah* and the Greek *dike*. *Torah* means law, *dike* means right, or order. What is the essence of law and order when the etymology of the Hebrew and Greek terms is taken seriously? *Torah* is derived from the root *jrh,* which means to direct, to point, and also to teach. *Dike* is a derivative of *deiknumi,* to show. Hebrews and Greeks agreed in considering the given law and the valid order as pointers that give direction and deserve the respect due to helpful instruments.

But the Bible itself does not elaborate on such a comparison. It has a better way of explaining that, although it contains many voices, they are related in different ways to one subject. Awareness of the variety of the voices of God's servants is most clearly expressed by the term "witness." In Israel's courts, as in most civilized courts, all grave matters require the presence and evidence of at least two, and possibly more, witnesses (Num 35:30; Deut 17:6; 19:15; Mt 18:16; 2 Cor 13:1; 1 Tim 5:19). The only natural witness of God, and the safest witness of all human affairs, is God himself (Job 5:32; Heb 7:17; 11:4; Gen 31:50); in addition, Jesus Christ is called "the faithful witness" (Rev 1:5; 3:14), and the Holy Spirit's function is to give witness (Jn 15:26). Inanimate things—a stone, or a heap or circle of stones, or an altar (Gen 31:48, 52; Josh 22:27; 24:27; 1 Sam 6:18)—but also heaven and earth (Deut 4:26), or a song (Deut 31:19)—may be considered witnesses. But most frequently the term "witness" is used to designate God's chosen men. "You are my witnesses" (Is 43:10, 12; 44:8; Acts 1:8, 22, 32; 1 Jn 1:1–4).

It is the task of the witness to give a faithful and convincing account of all he saw and heard at a certain moment. God's biblical witnesses give testimony to specific mighty acts which have been performed once in God's history with his people, but which must be made known to many because of their universal and perennial relevance. Whenever hints are given about the occasion and place where witness is to be given, a court situation seems to be presupposed. It may be God's own court, in which he acts as judge, and where his righteousness will be revealed and applauded. Or it may be a human court, in which an earthly judge and the people he rules are to pass judgment on events that have taken place and make decisions appropriate to their character and relevance. Scenes of God's lawsuit with man are described in Psalm 82; Isaiah 3:13–15; Micah 8:1–8; Jeremiah 2:4–13; and Isaiah 41:21–29; 44:5 ff. The position taken by God's servants before all manner of tribunals is most extensively narrated in the Book of Acts. There also exists in the Bible a series of important stories in which the divine and human lawsuits run concomitantly and cannot be separated. The sacrifice of Isaac by Abraham, the decision made on Mount Carmel, the Sacrifice of Jealousy, the trial and resurrection of Jesus, and the defense of the apostles before rulers and kings (Gen 22; 1 Kings 18; Num 5; Mk 14–16; Acts) should be mentioned as examples. In no case does the lawsuit take place without witnesses.

According to the Bible, God himself has appointed his chosen men to be his witnesses. In God's name they give testimony to the things which they saw happen. Virtually all men, at all times, are exposed to the voices of those witnesses. God's people, as well as the Gentiles, have to hear them. The Letter to the Hebrews speaks of a "cloud of witnesses" that "surrounds" us (12:1). In the Old Testament, the liberation from Egypt, the Babylonian exile, and the repatriation of Israel make the Gentiles realize Israel's function as a witness. According to the New Testament, the apostles are sent from Jerusalem to the ends of the earth because they are eyewitnesses, and Paul hurried through Asian and European cities to reach Rome for the same reason (Acts 1:8, 9, 12; 1 Cor 9:1). In Luke 10:1, Jesus sends out his disciples two by two; Acts describes the joint operation of the apostles Peter and John; Paul does not like to write his letters in his own name alone but prefers to mention coauthors; Revelation 11 describes the fall and rise of two witnesses.

Differences among the testimonies given are the result of the word of several witnesses who, on different occasions, attest to various great acts of God. The witnesses' utterances would be suspect if they contained unified presentations rather than highly individual ones. No two witnesses will describe the same event in exactly the same fashion. If their statements differ, the witnesses need not be liars. Even if angels could be called to the witness stand, their testimony might vary, since, according to 1 Peter 1:12, they do not possess knowledge of all hidden things. At any rate, if God wanted his acts to be retold and interpreted by persons rather than by recording machines, the risk of contradiction was not to be avoided. The Bible asserts that God wants a free, though perhaps fallible response rather than a mechanical repetition. The heavens, the stars, and the sun bear testimony to God's glory in their own way, which never errs; it is the privilege of man that, despite his fallibility, he is made a personal witness of God's work.

Therefore, it is not man's fault, but God's pleasure which brings into existence the variety of biblical voices. God wants many witnesses! The differences in their testimony look scandalous to man—but not to God. What both Testaments, but especially the New Testament, affirm must now be repeated: God is not the One who speaks only words of law or promise, of covenant or judgment, from Sinai or from heaven; neither does God speak on earth exclusively through Jesus Christ, whose words are words of perfect faith and obedience to both God and man. God is also the One who, through the Spirit's operation, causes different men, in different ways, to offer their prayers, to proclaim God's will, to be his witnesses to men.

"Filled with the Holy Spirit," the first witnesses are preaching and praying in forms that are far from uniform or stereotyped (Acts 4:8, 31; 6:3, etc.).

When they bring you before the synagogues and the rulers and the authorities, do not be anxious how or what you are to answer or what you are to say; for the Holy Spirit will teach you in that very hour what you ought to say. . . . We impart this in words not taught by human wisdom but taught by the Spirit. . . . No one can say 'Jesus is Lord' except by the Holy Spirit. . . . To each is given the manifestation of the Spirit for the common good. . . . Grace was given to each of us according to the measure of Christ's gift (Lk 12:11–12; Mk 13:11; 1 Cor 2:13; 12:3–4, 7; Eph 4:7).

The witness given through the Spirit's inspiration may sound like the babble of drunkards or madmen (Acts 2:13, 15; 26:24; 1 Cor 14:23; cf. 1 Sam 10:10–12); not even fellow Christians may always consider it edifying (1 Cor 14), and the Christians in Ephesus are warned not to substitute drunkenness for inspiration (Eph 4:18). The fact remains that, in the Bible, the diversity of the witnesses' statements is ascribed to the Holy Spirit.

A complete description of this "cloud of witnesses" cannot be given, but at least some of its features will be enumerated.

III *The Many Witnesses*

1) Different periods can be discerned in the history of God and man. There is the *Urgeschichte,* which cannot be dated; the time of the patriarchs (beginning with the eighteenth century before Christ?); the Exodus-Sinai migration period (thirteenth century B.C.); the slow conquest of the land (*ca.* 1250 B.C.); the troublesome period leading up to the beginning of the monarchy (1200–1000 B.C.); the period of Judah's and Israel's kings and classical prophets, ending with the deportation, first of the Northern, then of the Southern tribes (722 and 586 B.C.). Next follow the exile (until 538 B.C.); the different phases of the postexilic period; the time of John the Baptist and the public ministry of Jesus (A.D. 26–30?); the period of the first congregations of Jerusalem, Galilee, and Samaria; and the period of the expansion and fortification of churches, from the Black Sea to Rome, and from Macedonia to Ethiopia.

2) Naturally, the testimony of these different periods is rendered in many forms of speech and writing. The styles range from seemingly dry genealogies to the most appealing forms of epics and lyrics. Between these extremes we also find artful and legendary narration; songs composed for battle, well-digging, lamentation, or praise; biographical, national, or cultic historiography; and prophetic preaching. Ceremonial pedantry, ethical directives, reflective meditation, visionary prediction, and collections of prayers, proverbs, and anecdotes are all included. No form of speech or literature seems to be missing. There are even fragments of myth and fiction (e.g., Gen 1; Is 14; Jon; Rev), but they serve to describe specific acts of God which are understood as events that have taken place, or will occur in history.

3) The history told is basically the story of man's election and salvation by God. But this one great story is attested by many histories that are presupposed, reflected, announced, or factually recorded in the Bible. Not only the history of persons—of this or that patriarch, king, or prophet; of Jesus Christ, the church, and those living near or among God's people—but a manifold witness is heard in the Bible, resounding from the history of sanctuaries, the history of public and private worship, the history of traditions, the history of ideas and language, the history of idolatry and heresies, the history of ethics, laws, and politics, the history of jealously guarded separateness and cheap assimilation, and the history of one and of many religions. The purist who would like to exclude them in order to facilitate God's lawsuit or man's trial is put to shame. If he is impatient with the variety of stories and histories, God himself, and those who recognized the canonicity of the sixty-six biblical books, believe that, in the pursuit of truth, all the many witnesses should be given a hearing.

4) The central story of God and man, as well as the many supporting and conflicting stories just mentioned, is told and interpreted in many different ways. Yet none of the biblical writers

would have recognized the one great and continuing event of God's covenant unless, like the seer Balaam (Num 24:3–4), his eye had been opened. " 'What no eye has seen, nor ear heard, nor the heart of man conceived, what God has prepared for those who love him,' God has revealed to us as through the Spirit" (1 Cor 2:9–10). But because of their dependence upon every new act of revelation, the biblical writers bear different testimonies to God's mighty deeds. There is not only a difference between the Old and the New Testament, but also between prophets and priests, between the Deuteronomist and the Chronicler, between evangelists and writers of apostolic letters, between John and Matthew, between Peter and Paul, between Paul and James. Traditionalists and revolutionaries, ceremonialists and moralizers, centralizers and federalists, hunters for facts and pursuers of meaning, friends and foes of Israel's earthly king and stony temple, defenders of the law and antilegalists—all raise their voices.

Although the witnesses sometimes seem to demand that the reader decide finally for or against them, it is hard to group them into parties among which an easy choice may be made. A prophet like Ezekiel strongly fosters priestly interests, and the priestly Book of Leviticus calls for love of neighbor. In Matthew there is a passage that sounds Johannine (Mt 11:25–30); and in John's spiritual Gospel we are confronted with the "materialistic" statement, "The Word became flesh" (Jn 1:14). God's witnesses are not streamlined, not straight-jacketed, not goose-stepping—as Jesus said to a man inquiring for the rules of God's kingdom, "The wind blows where it wills . . . so it is with every one who is born of the Spirit" (Jn 3:8). A testimony to God's kingdom and guidance on entering it are given by the sober Books of Samuel and the Books of the Kings, and by the pedantic Books of the Chronicles; by prophetic blasts against wicked kings, and by the exuberant praise of the king to be enthroned which appears in some prophetic passages and in certain Psalms. There is only one "Good

News" of Christ's coming, but there are four Gospels. Luke takes pains to show that at each decisive step of Christ's ministry and the church's expansion, there were at least two similar parables, miracles, or experiences to ascertain an important event or doctrine.[16] If there were but one statement of a given event in the Bible, the reader might be inclined to consider it the result of an individual's imagination. Or he might be encouraged in a kind of presumption, thinking he had gained possession of an event, or perhaps even of God, through a single description. The manifold witness warns him against both temptations. The Bible can only point; it is left to man to respond. It does not hand out its contents in streamlined or undialectical form.

5) Finally, the biblical witness is manifold because it was written down, or composed, by different individuals whose personalities are distinct. The first five books of the Bible, often called the Books of Moses, contain elements that are today ascribed to authors, or schools, called the Yahwist (before 850 B.C., in or near Jerusalem), the Elohist (*ca.* 750, in Samaria?), the Deuteronomist (*ca.* 625 in Jerusalem?), the Priestly Writer (postexilic?). Each of these writers and schools has special linguistic characteristics, special information, special interests, and special predilections. Different authors have also contributed the material gathered in the Books of the Kings. The first three Gospels are not the completely original work of Matthew, Mark, and Luke. We learn from Luke 1:1–4 that before the canonical Gospels were written, there existed oral or written collections of the words and stories of Jesus Christ; such "gospels before the Gospel" were obviously used by the evangelists. In many cases, of course, prophets, scribes, evangelists, and apostles described and interpreted different events, but they also differ in the judgments they pass on similar or identical events.

There are further complications. Under the name of one biblical author, several authors may be hidden. Comments, elucidations—

and perhaps obfuscations—were added by editors who were more or less convinced they could speak in their master's voice. What the rabbis and the church received as a canonical text was frequently the result of an extended oral and literary tradition. It is possible that the anonymous redactors often deserve much more credit for the character, unity, and influence of a biblical book than the celebrated prophet or apostle whose name it bears. Biblical historical research of the last forty years has made it seem probable that most of the so-called biblical authors were not "authors" in the current sense of the term, but rather spokesmen, gatherers, and editors of specific traditions, whether of a legal, hymnic, narrative, festival, or proclamatory character. Traditions of one or more of the twelve tribes of Israel; formulae used at the conventions of the tribal confederation; the liturgy of a festival like the Passover; the sayings of Jesus that were collected by one group and the stories of his miracles that were told by another; the death and resurrection of Jesus Christ as retold and celebrated during the Christians' community meal; forms of preaching used at baptismal services—such varied material was selected, arranged, retold, and applied to different congregations and generations by the writers and redactors of the biblical books.

Under these circumstances, it is less surprising that the Bible contains so many differences than that it still contains so much of common remembrance, affirmation, and understanding. The unity of the Bible will be found, not in a solo performance, but in the harmony of many more or less pure voices. Nor is there any way to single out the language of God, the diction of Jesus, or the sound of the Spirit from among these voices, for, as we have seen, not only man's answer to God, but God's own words to man are delivered exclusively through the witness of many human voices. It makes little sense, therefore, to eliminate alleged human interpolations, to try to isolate the genuine words of God, or to edit the parables and discourses found in the four Gospels in such a way as to reconstruct the supposedly "authentic" words of the "historic Jesus." All the words written in God's name bear the marks of the witnesses' humanity. The Bible is not God's revelation on paper. It is a collection of testimonies to God's words and deeds. In it we are confronted with a dialogue in which different people use different words to speak about the same subject.

It is obvious that this variety of witnessing voices requires that we seek a special way of understanding.

IV *The Way to Truth*

The reader of the Bible is like a man in court, where a judgment will be passed that affects him. He has to make wise use of his reason. Whether he considers himself judge, juror, attorney, defendant, or a member of the public, he has to co-operate by listening carefully, and by evaluating what he hears and reads. He cannot neglect the possibility of error; he will try to grasp what is in the events at issue.

The Bible does not offer undisputed facts, as a historical or technical textbook does. It contains neither incontestable propositions nor a perfect system; neither a set of instructions that promises success, nor an example whose slavish imitation guarantees happiness. Rather, the Bible as a whole points to something, to somebody, to a life that has to be found out. The perception and description of God and his acts involve the same risk of error that is involved in the final opinion of the judge, the jury, or the public in a court of law. The parables of the Bible merely call attention to specific features of God's kingdom. They do not make its mystery profane but ask the listener for careful thought, application—and decision. The Bible is like a puzzle or wise saying (the Hebrew *mashal*) which points to the right answer and promises joy to the finder of the solution; but it requires thought and work. An attentive reader of the Bible will not be spared confusion and irritation; but he will try to proceed to a possible understanding of the unity within the diversity, of the light shining in the darkness.

Nothing less than the truth is at stake. If the biblical witnesses offer any aid to finding it, intensive study will be worthwhile. It is impossible to answer the question[17] whether a given statement is true because it is in the Bible, or whether it is found in the Bible because it is true. We should not consider Bible and truth as two propositions whose respective priority or interdependence we may measure and adjudicate. Every man is measured and judged by the truth; no one has the right or the power to confine it. That man respects the truth who remains prepared to learn about it, to be surprised by it, and to walk in it wherever it is found and whatever the cost. The Bible's usefulness is as great or as small as its witness to truth. Its uniqueness and authority depend on the result of a trial that has often taken place, and is still going on in the presence of every Bible reader. He is challenged to discover whether the biblical witnesses give glimpses of a truth—and joy in that truth—that are different from what might be learned from other secular or religious books. If the truth attested to by the Bible does not speak for itself, all arguments for establishing the Bible's unity, uniqueness, and usefulness will be futile. And if the Bible reader shuns the labor of the search, because he imagines he already possesses the truth, he betrays his lack of respect for its awesome mystery.

What is that truth of which the Bible speaks in a unique way? In the Gospel of John (18:38), we discover not only the perennial question, "What is truth?" but also a series of utterances about the way of truth this is both striking and compelling. Truth appears in fullness only when God's glory is manifested; it is inseparable from grace, Spirit, and life; it comes via the messenger of God; it is "attested" and "spoken" only by God's Son and by certain chosen men. Those chosen are "of the truth," "do the truth," "stay in the truth"; they are "sanctified" in the truth; only the Spirit sent from God will "guide you into all the truth"; truth will make free those who "know the truth" (1:14, 17; 3:21; 4:23, 24; 5:33; 8:32, 40, 44–46; 14:17; 15:26; 16:7, 13; 17:17; 18:37; 19:35, etc.). Finally, this Gospel contains a bold identification of Jesus Christ and the truth: "Jesus said to him, 'I am the way, and the truth, and the life; no one comes to the Father, but by me'" (14:6).

In an uncompromising manner, this Gospel treats of the one truth rather than of many truths or half-truths. The Evangelist's concern proves to be existential rather than intellectual; he relates sayings of Jesus Christ in which knowledge of the truth is identified with living it; the promise is given that the truth will make free and that its witness leads to God. This clearly shows that, at least for the Gospel of John, truth cannot be captured in propositions, a book, or a system. The truth of which this Gospel speaks has a strictly personal and relational character. It is from God; Jesus Christ is not only its chief witness but its embodiment. It will liberate man. Truth is the way God deals with man and man comes to God. Truth is the Spirit that Jesus Christ communicates to his disciples.

These things are less explicit in biblical books that put more emphasis on laws and statutes, on serving God through institutions, or on the role of "sound doctrine." But whenever petrification seems to triumph, prophetic voices call God's people back to worship him "in spirit and truth" (cf. Jn 4:23–24). It is the circumcision of the heart that pleases the Lord (Lev 26:41; Deut 10:16; 30:6; Jer 4:4; Rom 2:29); the Law written on stone tablets is not the end of all things, for the Law will be written upon the hearts of men (Ex 32:16, 19; 34:1; Jer 31:31–35; 32:38–40; Rom 2:14–15); the temple and the institutional sacrifice do not guarantee the presence of the Lord; God chooses to dwell with a broken heart and a penitent people (1 Sam 4–5; Jer 7; Is 66:2; 2 Sam 6:5 ff.; 1 Kings 8:27 ff.; Acts 7:44–51; 1 Cor 3:16–17).

As Plato's philosophy is unfolded in dialogues, so the testimony for biblical truth is given in the form of conversations. By recording the many exchanges between God and man, priest (or king) and prophet, Job and his friends, Jesus and Pilate, and Peter and Paul, the Bible calls us to the recognition of the true God, the true mediator, the true people of God, and the true life. The absence of a propositional or casuistic conception of truth, and the presence of multiple invitations to look for truth within a specific history—the history of the covenant between God and man—is both remarkable and consistent. The reader of the Bible is asked to find out by experience "what is the will of God, what is good and acceptable and perfect" (Rom 12:2). Jesus urges his listeners to "judge for yourselves what is right" (Lk 12:57). Man is expected to act as a free child and a fair judge.

But how can discernment, courage, and freedom be expected from those who listen to the Old and New Testament witnesses? If (with 2 Tim 3:16; 2 Pet 1:21; 1 Cor 7:40, etc.) we call the biblical writings or authors "inspired," how is inspiration perceived by those who do not know of inspiration? An explicit answer to this question is given in the Bible at least once: Paul writes, "The unspiritual man does not receive the gifts of the Spirit of God, for they are folly to him, and he is not able to understand them because they are spiritually discerned. The spiritual man judges all things" (1 Cor 2:14–15). It follows that a second inspiration must follow the first: the hearer and reader of the Bible needs inspiration just as much as did the original biblical witnesses. The same Spirit must inspire him. The letter alone, even the letter of God's holy Law, can and will kill (2 Cor 3:6; Rom 7:6). "Where the Spirit of the Lord is there is freedom" to recognize the truth of the Bible (2 Cor 3:17). Luke's Gospel contains a saying of Jesus according to which "the heavenly Father will give the Holy Spirit to those who ask him" (Lk 11:13). The Bible reader is dependent upon this promise.

According to both Testaments, however, the gift of the Spirit is not a magical power that makes it possible to pierce all secrets at all times, but has to be renewed day after day. It is misused when it results in possessive claims rather than a child's humble prayer and the service of others (1 Cor 12; 14; Rom 8:14–16; Gal 4:6–7). It drives man to search endlessly for better insight into truth and obedience. "The Spirit searches everything, even the depths of God" (1 Cor 2:10).

What will this search achieve? By giving insight into the mystery of the witnesses' testimony, the Spirit brings man to nothing less than the knowledge of God.

The Knowledge of Truth

When an old rabbi was once asked, "Can you say briefly what the knowledge of God is?" he replied, "Having God for a husband!" However perplexing, this answer is a beautiful summary of how the prophets Hosea (1–3), Jeremiah (especially 31:31–34), and Ezekiel (especially in Chapter 16) describe the experience, the hope, and the necessity of the knowledge of God. In the Bible, the verb "to know" is sometimes used to indicate the most intimate relationship between man and woman (Gen 4:1, 17, 25, etc.); it describes a personal relationship, an act not only of intellectual perception but also of existential acknowledgment and mutual respect. According to Augustine, to understand is to encounter love and to respond with love. The Bible indeed teaches that he alone knows God who enjoys his steadfast love and responds to his faithfulness with faith.

In recent biblical study there has been an increasingly dominant tendency to draw a sharp line between the Hebrew (or biblical) and a so-called "Greek" concept of knowledge.[18] Greek knowledge means, if we follow current definitions, the acquisition of an objective outlook (*theoria*) on a given subject matter, the ability to state what it is in reality, and to gain a certain amount of control over it. Even the gods do not seem secure in the face of such knowledge, and the world becomes subject to its domination. The New Testament's affirmations that Christians "walk by faith, not by sight" (2 Cor 5:7; Jn 20:29; 1 Pet 1:8; Heb 11:1) point to a different concept of knowledge. In the knowledge of faith there is nothing purely objective. Instead, there is passionate subjectivity, involvement, and submission. To know someone is to enjoy a personal bond; it is to care for another; it is the wisdom displayed in living with others in faithfulness and respect. The man who says, "I don't know you," severs and denies all personal relationship and care (Deut 33:9; Mt 25:12).

Although there are real differences between biblical and Greek thought, it is doubtful whether Heraclitus, Parmenides, Plato, or Aristotle would recognize their search for truth in the description just given of Greek knowledge. It seems that the Greeks also strove for more than intellectual perception and control; in their quest for knowledge, they too were searching for understanding, recognition, and wisdom. Is there anything original, then, which the biblical writers contribute to the philosophical search spearheaded in the West by the great Greek philosophers, and in the East by wise men of all ages? Or, does the Bible offer a viable alternative? A simple answer to such questions is impossible. Each reader of the Bible and each student of philosophy has the right and the duty to answer for himself whenever he feels able to make a decision. In the following, no more will be attempted than to convey some hints as to how the biblical writers themselves treat such fundamental questions as: How is it possible to know the true God? Why should human beings know him? What has knowledge to do with words? What good is achieved by knowing God?

1 *God's Knowledge of Himself*

It is characteristic of the thought of most biblical writers that, rather than ask whether or how an event or statement is possible, they describe it as real and relevant. They start from the factuality of creation, election, exodus, law, incarnation, resurrection—and in the light of experienced or promised reality they point out its meaning and relevance. They may also make statements concerning the appropriateness, necessity—and perhaps the beauty—of these events. In every case the factual prevails over the possible. The outstanding example of this is that the Bible does not unfold a doctrine of God's knowability before making statements about his revelation. Just as the place of ontology was taken by the witness to the Trinity of the living God, so the place occupied by epistemology in a philosophical system is not left empty. Distinct hints of the origin, necessity, and appropriateness of authentic knowledge of God are found in the Bible. The man who knows God is not applying to God something unnatural or essentially fallacious—he is not projecting his own concepts, emotions, or modes of perception onto God. Nor is he presuming to know things that cannot be known. Knowledge of God is considered a good and necessary thing, without which man cannot live decently.

According to Proverbs 8:22–31 (cf. the apocryphal *Wisdom of Solomon* 8), wisdom was made by God, and existed joyfully in his presence before men were called to listen and become wise. That is, wisdom is not a human invention applied to God. When Jesus says that he knows the Father, this knowledge of God is not dependent on the existence of the world or of human knowledge; for Jesus Christ knew God "before the world was made," while "the world has not known [him]" (Jn 17:5, 25). According to John 1:1–18, the Word is "with God" ("directed *toward* God," seems an even more appropriate translation) before it becomes flesh among men and is received by those chosen. In Matthew 11:25–27, it is stated that only the Son knows the Father, and the Father the Son—knowledge of God is hidden even from the world's wise men. This recalls a passage in Paul referred to earlier, in which he states that the depths of God are revealed exclusively by the Spirit because only the Spirit knows (in eternity and time) the things of God (1 Cor 2:9 ff.). Paul also insists that only the Spirit of God can make man confess that Jesus is Lord; only by the Spirit can he understand that to be human is to be God's child; only by the Spirit does he learn to call God Father (1 Cor 12:3; Rom 8:15–16). When Peter had made his surprising confession to Jesus, "You are the Christ, the Son of the Living God!" he may not have been aware of how truly he spoke; then Jesus congratulates him, and adds, "Flesh and blood have not revealed this to you, but my Father who is in heaven" (Mt 16:16–17). Just as, here, the Father instructs man how to speak to the Son, according to Matthew 6:7–15, the Son alone teaches man how to pray to God. The author of Hebrews knows no better way to substantiate his teaching about Christ than to quote Old Testament utterances which he understands to be affirmations made by the Father to his chosen priest, or by the Servant of the Lord to God.

All these passages reveal that there is knowledge among Father, Son, and Holy Spirit—above and before any and all knowledge of God given to man. God becomes perceptible and recognizable to man because, in eternity and time, he is three in one and knows himself. According to the Bible, knowledge of God will be true knowledge of the true God only when it is participation in God's self-knowledge.

To the wise men who inscribed "Know thyself" upon the temple at Delphi; to the classical philosophers who respected that axiom; to the Sophists, Descartes, and some of today's existentialists, man's understanding *of himself* may appear to be the key to all knowledge. If they are right, man is subject and object of knowledge at the same time, and the distinction between subject and object in the process of knowing must be considered a basic fallacy.[19]

The Bible agrees that self-understanding is behind all understanding; but it is God's, not man's, self-knowledge that is presupposed, proclaimed, and respected as the basis of all true knowledge. If God's knowledge underlies all knowledge found among men, then the distinction between him, the subject, and man, the object, or between two subjects, can no more be eliminated than that between different members of a covenant. If there were not two different partners, it would be meaningless to speak of a covenant. If there are not these two—God who knows and gives himself to be known, and man who is given the privilege of being known and of participating in knowledge—there is no knowledge or understanding of anything that is treated in the Bible.

II *Participation in God's Knowledge*

Most of the biblical allusions to God's self-knowledge suggest amazement and gratitude that God imparts knowledge of himself to others. Obviously, God does not know only himself; he also knows all things, and he knows man. With this knowledge, he chooses man to be his acknowledged child; he enlightens him so that he may know God and convey knowledge of God to others as a witness. This spreading of the knowledge of God to all lands is what the Bible calls God's glorification or revelation.[20]

In the Old Testament, when the Trinity was not yet clearly manifested, there are innumerable promises that Israel and others shall know God; in addition, God's people are severely scolded for not knowing God—that is, for ignoring him (Jer 31:34; Ezek

6:7; Hos 4:1). But the actual statement that anyone "knows the Lord" is not found. It is the New Testament that indicates, after the coming of Christ and the outpouring of the Spirit, that man will be given a knowledge of God corresponding fully to God's knowledge of man. "If anyone imagines that he knows something, he does not yet know as he ought to know. . . . I shall understand fully, even as I have been fully understood. . . . The Lord knows those who are his. . . . To you it has been given to know the secrets of the kingdom of heaven. . . . I am the good shepherd; I know my own and my own know me. . . . You have come to know God, or rather to be known by God" (1 Cor 8:2–3; 13:12; 2 Tim 2:19; Mt 13:11; Jn 10:14; Gal 4:9).

The Gospel of John and the Letter to the Ephesians put specific emphasis upon knowledge. Those whom God has given, from eternity, to Jesus Christ, or those elected in Jesus Christ, are described as people who have received, through the Son—and are still receiving through the Spirit—knowledge of the true God. They receive enlightenment, not in individual meditation, but in their encounter with Him and in community with Jesus Christ. They form a community whose head is Jesus Christ; a community which is called his flock, his body, God's house, or the church. The eyewitnesses of Jesus Christ play a dominant and lasting role in that community; through their witness and upon their foundation, all later Christians receive and retain their faith. The whole community has received enlightenment in order to be bearers of God's grace to the world. Christians are admonished to grow in their knowledge of God and Christ; this growth is inseparable from the witness they render to others. Through it they hope to "attain to the unity of the faith and of the knowledge of the Son of God" (Eph 4:13).

Our participation in God's knowledge is obviously an unfinished business as long as we live. Like the column of fire that conducted and protected the Israelites on their migration through the wilderness, Jesus Christ is the leader and protector of those who walk on the way of faith (cf. Heb 12:2).

III *The Role of Language*

Biblical writers make us aware that revelation and knowledge of God may defy definition but are never without words. Epiphanies of God are seldom simply extraordinary visual exhibitions; the words spoken by God, and man's reply, are mostly connected with them. "How are men to call upon him in whom they have not believed? And how are they to believe in him of whom they have never heard? And how are they to hear without a preacher?" (Rom 10:14) "He sent forth his word" (Acts 10:36; 13:26; Ps 107:20). There is no greater expression of the word's relevance than the Gospel of John and the Book of Revelation; in both, Jesus Christ is called "the word of God" (Jn 1:1 ff.; Rev 19:13; Heb 4:12). It is important to remember that Jesus Christ bears this title not only as the spokesman of all the messages God has given to man but also as God's commissioned intermediary on behalf of man—that is, as the epitome of man's amen to God and of man's praise of God before his fellow men (2 Cor 1:20; Heb 2:1–3; 3:1). Knowledge of God is conveyed as much by the terrifying cry, "My God, my God, why hast thou forsaken me," as by the consoling admonition, "[The Most High] is kind to the ungrateful and the selfish. Be merciful, even as your Father is merciful" (Mk 15:34; Lk 6:34–35).

The problematic character of human language, however, is fully sensed when Moses (for whatever reason) states that he is not "eloquent" but "slow of speech and of tongue"; when Isaiah confesses that his lips are unclean; when Job admits that he has uttered things he did not understand; when parables of Jesus are intended to conceal rather than to reveal; and finally, when Paul asserts that he has heard words that "cannot be told," and bows before the depth of God's wisdom and his unsearchable judgments (Ex 4:10;

Is 6:5; Job 42:3; Mk 4:10–12; 2 Cor 12:4; Rom 11:33). The occurrence of the phrase, "speaking in human terms" (Rom 6:19; Gal 3:15, etc.), is one among many indications that the biblical writers acknowledged their inadequacy to express what they wanted to say.

Nevertheless, the Bible does not exhibit a general skepticism regarding the use of all language. Psalmists worry when God does not answer prayer; prophets are dismayed when their preaching is neglected. God scolds the man who "darkens counsel by words without knowledge" (Job 38:2). But the failure to achieve hoped-for results by means of words does not make men cynics. There are times when they are to be silent, when God is silent, when it is not a time to converse. Still, language, as such, is not mistrusted.

Neither do the biblical writers try to develop an impeccable superlanguage whose logic and structure would exhaust, and perhaps replace, a given object. They are not logical positivists and have different ways of using language and aiming at understanding. Some show a preference for statistics and genealogies; others may consider the description of God-given visions, or the constant use of metaphors, parables, and analogies the most appropriate method of witnessing God's dealings with man. In the Letter of James, the imperative form of the verb is preferred to other moods; other books make extra use of the historical present (Mark), the kerygmatic aorist (Paul) or the parenetic participle (1 Peter). But no one pretends to have found out the one language which might eliminate all others. Mixed forms of language prevail within the same books. The Gospel of Matthew, for instance, combines genealogy and short, crisp sayings, pointed discussions in rabbinical style and intricate parables, allegorical interpretations and anecdotes, the many little details of the Passion and the visionary stories of Christ's baptism, transfiguration, and resurrection. Almost all of the sixty-six biblical books, except for some of the shortest, show the greatest freedom in the choice of forms of expression. In the Old Testament, texts written in good Hebrew stand beside passages written partly in Aramaic; attempts to recover Attic Greek in Luke and Hebrews stand beside the rather vulgar diction of Mark, the extremely incorrect Greek of Revelation, and Paul's Greek, which a modern linguist described as a sort of Yiddish!

Several observations may help to explain why the biblical authors gladly accept the role words play in God's revelation, and why they call for a response in words. Language is described and accepted as a gift of God. Israel is happy to have a God unlike an idol, which has a mouth and does not speak (Ps 94:8–11; 115:5–8; 135:16–18). The whole creation, and even man, came into being because, by his word, God called it forth. Man calls day and night by the names God first used; he gives names to the animals because God gave him dominion over them. Through his revelation and inspiration, God has made man capable of calling on his name and of speaking in his name (Gen 1:3 ff.; 2:19–20; 12:1–3, 8; Ex 3:14; Jer 1; Is 6; Lk 12:12; Rom 8:26; Jn 20:22–23). This is why the prophets can dare to say, "Thus says the Lord." For the same reason Paul is "not ashamed" of his preaching, but calls it "the power of God for salvation" (Rom 1:16). Certainly, we may err in receiving man's word for God's word (e.g., Jer 14:14; Acts 12:22), but although some speakers are deceivers, the God-given power of preaching in human words is not defeated.

Paul expresses his thanks to God that the Thessalonians accepted his preaching "not as the word of man but as what it really is, the word of God" (1 Thess 2:13). The individual character of the various books of the Bible, their authors' accommodations to the listeners' ability to understand, their potential and actual misuse of law, prophecy, and preaching does not prevent human words from being useful means to convey knowledge of God. Words are, like those who use them, nothing but witnesses. That words have pointed to God and still point to him—this is the testimony of the

Bible. God himself has chosen men not for their hearts and hands alone, but also for their mouths, and sometimes their pens (1 Sam 10:25; Is 8:16; Jer 29; 36; Gal 6:11; Jn 5:39, 46, 47; 1 Jn 1:4, etc.).

Language primarily serves the purpose of introducing God and man to each other and maintaining their personal union. By the use of language—whether in epiphanies, giving promises, declaring law, or delivering judgments, God announces that he is. By speech he reveals his presence. Words proclaim his help in the most desperate moments of human life. Certainly, what God says is implemented by deeds, but they would not be understood as *his* deeds unless he had announced them beforehand, and unless he commented on them afterward, and his prophets continued to speak of them. To God's speech, authenticated by the history of Israel, man is to reply with a simple, "Here I am," or "Amen," or in more lengthy forms of supplication and thanks. The conduct of his whole life is destined to be a response to God's address. Hence, neither God's communion with man nor man's communion with God takes place without the use of language. Of course, language has other functions than that of binding together I and Thou. But it appears that the Old and New Testament witnesses did not consider language primarily as a tool for giving infallible descriptions of nature, history, or ideals. By God's grace, God and man are "on speaking terms," and they reveal their mutual knowledge and care for each other through the words they exchange.

Finally, when thoughts are crystallized, when words are formed and speech is uttered, events are called into being, hidden facts are revealed, new relationships are created, and truth is gradually brought to light. The result is respect or joy in God's presence. Language is not only a preparation for, or commentary on events; it is itself an event.[21] The biblical authors would not dare to be so detailed in their narratives and their explication of the laws, so imaginative in their threats and promises, so repetitive in their emphasis on God's mighty acts, unless they were convinced that man's witness to God is a meaningful act. We repeat, for them, man is truly man only to the extent that his life is a response to God. The proper use of language is to create, augment, and spread abroad the awareness of God's communion with man and man's communion with God.

It should now be evident that the manifold verbal witness of the Bible to God and his covenant with man does not limit man's knowledge of truth. Rather, this witness is, in content and form, a demonstration of the freedom truth grants to those seeking truth. Each of the biblical writers was brought to truth—and gave witness to it in his own way. We are invited to enjoy their experiences, to respect their priority, to walk on the path which they point out, and to respond with the discernment and daring of a free child of God.

IV *Knowledge and Love*

It will be remembered that in the Bible the term "knowledge" serves occasionally to describe the most intimate relationship between man and woman as well as that between God and man. Indeed, knowledge and love are equivalent. This insight is not a monopoly of prophets and apostles. Plato makes the same point in his *Symposium,* although the *eros* of which he speaks is, in many respects, distinct from the *agape* shown by God.[22] As Plato describes him, Socrates exemplifies, more aptly than many Jewish or Christian zealots, the man who, despite his earthly bonds, is free to seek, proclaim, and assist in unfolding the knowledge of truth. The Hindus and mystics, too, although they renounce all articulate or conceptual knowledge of God, love their god with all their heart. But what the Bible calls knowledge or love of God, what the man freed by God enjoys as an undeserved gift of God, contains distinct features of its own.

Like all true love, the knowledge of God attested by the Bible is linked to specific encounters and events in time and space. It joins together not a known thing with an unknown, but two partners who are to become known to each other. On the basis of what has been made known, it seeks and grants deeper and fuller understanding. Knowledge or love of God is not afraid to wait and to suffer. But it keeps faith; it prays for, and expects the best; it enjoys the smallest signs. On one occasion it respects or keeps a secret; on another, the heart overflows and the mouth shouts with joy. This is the love of God that is experienced, described, and exemplified by the biblical witnesses. They insist upon the unshakable priority of God's love for man. The superiority and perfection of God's knowledge is tirelessly affirmed. But they also disclose that God's grace, given to his chosen witnesses, is not given in vain. Knowledge, and love, and faith are kindled in them. Paul praises faith, and hope, and love, but insists that love is the greatest of the three (1 Cor 13).

As love lives in the joy that one person has been found by another and has found the other, so knowledge and understanding live in the distinction and companionship of a subject and an object. To claim that the Bible expresses only man's understanding of himself is to claim that God and man can ultimately love only themselves. Man's self-love is conceded by Levitical law, and also by Jesus and Paul: "Love your neighbor as yourself" (Lev 19:18; Lk 10:25–37; Mk 12:28–34; Rom 13:9; Eph 5:28). But God's sacrificial love stands in clear opposition to that selfish love. The love story of the Bible does not culminate in the description of mutually exclusive or dispensable partners or actions. It is the story of God's love poured out into human hearts—despite their hardness and blindness, despite their rebellion and acts of unfaithfulness, despite their laziness and deadness to all that is good and true. To seek and gain knowledge of truth with the help of the biblical witnesses means to become involved in the gift, the suffering, the surprise, and the praise of that love.

If the Bible has a unique character or a special authority, it must be located in the authentic, original, and exemplary description of different partners, events, and words, bound together and informed by love. Love's victory over rebellion, division, and foolishness is the truth that makes man free. What is told of the power and the ways of such love deserves to be remembered, imitated, and celebrated. The Bible deserves a hearing because it is a record and witness of partners who are enjoying that love.

Our survey of the Bible's contents and formal characteristics has emphasized that this book is a record of a dialogue, even of the conversation of lovers. The purpose of the following chapters is to show why and how the conversation going on *in* the Bible is continued, applied, enjoyed—or disturbed—by a dialogue *with* the Bible, by a conversation between the Bible and its readers. It is obvious that participation in the second dialogue can only be meaningful when instructed and inspired by the characteristics of the first.

PART TWO

THE AUTHORITY OF THE BIBLE

It is impossible to count the number of books, essays, and sermons devoted to defending the authority of the Bible. In all such efforts we distinguish a theological, an anthropological, and a Christological way of arguing for this authority. All three approaches are efforts to promote what may be called "biblicism,"[23] and all of them serve—more or less explicitly and successfully—a threefold purpose. They give an account of the faith of believers; their reasoning strengthens those who have accepted the Bible as "God's Word"; they attempt to persuade unbelievers that there is value, or even necessity, in the words of the Bible. After these three ways of arguing for biblical authority have been discussed, we shall search for an alternative approach.

CHAPTER III

THEOLOGICAL REASONING FOR DIVINITY

The High Doctrine of the Bible

Despite serious disagreements in dogma, ethics, and ecclesiology, ancient Jewish scholars, some early Christian thinkers, more or less recent Roman Catholic official statements, and many Protestants use a common argument in regard to biblical authority. They derive it from "God the author of Scriptures." Each event, as well as the sum of events by which God discloses himself—whether by word, deed, or appearance—is called "revelation." The specific action by which God, in his revelation, enables and directs men to think, to say, and to put into writing exactly what he wants said and written is called "inspiration." If asked why the Bible possesses an authority "useful for teaching, for reproach, for correction, for training in righteousness," all these different groups can answer, "Because 'all scripture is inspired by God' " (2 Tim 3:16).

They may choose different ways of defining what they mean by God's authorship; there is little uniformity among the spokesmen of these groups when specific utterances are made about the limits of revelation, the essence of inspiration, and the differences and connections among them. But the representatives of each group certainly intend to distinguish inspiration as it occurs in the Bible from a pagan concept of inspiration. Greek writers ascribed the words of poets, and of some philosophers and orators, to the inspiration of the Muses. Among Jews and Christians who respect the Bible, it is God's own dictation or the Holy Spirit's direct action by which God's will and the words of chosen men become identified as the Word of God.

Let us look more closely at how this point is made by Jews, early Christian apologists, the Catholic Church, and some Protestants.

Jewish theologians differ widely among themselves—from Philo of Alexandria to Rabbi Akiba, from medieval Talmudists to modern scholars—but all take as their beginning the law which was God's gift to Moses on Mount Sinai.[24] This revelation consisted of both the written and the oral Law (Torah). The oral Torah is the basis of that tradition which cannot be exhausted or defined, but lives in prophetic and other holy writings, in the Mishnah, in the Talmud, in Haggada and Halakah, and in the theological, liturgical, devotional, and ethical utterances of all times. The written Torah is identified with the five books of the Bible which are called the Law—the Books of Moses, or the Pentateuch. If we follow Jewish legends and early scholarly opinions, Moses was either miraculously instructed what to write by God; or he was given the written heavenly original of the Law in order to make a copy; or he was following a word-by-word dictation when he wrote the five books. Angels are said to have been present when the Law was given. Their role was to enhance the glory of the Torah or of Israel; they were to threaten the trespasser and reward the obedient.

It is obvious that such theories and legends were formed before historical and literary research made it appear that extensive portions of the Books of Moses were put into writing not during Israel's migration from Egypt to the promised land but in the time of the kings and prophets and in later periods of Israel's history. The Pentateuch's present form probably dates from the period after 538 B.C.—that is, from the time of the reconstruction of the temple and of Jerusalem, after parts of Israel had returned from the Babylonian exile. While substantial parts of the Law are older than the prophetic documents, some elements of the Books of Moses are later than the period of Israel's classical prophets.

According to orthodox Jewish teaching, the words of the prophets are an addition to, and an interpretation of the written Law. The prophetic books of the Bible do not create law; they interpret and apply the ancient covenant traditions of Israel to the requirements of different situations. The prophetic writings are considered a less immediate expression of God's will, for they are mediated by that spirit which, according to Jewish teaching, is not God, although it is of God. There are Jews who hold that the prophetic words are, like the Torah, "spoken out of the mouth of the Lord." But the authority of those words is treated as minor, and is subject to that of the written Torah. The rank of Psalms and the other Writings included in the Jewish canon is even lower. A hierarchy exists within the Jewish Bible; the Moses books form the highest, the prophetic books the middle, and the Writings the lowest level of authority.

It is characteristic of Jewish outsiders and heretical groups to change the rank of these three groups of canonical books. Some (Philo of Alexandria, the Sadducees, and the Samaritans) recognized only the Pentateuch as canonical. Others (the Qumran community and some authors of apocalyptic books) seem to have given great weight to a selection of prophetic books. But no one can remain a Jew and at the same time doubt the supreme authority of the Law.

In sum, it is remarkable that, whenever Jews affirm the authority of their Bible, different levels or grades of canonicity are distinguished; and all that is written is matched by the authority of living tradition. Some Jews pay respect to new "revelation"; among the sectarian group of Qumran, the interpretation of Scripture given by the Teacher of Righteousness was respected as such.[25]

The Christian apologists of the second and third centuries and the classical Roman Catholic official position may be introduced together, for the decisive elements of their arguments are almost identical. Roman Catholic writers and official declarations like to call God the *auctor* of Holy Writ. Originally,[26] God was called the author of the whole Bible, in opposition to the belief and practice of certain Christian groups. Since some Gnostic heretics repudiated the Old Testament in favor of secret or public "Sayings of Jesus," and of the equally secret or public "Tradition" of one or several of the apostles, they were told that God is the author not only of the New Testament but also of the Old. "Orthodox" Christian writers and churches were in agreement with Jewish teachers in emphasizing, as the reason for the Bible's authority, that God is the giver of all holy Law, whether Israel's law or the "new law" given by Jesus Christ and proclaimed by his apostles. But by including the Gospels, the apostolic Letters, and the Book of Revelation, the orthodox Christians formed a more extensive canon. Gnostic heretical groups fostered a much narrower canon, consisting principally of books found in the New Testament or ascribed to certain apostles.

The similarity between Jewish and second century and later orthodox Christian argumentation may be further illustrated by reference to the role of tradition. Irenaeus' suggestion concerning the supporting role of tradition,[27] was elaborated upon and became law in Roman Catholicism. It was repeatedly confirmed[28] that a specific oral tradition (as found in more or less official documents produced by outstanding assemblies and teachers) was, along with the Scriptures, "being received and venerated with equal piety and reverence." Roman Catholics show the same respect for tradition as the Jews, but the contents and carriers of their tradition are different. Instead of rabbinical dicta concerning the law and synagogical practice, the words of Jesus and the apostles, together with the experience of the worshiping and teaching church of Rome, confirm and complement the authority of the Bible. Conflicts within Christianity had to arise, and this occurred when the traditions of Ephesus, Byzantium, or other metropolitan churches were set up against the claims made for the universal validity of decisions made in Rome and the infallibility of the bishop of that city. But most Christian churches, except those of the Reformation, have, *de facto* or *de jure,* attributed to one or another oral tradition a value similar to the value oral tradition had for the Jews.

However, not even within the Roman Catholic Church is all teaching on the authority of the Bible and tradition a parallel to Jewish theory and practice. The affirmation that God is the author of the Bible can also be made to attest the unique authority of the Bible. Some recent Catholic scholars[29] reject the idea that the co-ordination of Scripture and tradition implies a "two-source theory" of divine revelation. Other Catholics have spoken explicitly of the two sources of revelation.[30]

If no agreement or final statement on the relation of Scripture and tradition is yet in existence, there nevertheless exist official statements and considerable agreement in regard to the reliability of the Bible. It is stated by Irenaeus,[31] Hippolytus,[32] Epiphanius,[33] and Augustine[34]—and endorsed by modern Encyclicals[35]—that the Scriptures are free of contradictions and contain no error. God, the author of the Bible, does not lie or contradict himself. The infallibility of Scripture is not restricted to the Bible's utterances concerning faith and morals, but pertains to all the Scriptures say.

The infallibility of the whole Bible is unanimously ascribed to the inspiration of its writers. But the views held among Catholics on the mode of inspiration and the contribution of the hagiographers vary. They range from a technical-mechanical understanding of inspiration, which looks on the writers as secretaries of God, to a high estimation of the contribution made to God's revelation by human "coauthors."

A theory of mechanical inspiration was developed by such early apologists as Justin the Martyr, Theophilus of Antioch, and Athenagoras. Their view is based on the conviction that the writers contributed nothing of their own, since they wrote in an ecstatic condition comparable to, though by no means identical with that of the mantics at Delphi and Cumae. The writers were but the zither or flute on which God played.[36] The Montanist movement may have helped to discredit this view; with its supposedly new revelations, the idea of uncontrolled onrushes of the Spirit, which eventually eliminate responsibility, became suspect.

At the other extreme, we find a theory of inspiration which includes the consciousness of the writer and co-operation between God and man in the production of a biblical book. This co-operation is sometimes explained by reference to that providential concursus of God and man which is effectively at work in all historical events; or reference is made to the miracles wrought by God, both for man and through him, whenever the divine economy of salvation (*Heilsgeschichte*) made a special intervention of God and an exceptional authorization of a chosen man possible and necessary. It is therefore held that inspiration does not obliterate the human will, or imply that man's capacities are momentarily put to sleep. Rather, it stimulates and uses the best in man.

No decision on behalf of either the mechanical or the co-operative theory of inspiration has been incorporated into official Roman Catholic teaching. Origen himself sometimes describes inspiration as ecstasy; elsewhere he maintains that inspiration does not paralyze the rational faculties of the writers.[37]

Whatever view on inspiration may one day prevail in Catholic teaching, a conclusion is derived from the three principles of divine authorship, operation of the Spirit, and infallibility of the Bible. The Bible is considered to possess unshakable validity as *divine law*. Since Tertullian,[38] the Bible and its parts have been called (legal) "instruments," and employed accordingly. Theologians using the Bible begin to resemble lawyers who argue by reference to the law and its statutes. Not only the Old Testament but also "the New Law" is now recognized as having a legal status and function in the church. It is noteworthy, first, that late in the second century the "Rule of Faith," or "Rule of Truth" (i.e., early confessional statements), was given the name and legal function of a "canon"; that in 325 the decisions of church synods and councils received this rank; and that finally (*ca.* 360) the Bible was called "canon." In the ninth century, papal decrees were honored with the same title, and "canon law" began to flourish.

It is obvious that a law, or canon, of as positive a character as the Bible needs a court, judges, and officers to state, enforce, and apply it. For a Catholic, it is the church's privilege and duty to describe, define, and judge what this law actually contains. The church declares herself to be the universal teacher of the inspired word: *Ecclesiae est judicare*.[39] The church's judgment is held to possess the same infallibility as the Bible, but its range is narrower. What the church declares through the mouth of the Pope is infallible solely in matters of faith and morals.[40] In its struggle against Reformation theology and the Reformation churches, official Roman Catholic teaching has assumed a rigorous and legalistic undertone which is today regretted even by Catholics.

What, finally, is Protestant teaching on the authority of the Bible? Of the many, often conflicting Protestant views of biblical authority, we will describe only one, the so-called "high doctrine of the Bible," as it was developed and is maintained by the Fundamentalists.

The members of this group prefer to call themselves Conservatives or Evangelicals, but do not always resent their nickname. Fundamentalists claim that their doctrine is based solely on the Bible's own teaching, and harmonizes with the original consensus of Jewish and Christian interpreters, the understanding of the Word of God common to both Luther and Calvin, and some post-Reformation orthodox synodal decisions.[41]

There are Fundamentalists who endorse, without the slightest hesitation, decisive features of the ancient Jewish (that is, Philonic and Rabbinical) teaching, the early apologists' teaching, and the post-Reformation Roman Catholic teaching on the Bible. For them, as for Jews and Roman canonists, the Bible is basically the law given by God. They hold that, by a mysterious operation of the Holy Spirit, even by inspiration, God's revelation has assumed the form of a book of oracles and statutes. However, little agreement exists among Fundamentalists in regard to the method by which God's revelation was transmitted. Some speak of dictation and use a mechanical terminology. The role of the hagiographers is then considered to be that of more or less passive instruments of God. For, it is argued, how could the Bible be infallible if men made a contribution of their own to its content?

But writers such as B. B. Warfield[42] and J. J. Packer[43] feel free, each in his own way, to attack a mechanical understanding of inspiration. They both attempt to elaborate a theory of the concursus between the creator and creature which does not limit inspiration to the moment of writing, but sees it operating in the whole life, experience, and specific situation of the hagiographers. The writers of the Bible made use of their experiences and formulated their convictions, not according to their own pleasure, but following the guidance of God; nevertheless, they acted as thinking, learning, and responsible men. While writing they obeyed God out of a whole life's experience; they did not become holy typewriters or Dictaphones.

Regardless of the differences in regard to the mode of inspiration, Fundamentalists appear to agree that revelation and inspiration are almost, if not completely, identical. The Bible is accepted as an accurate record of revelation; therefore it is revelation. Since God cannot lie, the Bible possesses "indefectable authority" and "divine trustworthiness"; it is infallible in every detail.[44] The inspiraton of the prophets, of which the synagogue and the New Testament speak, is also the basis for the authority of the whole Bible. Law, prophecy, and Scripture are said to be "strict synonyms."[45] As with Tertullian, the whole Bible is again put to use, both as legal evidence for the truth of orthodox faith, and in refutation of heresy.

However, as soon as the Bible is considered as juridical evidence, its interpretation almost unavoidably assumes the character of the explanation and application of human statutes. Its commentators begin to resemble—and even to imitate—lawyers who place evidence against evidence. Unlike the Catholics, the Fundamentalists have developed neither a canon law nor the scholarship to explain and enforce it, but their esteem and use of the Bible is similar.

The Bible itself knows of such legalist use of biblical words. Jeremiah (8:8) denounces "the false pen of the scribes" who, after "discovering" Deuteronomy, seem to have pounced upon it in order to introduce a reformation. They boast, "We are wise, and the law of the Lord is with us." The New Testament story of Jesus' temptation by Satan also offers a striking example of legalistic interpretation. The devil quotes the Scriptures (Ps 91:11–12, in Mt 4:6) in order to make Jesus act according to a satanic notion of what a "Son of God" ought to be. But Jesus answers the devil by quoting the Law (Deut 8:3; 6:16; 5:9, etc., in Mt 4:4, 7, 10);

the rabbinical principle that the Law overrules the other books of the Bible is effectively applied. As for the New Testament authors, Matthew and Paul bear the most obvious resemblance to Jewish biblical interpretation. It cannot be denied that Jesus' reference to Moses and the creation story (Mt 19:3–8), Paul's harking back from Moses to Abraham (Rom 4; Gal 3), and Hebrews' appeal to the order of Melchizedek, which precedes and supersedes the institution of Levitical priesthood (Heb 7), remind us of the appeal Supreme Court lawyers make to the Constitution.

But Matthew, Paul, and Hebrews do not always handle their Bible in this way; in most cases they quote it as witness to the Gospel, as good news rather than law (Rom 1:17; 4; 9–11; Mt 8:17; 12:18 ff.; Lk 4:18–19; 1 Pet 1:11; Heb 4:2, 6, 12). The most explicit statements against a legalist use of the Scriptures are found in the Fourth Gospel. The Law is employed by the Jews to urge the execution of sinners, and even of Jesus himself (Jn 8:5; 19:7). But the "fulfillment" of the Scriptures by Jesus Christ (19:36 ff.) is "grace and truth" (1:17), "spirit and life" (6:63). Testimony to Christ is the true purpose of the Law (Jn 5:39, 45–47).

Present-day Fundamentalists, however, establish a final equation of Scripture, prophecy, and law. Although Old Testament writings were used for legal purposes before the New Testament was written, the Fundamentalists' biblical legalism must be considered an innovation. For it is inseparably connected with an insistence upon the most minutely literal interpretation of the inspired text. In the time of the early church, those who believed in the inspiration of a given text were convinced that only an allegorical or spiritual interpretation would do it justice. Inspiration was for them a reason to transcend what they considered a fleshly, outdated literalism.[46] For Greeks, Jews, and Christians, the belief in plenary inspiration was an invitation to assimilate the "subsense" of the writings to the requirements and standards of a modern age.

For the Fundamentalists, however, literal inspiration calls for literal interpretation. The legal elements they find in the Bible make them assume it contains a timeless, absolute, and definable system of truth.[47] It becomes the interpreter's task to display and uphold this system—much as a judge is supposed to uphold law and constitution. If ancient believers in inspiration sailed on wings of imaginative (if not fantastic) interpretation, the Fundamentalist attorneys of inspiration engage in a more pedestrian mode of exegesis. They use the Bible to confirm the five fundamentals to which they owe their name: the inspiration and infallibility of Scripture, the divinity of Christ, the virgin birth and the miracles of Christ, his atoning death, and his bodily resurrection and second coming.

While the Catholic church is probably the greatest master of accommodation to the demands of different regions and periods, the Fundamentalists claim to be the most faithful, if not the only guardians of the ancient landmarks that must not be removed (cf. Prov 22:28; 23:10). Jewish teaching emphasizes the legal, personal, and binding character of revelation; it therefore relies upon the books of the Law; it makes the Torah the standard of all canonical books. Its interpretation is not dogmatic, but halachic (concerning man's conduct). Roman doctrine puts greater emphasis upon the institution of the church and its dogmatic and moral discipline; the Church of Rome is declared the only authorized judge of biblical authority. The Fundamentalists stress the infallibility of the autographs of the biblical books, words, and letters; anything but literal interpretation is forbidden.

A more detailed study of these three groups would bring to light many other important traits, but the relative harmony among them may be even more important than their distinctive individual features. How are we to explain this amazing accord among such radically divided brethren?

The Dignity of Law

The common denominator of the Jewish, Catholic, and Fundamentalist teaching on the Bible is a well-meant legalism. All of them want to affirm that God alone is king of kings, the supreme lawgiver, the wise, righteous, and gracious judge of Jews and Gentiles alike. For this reason they insist that the Bible does not reproduce human laws like those pronounced by Hammurabi or Napoleon, or man-made oracles like those that might be received in any sanctuary, or magic invocations like those found wherever a religious tradition is alive. Their lofty aim is to explain, to the sophisticated and the uneducated, to members of the congregation and non-Christians alike, that this book deserves reverence, obedience, and faith. Thanks to their insistence, the Bible was heard as "the good book" by millions of people, both high and low, on good and on evil days. Above all, the promoters of this doctrine have searched the Bible's testimony; they believe they have done nothing but submit themselves to its pronouncements and judgments.

What does the Bible say about itself? A great deal that sounds like obvious support of the high doctrine of the Bible! More than three thousand passages, both short and long, are introduced by formulae such as, "Thus says the Lord." The Old Testament abounds in laws and prophecies uttered in the name of God, and the New Testament reaffirms that "God spoke of old to our fathers by the prophets" (Heb 1:1). Sometimes, when New Testament writers quote the Old Testament, they even introduce, as words of God, sayings that are not necessarily spoken by God in their Old Testament context (see, for example, Gen 2:24 in Mt 19:5; Is 8:17 in Heb 2:13; Ps 95:7 in Heb 3:7). Though the classical prophets of Israel seldom speak of the Spirit as given to them (e.g., Mic 3:8; Is 61:1), the New Testament states that all prophets are "men moved by the Holy Spirit" (2 Pet 1:21); indeed, "all Scripture" is called "inspired by God" (2 Tim 3:16). Jesus bids friends and foes to search the Scriptures and to believe in Moses in order to find, in them, eternal life, and by them, faith in Jesus Christ (Jn 5:39, 46, 47). According to the Acts of the Apostles and the Epistles, the apostles taught in a similar way (Acts 3:21; Rom 3:21). "Learn this from us: Never beyond what is written [Live according to scripture]" (1 Cor 4:6).

What the New Testament says about the authority of the Old is also applied to the words of Jesus and the apostolic writings. Jesus himself says, "The word which you hear is not mine but the Father's who sent me" (Jn 14:24). Sometimes Jesus sets himself in opposition to ancient tradition or current piety; he announces boldly, "But I say unto you. . . . Then will I declare to them. . . . For the sake of your tradition, you have made void the word of God" (Mt 5:22, 28, etc.; 7:23; 15:6). Jesus' words demand more respect than anything said before his coming; he alone knows and makes known the Father's nature and will (Jn 6:63; cf. 12:27–49). Not only are the promises and commandments of the Old Testament "fulfilled" (Jn 12:38; 13:18; 17:12; 19:24, 36), but also the words of Jesus (Jn 18:9, 32). Some New Testament writers assert explicitly that Jesus Christ is in eternity the divine Word, even before and in the act of creation (Jn 1:3; Heb 1:3). He brought the message of salvation to the generation of Noah (1 Pet 3:19–20), and his Spirit made the prophets speak of his sufferings and subsequent glory (1 Pet 1:11). "Before Abraham was, I am" (Jn 8:58). Because the Bible gives expression to Jesus Christ's word, it has a share in his unique authority.

According to the New Testament, Jesus, in turn, authorized his disciples to speak in his name. "An apostle is like the one who sent him"—this maxim of Jewish legal and communal administration is reflected in both the Gospels and the Epistles. Jesus delegates special authority to some of his disciples. "He appointed twelve, to be with him, and to be sent out to preach and have authority. . . . [Father,] as thou didst send me into the world, so I have sent them into the world. . . . He who hears you hears me. . . . He who receives you receives me. . . . Whatever you bind on earth shall be bound in heaven. . . . It is not you who speak, but the Holy Spirit" (Mk 3:14–15; Jn 17:18; Lk 10:16; Mt 10:40; 16:19; 18:28; cf. Jn 20:23; Mk 13:11). In reporting the work of the apostles, it is said that "they proclaimed the word of God"; people wanted to hear from them precisely this "word of God" (Acts 13:5, 7, 44).

Of all the apostles, it is especially Paul who claims an authority equal to that of Moses and the prophets (2 Cor 3; Eph 2:20). Like Moses, the prophets and the rabbis—as well as the Mishnah, the Talmud, and those Jewish sects about which we have some knowledge—Paul recognized no authority "except from God" (Rom 13:1). He insists upon stating that he was made an apostle by God himself (Gal 1:1; 1 Cor 11:23). He asks the hearers and readers of his words for nothing less than obedience. Even when his words are not the Lord's explicit command, they are still the judgment of a man who believes he has the "Spirit of God" (Rom 6:17; 1 Cor 7:25, 40; 14:37; Phil 2:12). His message is to be received "not as the word of men but as what it really is, the word of God" (1 Thess 2:13).

Paul explains that he represents the Lord's own authority even when he is bodily absent. He is "present in spirit" when he prays for a church or when his letters are being read (1 Cor 5:3; Phil 2:12; 2 Cor 10:11; 13:2). The same idea is found in the fourth-century church historian, Eusebius, when he is speaking of the author of the Gospel according to Matthew: "After he had first preached . . . he wrote . . . in order to replace by the writing what was lost by his departure."[48] Isaiah 8:16 and 30:8, and Jeremiah 29 and 36 explain the origin and purpose of some of the prophetic books in the same way. The New Testament contains statements that express the equal authority of apostles and prophets (Eph 2:20; 2 Pet 3:2); other statements indicate the eminence of the apostles over the prophets (Mt 10:16–17; Lk 16:16; Rev 21:12–14); in one instance the ministry of the new covenant is called even more glorious than that of the old (2 Cor 3:7–11).

These references indicate the biblical testimony on which the Jewish-Catholic-Fundamentalist consensus (except for the rejection of the New Testament by the Jews) is built. The (Presbyterian) Westminster Confession of 1647 (I, 4) states, with classical brevity and clarity: "The authority of the holy scripture . . . dependeth . . . wholly upon God . . . the author thereof; and therefore it is to be received, because it is the word of God." Its argument consists of three statements: first, the Bible possesses supreme authority because it is the word of God; second, it is the word of God because it says so; and third, it says this with supreme authority. A note of grandeur is perceived in this argument. An invitation to humility before the Law laid down by God is extended. Conviction, and perhaps faith, stands behind such reasoning. What more can a man or a community ultimately do, but bravely make a confession and simply inform others of what they have "received" as true?

The Weakness of Legalism

Different objections can be raised to the literalist and legalist insistence upon the Bible's divinity. They all point to a common misunderstanding: the Bible is mistaken for a law.

1) We have already seen that not all biblical statements are introduced as word of God. "O that we had meat to eat! We remember the fish we ate in Egypt for nothing, the cucumbers, the melons, the leeks, the onions, and the garlic. . . . Why have I not found favor in thy sight, that thou dost lay the burden of all this

people upon me? . . . My God, why hast thou forsaken me. . . . There is no God . . . I say [it], not the Lord. . . . I speak in a human way. . . . I shall not be a fool. . . . I have been a fool!" (Num 11:5, 11; Ps 22:1; 53:1; 1 Cor 7:12; Rom 3:5; 2 Cor 12:6, 11) If these words can hardly be identified with God's own word and are yet found in the Bible, they seem to prove that perhaps only a Bible purified of human background noises and dubious accretions should be equated with the divine word. The problem of where to stop eliminating the human factor then becomes an enterprise that throws the word of God at the mercy of its critical purifiers.

2) The Bible itself treats of false prophets and apostles (1 Kings 22:22–23; 2 Cor 11:4, 13). They pretend to have seen visions, to have received auditions, and to speak the word of God. Even if various criteria for the detection of liars are given (as in Jer 28; Deut 18:20–22; Mt 24:23–26; Gal 1:8; 1 Jn 4:1–3), the misuse of the formula, "Thus says the Lord," cannot be prevented. Since the same, or a similar formula is also found in the Koran, Jews and Christians had better build their doctrine of the Bible's specific authority upon less shaky ground. A speaker's or writer's assertion that he speaks in God's name may point to the direction from which he received his commission, and may indicate how his message should be received. But the content and consequence of his message must vindicate his claim; his formula is no authentication—no matter how often it is used.

Jesus himself is the decisive witness in this matter: "If I bear witness to myself, my testimony is not true; there is another who bears witness to me. . . . If I glorify myself, my glory is nothing; it is my Father who glorifies me . . ." (Jn 5:31–32; 8:54; cf. Heb 5:4–5). Is the Bible more than Christ? If *his* authority was neither established nor proved by his assertion that he was the Son of God and had all authority, then the Bible's authority cannot be proved just by reference to texts which claim to be the word of God. Jesus

Christ was satisfied to fulfill his servant ministry in humility. If the apostles are not above their master, neither are their writings.

3) All too often the Scripture-quoting apologists of the Bible's authority create the impression that they themselves are not truly subject to the Bible, but wish to subject others to their own authority. Would not the humble, joyful, liberal attitude of a man who respects the Bible—and a corresponding application of its contents to his dealings with fellow men—speak much more eloquently than the bitter zeal of fanatics and lawyers who pretend to know all about authority?

Defenders of the "high doctrine of the Bible" are on safe ground when they seek the root of all authority in God himself, but when they assume they have God's revelation and authority in their hands because they handle and quote the Bible, they are guilty of presumption. The authority of the Bible is not theirs. They have not been standing "in the council of the Lord" (Jer 23:18); they are in no position to judge or to assert the Bible's infallibility. Those speaking of the Bible's infallibility inevitably assume that they are in a position to pass judgment over both the truth and the Bible. The biblical witnesses appear to be more humble and mysterious than their Catholic and Protestant apologists. Only that sort of reasoning about the Bible which, in deed and word, discloses a humble submission to authority rather than an attempt to master it, is truly theological.

4) In any case, the Bible simply does not yield to legalist understanding and treatment. Not only is it too full of contradictions which simply cannot be resolved but, more important, even in its legal parts, it is a call to freedom, an announcement of the presence and help of the good Lord. A man would have to be insensitive to the "good news" preached in the Old and New Testaments (as Heb 4:2, 6 states) to degrade it to the status of a legal "instrument." A theologian, in the biblical sense, always speaks of the Lord of Israel, the Father of Jesus Christ, the giver of the Holy Spirit; if he

remains close to the testimony of God in the Bible, he cannot become a grim advocate of a divine law against man, but will serve as a messenger of joy. The Bible has raised its voice, and despite legalistic misinterpretation, it has been heard as God's good news for man.

Attempts at a legalistic apologetics appear doomed to failure. No one has succeeded in establishing the Bible as the sole and sufficient law for either synagogue or church. No theology, whether Jewish, Catholic, or Protestant, which speaks of the supreme authority of the Bible has failed to place another, competing authority beside it! As we saw earlier, according to Jewish legends and teaching, the oral Torah, or living tradition, is as much "from God" as the written Torah. Among orthodox Christians of the second and third centuries, the authority of the "rule of faith" (the church's Creed) and of the episcopal office was established along with the authority of the biblical canon. Since the Reform Councils of the fifteenth century, Catholics have attempted to maintain a subtle balance between the authority of tradition and the authority of the Bible; but in the heat of anti-Reformation polemic, some of them went so far as to argue that the Bible would have no authority unless it were given by the church![49] Whether in Roman Catholic, Anglican, or Protestant quarters, the juxtaposition of natural law (i.e., natural theology) and supernatural revelation necessarily imposes a certain limitation on biblical authority. Fundamentalists, in turn, bow down to another competitor. Before their Bible studies start, they seem convinced of their five Fundamentals; the result of their Bible study has to support them. In this way a certain selection of biblical truths defined by man stands as a criterion of truth above the Bible and its interpretation.

The Reformers are no exception. When they rose to uphold the principle of *sola Scriptura* against a codominion of church and tradition, they saw no reason to abandon all elements of natural theology and law. More important is the fact that they and their successors explicitly acknowledged that there exists another authority besides, if not above, the Bible. Only by the testimony of the Holy Spirit did it please God to vindicate the authority of the Bible and the truth of its contents.[50] This testimony guarantees important things: the immediate subjection of the Bible to the authority of God, and the independence of the Bible's authority from the judgment of the church. It also made sure that rational arguments for the authority of the Bible (e.g., the criteria of its antiquity, consistency, and clarity) were given that secondary or tertiary rank which they deserve.

In the nineteenth century, this testimony of the Spirit received an entirely new meaning. It was boldly equated with the religious experience of the individual or of the believing community, and was employed against both the Catholic belief in an authoritarian church and the orthodox Protestant belief in the authoritative Bible.[51] Despite misuse, this testimony of the Spirit seems to come closest to the Bible's own attitude to the authority of prophets and apostles, or to the sources, usefulness, and purpose of their words. If that testimony exists and is still being given, it may be much more convincing than the tireless but highly fatiguing recital of those biblical verses that equate the words of Scripture with words of God. "The written code kills, but the Spirit gives life" says Paul (in 2 Cor 3:6)—surely this applies to the authority of the Bible! According to Paul, it is God's Spirit alone that can and will uphold the authority of God's witnesses and the truth of their words.

When the Bible's authority is defended by reference to a formula like "Thus saith the Lord," without reference to the Spirit's ongoing testimony, it is done to compete with those books of the world's literature that claim supernatural origin, or are said to have fallen from heaven in complete and final form—much as Athene came forth from Zeus' head. Such writings are supposed to make a temple or shrine holy, to turn a bad man or society to the good, to heal a sick person, to give victory in battle, to insure the stability of oaths, and to accompany the dead on their journey. But the more that is said of them, the greater is their contrast to the testimony of the Bible. The attributes and predicates which adorn them may fit God, but they do not fit the Bible. The Bible is holy because it is useful for God's own work of sanctifying sinful people. Therefore, a truly theological approach to the Bible abstains from deifying the Bible. It recognizes the humility and humanity of the biblical witnesses and words.

This observation makes us turn to an entirely different way of describing the Bible's authority, a way that should help us see the book more clearly in its human character.

CHAPTER IV

ANTHROPOLOGICAL ARGUMENTS FOR HUMANITY

The Bible's Aesthetic Value

There is a famous saying that unless man's eye is sunlike it cannot see the sun. If we apply this to the question of biblical authority, it means that the Bible possesses authority only inasmuch as there is something in man that makes him susceptible to its influence. The mystery and seal of the Bible's authority, therefore, is a condition of man rather than of the book; its hearers and readers have to be alive and responsive. It acts compellingly on many men because it meets with specifically human, personal, and existential needs. For this reason it is held that, if we wish to demonstrate the Bible's unique authority, we should start with an analysis of man's strength and weakness, his finitude and his yearning for eternity.

Many attempts have been made either to complement the high doctrine of Scripture or to create a substitute for it. This often resulted in an affirmation of the Bible's internal and subjective authority. Why should not the internal and subjective be of much higher value and deeper impact than anything external to man—even if the external object shows signs of supernatural qualities? If the reader has even a minimum of aesthetic sensitivity and can perceive the beauty that belongs to the Bible, should not the Bible's authority be much greater than when it is imposed as a rigorous law? Since the eighteenth century, theologians have tried to do justice to the literary, historical, and human character of the Bible. No dogma or prejudice was to overrule the results of psychological observation, objective literary and historical research, and systematic reasoning. The historical character of the Bible was to be given greater consideration. The reader's capacity to evaluate critically everything in the Bible was made the touchstone of its value. A new dogma was proudly proclaimed: that the criterion for knowing whether, and how, "God touches us . . . lies within ourselves, in the response of our own spirit to the Spirit that utters itself in the Scriptures. . . . In morals and religion no purely objective evidence is obtainable."[52] Schleiermacher[53] and Kierkegaard[54] are the nineteenth-century fathers of this attitude; thinkers who follow this approach are often called "liberal" theologians. They have built upon the foundations of the eighteenth-century Enlightenment, and frequently take a radical stand against the high orthodox teaching. They are supposedly outmoded in our time,[55] since their opponent, the ultraconservative view of the Bible, is also said to have become obsolete. But their arguments are as old as the Bible, and anything but dead.

We shall consider three representative anthropological arguments.

In the first, observations concerning man *in genere* are made the basis of argument. The individual man, or the man's reason, may be considered the measure of all things, including the authority of the Bible. Following the reasoning of some Greek (especially Stoic) thinkers, it is taught that the logical or rational faculties with which man is endowed—or for which he strives—reveal a pre-established harmony between man's mind and the order of the universe. If the same logos, or spirit, is working both outside and inside man—in nature or history as well as in human thought—objective and subjective truth cannot be different things. Nothing is required to demonstrate the Bible's authority but evidence of its harmony with the nature and demands of spirit or reason. Justin the Martyr, Clement of Alexandria, and innumerable later Christian scholars were convinced that this harmony could be proved.

But the nature and capacities of man may also be described in another way. His self-consciousness, his awareness of history, and his will may be shifted into the foreground. It was Augustine[56] who opened the minds of Western thinkers to the mysteries of man's dialogue with himself, and to an interpretation of human history that went beyond the limits of rationalism. For him—as for some of his Neoplatonist teachers—the "word" is essentially a sign that directs man's will toward those things that have true being, even to being itself. Full understanding is identified with love of the object that is manifested.[57] It can then be argued that since the Bible contains that signifying word which instills ultimate love, its authority for man cannot be questioned.

Again, man may be understood as conditioned not only by reason and will, but by either the hard facts of biological and economic development, or the challenges life offers him and the possibilities the future throws open to him. This corresponds to the materialist and existentialist view of man. If it could be proved, either that the Bible is built upon the conditions that shape every man's life, or that, unlike other books, it mediates an encounter with truth and opens a future to man, its unique authority might be solidly established. Popular archaeological books on the Bible attempt to prove that the Bible is much truer to verifiable historical facts than was often assumed. Similarly, a widespread psychological interpretation emphasizes that the stories of the Bible fit beautifully among the "varieties of religious experience."

Finally, man may be characterized not by things he controls or the facts and events that can be shown to control him, but by a power, a truth, a history that lies beyond the grasp of reason, will, or self-consciousness. In Plato, myths are used not only for indicating the limits of the logos but also for hinting at the indispensable, mysterious background of all logical argument. Kant teaches us that religion is not restricted to pure reason, though some of its postulates are rationally explicable. Some linguistic analysts acknowledge that the descriptive language of the natural sciences (which is appropriate for the definition of things that can be touched, or rules that can be verified) is not the only language that makes sense; the language of conviction and confession may also present just claims.[58] Tillich rejoices in the power that belongs to symbols and symbolic diction and he warns of its misuse. If it could be shown that the Bible fills the necessary role of mythical, symbolic, or convictional speech, it would surely possess great authority. Augustine[59] argues in just this way. Two modes of knowledge have to be distinguished—the way of reason used by science, and the way of authority recognized by faith. They need not exclude each other. The Bible deals with matters of faith, not of science. It makes sense to accept its direction, precisely because it points out things reason and science cannot grasp.

This kind of apologetics may be summed up in more recent terms: man's ultimate concern, man's need to experience love, man's selfhood in historic existence, or man's encounter with the totally Other, the Holy, the *mysterium fascinans et tremendum* find stimulus, expression, and verification in the Bible. Here is a love (*agape*) distinct from either a Platonic or sexual *eros*. Here we have at least a few hard facts—the exodus of certain tribes from Egypt, the conquest of a heathen land, the establishment of a

Davidic dynasty, the destruction of Jerusalem, the death of Jesus of Nazareth, the mission work of some of the apostles. No historian can doubt that these events have great historical and symbolic power. Here a challenge is presented to humanity: behold, and encounter your God! A prophetic historiography that calls for participation in authentic historical existence is offered. The myths and symbols expressed are often those common to almost all religions or present in the subconscious mind of every man. Here are a record and source of religious experience that have proved—and are still proving—both impressive and effective. Therefore, the need of humanity is met and the highest potential of man is displayed when the authority of the Bible is recognized.

Such reasoning based on the need, concern, and experience of man need not totally exclude those arguments described earlier as typically Jewish, Catholic, and Fundamentalist. The anthropological reasons for the Scriptures' authority have sometimes been set in opposition to theological reasoning, but they need not always oppose them. Augustine's great influence upon Western Christianity may be due to the subtle way in which he combined theological, metaphysical, existentialist, and psychological arguments. In Thomas Aquinas, reason and faith are far from mutually exclusive: faith perfects the work begun by reason. Among orthodox Protestant scholars, rational grounds for proving the Bible's authority were readily accepted. The eighteenth-century struggle of Lessing with his orthodox antagonist Goeze, or similarly fierce nineteenth-century disputes have no present-day counterparts. Scholars of our time are inclined to reconcile the extreme positions: "The moral passion for social righteousness cherished by the Hebrew Prophet was a genuine 'revelation' of higher values, yet it was not less a personal 'discovery,' and these were blended into the unity of an experience which underlies the prophet's 'Thus says the Lord.' We can give a psychological analysis of that experience which yields us no more than 'Thus says the prophet,' whilst a dogmatic theory of inspiration has sometimes claimed that the message was wholly divine. The truth does not lie between these extremes but above them, in the unity of the fellowship of the human spirit with the divine."[60] Enlightened orthodoxy and conservative pietism can thus combine in a higher unity decisive features of both the theological and anthropological approaches. The distinctive features of the two ways of reasoning no longer appear divisive. Whenever one way proves too steep or dangerous, a change-over to the other takes place. Reconciliation rather than division is the goal of anthropological reasoning for the Bible's authority.

However, there are other anthropological arguments for biblical authority that seem no less respectable. One approach would stress that the universal characteristics, needs, and experiences of man do not exhaust the essence of humanity. There are also the characteristics and deeds of special men—that is, of *great men*. The history of civilization and culture, of nations and sciences, of art and literature, is unthinkable without the lives and works of heroes, sages, and artists. Men make history; the fact that many people may not know their achievements or care to respect their authority cannot diminish their real impact.

Jesus of Nazareth has sometimes been presented as an outstanding member of a group of prophets composed of Moses, Gautama, Zoroaster, Mohammed, and others. It is equally feasible to consider Jeremiah and Paul, the author of the Fourth Gospel, and perhaps even Daniel as religious heroes of the same rank as the greatest philosophers or inspired artists. C. H. Dodd[61] compares the scriptural authors to great artists and the Bible's uniqueness to that of a work of art; he speaks of the "authority of individual inspiration" which is felt in both. Although a parallel ranking of religion and art seems to disregard the superior character of religion, an ascending line, leading from science to art, and onward to religion, has frequently been constructed.[62] Since there are undoubtedly experts in the fields of science and art, the Bible was considered an accumulation of the experience, words, and works of experts in religion. Not all biblical authors need have reached the same altitude; the Bible may illustrate the process from primitive to purified ideas of God. If the purification of religious thought and practice is the great thrust of the Bible, man's debt to the heroes that helped to achieve it is incalculable.

Among the creative ideas of the biblical authors, there is one of special importance. They themselves insist that something happened to them before they became creators; what happened is commonly called "a revelation of God." It was given to them to see visions, to understand events, to plant hope, and to give guidance. Their personal authority is to be located in the manner in which they experienced, evaluated, and shaped given events, and in the power with which they proclaimed what they considered crucial. "[The Lord] has showed you, O man, what is good; and what does the Lord require of you but to do justice, and to love kindness, and to walk humbly with your God?" (Mic 6:8) Prophets and apostles were men who responded promptly and nobly to the challenge of their environment.

Little wonder that by the study of the books of the Law, of Isaiah, the Psalms, John, or Paul, other spirits were kindled and new geniuses (like Philo, Origen, Augustine, Luther) were begotten. One fire kindles another; but in order to burn, there has to be combustible material. Consequently, the Bible's authority may well be that it is a burning fire for all that are able to be inflamed by it!

It is obvious that this kind of argument has a distinctly aristocratic flavor. Giant spirits are distinguished from the masses, and an appeal is made to those able or willing to participate in the higher levels of existence. What sensible man can deny or belittle the beauty and incisiveness of the prophets' language, the social and religious concern and the wisdom of the Deuteronomic legislation, the immediate appeal of the Sermon on the Mount's radicalism, and the depth and warmth of Pauline and Johannine thought?

But there are less uplifting biblical passages. According to humanistic Bible students, they belong to a more primitive level of religious development which, in turn, is successively and successfully overcome by the spiritual evolution manifested in those texts which achieve an increasingly universal character. The widespread notion of "progressive revelation" seems both to establish the Bible's authority and to account for its weaknesses. The Bible was understood to show, to inspire—and perhaps to guarantee—the ascent of the soul from fleshly captivity in primitive religious notions to the pure vision of God. Philo of Alexandria was already convinced that the archaic ritual laws and ancient stories of the patriarchs, and even Israel's liberation from Egypt, were to be understood not only in their "fleshly meaning" but also as an image of the ascent of the soul to God on the "King's Highway" (Num 20:17).

Before making any attempt at criticizing this claim for biblical authority, we have to consider a third kind of anthropological reasoning, designed to avoid the limitations of the aristocratic approach. After the nineteenth-century celebration of the individual hero, another mode of thinking gained the upper hand. It was rediscovered and asserted with great vehemence that *man is a social being,* and that he has to be analyzed and understood as such. Sociological studies and arguments did not replace, but began to reshape and enrich a predominantly psychological, aesthetic, or idealist interpretation of man, history, and religion. Instead of valuing only the contribution of individuals to the history and culture of mankind, the people's feelings, needs, yearnings, and wisdom were again given a place. J. G. v. Herder and the brothers Grimm prepared the way for what today is called the form-critical, or traditio-historical, school of Bible interpretation.

If literature can be traced back to the family assembling around the hearth, the tribe meeting at the campfire, or the religious, political, and judicial assemblies of the people at holy trees, historic sites, and sanctuaries, the deepest roots of the Bible's special power may also lie in the beliefs, the tales, and the ceremonies of a community.

The community out of which the Bible grew is that of Israel and the early church. The reader of the Old Testament is confronted with the experiences, the celebrations, and the longings of nomadic tribes, of settlers conquering the land, of a growing nation seeking stability in a monarchic constitution, of country people in conflict with developing urban capitalism, of prophetic movements resisting both political absolutism and ceremonial formalism, of priests and scribes concerned with timeless order and law, and of visionaries trusting in a redemption that comes from supernatural interference. This community goes through diverse phases; at times its identity is obscured or becomes questionable. But the diversity of the different strands and strata of Old Testament literature reveals that a living community rather than a timeless idea stands behind all that is written. Similarly, the New Testament reflects the life and thought of groups that, despite all differences, form one body. There are Jewish groups; the austere John the Baptist and his disciples; the prophetic and puritan Pharisees, rigorously resisting the indifference of the "people of the land"; the assimilationist Sadducees; the zealots, with their underground movement; the ever-suspected and scorned Samaritans; the ambiguous Galileans; and Jesus and his disciples. And there are the churches of Jerusalem and Samaria, of Antioch and Ephesus, of Corinth and of Rome. Besides the many different Jewish factions, each of the Christian groups may also have included clusters of conservative Judaists, enlightened Hellenists, radically dualistic ascetics, or cynical libertines. To a large extent, the various New Testament books present either the voice *of* one of these groups or the challenge extended *to* them.

If biblical religion is based upon the changing experiences of such groups, why were the contents of the Old and New Testaments fixed in writing? Someone influenced by form-criticism or by the importance of the sociological context of the Bible might say that it was because the sum of what the community of worshipers had received, experienced, and celebrated was considered worthy of written form. Consequently, the Bible is not to be considered an external norm imposed upon believers; originally and of its nature, it is nothing but the remembrance of the very life lived by religious people. The biblical books were recognized as canonical because they expressed the accepted (or acceptable) tradition of the community. Not an external authority, but the immanent richness and relevance of the group experience was acknowledged. What was actually *vox populi* was now hailed as *vox Dei*.

Therefore, regardless of whether a given biblical passage seems mythological, historical, biographical, legalistic, ceremonial, or moral, it may possess authority, because it is true to some sort of genuine piety. The very changes, adaptations, and reformations which are typical of a community's life—and of all real life—may possess a power that convinces the susceptible reader better than statements made in the name of a transcendent power. As long as the Bible is considered a representation of the ongoing vitality of religious life, its authority need not be based on an upward evolution or progressive purification. The ups and downs of nomadic, monarchic, prophetic, priestly, institutionalist, and spiritualist communities and their leaders can be sincerely appreciated only if the reader is looking for something more than drab facts or evolutionary charts and can show some understanding for people as they actually live! C. H. Dodd's *The Authority of the Bible* combines belief in "the authority of individual inspiration" and "the authority of corporate experience."[63] The individualistic and the sociological reasons for the authority of the Bible obviously do not exclude one another.

What was begun by poets and professors enamored of folklore, and avidly taken up by Protestant biblical scholars, has now been adopted by Catholic theologians like K. Rahner and G. Tavard.[64] Their treatment of the relationship of the Bible's authority to the authority of the Church is intended to ease the age-old Protestant-Catholic dispute on Scripture and tradition. Both before and since the Reformation of the sixteenth century, official and private Roman Catholic documents have spoken of Scripture and tradition as two sources of revelation available to the Church. Against this view, orthodox and conservative Protestants pointed to the slogan, *sola Scriptura,* often called the formal principle of the Reformation. Rahner and Tavard, however, now argue that the Bible is the sum and expression of the church's self-consciousness. "The archetypal memory of the Church . . . adequately embodies itself into the Scripture." The Scripture is both "God's word" and "genuine self-manifestation of the Church's faith." The Bible cannot be word of God if it is severed from the church. An "inclusive concept of Scripture and Church" is necessary because they are "mutually inherent."

What makes Scripture authoritative in such an interpretation? The unique and decisive role of the early church! In the period ending with the death of the last of the apostles, the church received God's final revelation; by his grace, the Apostolic Church became the standard for future generations, and the Bible became the adequate, objective record of revelation. Therefore, the Bible is normative at all times and places for the whole church. It is the epitome of the delivered message *and* the received faith, the essence of tradition *and* interpretation. It cannot be set in opposition to tradition; for the living tradition and interpretation of the church are inherent in the Scriptures, and the Scriptures inhere in the living church. Accordingly, the witness of the Bible is not inferior to that of any oral tradition or proclamation; the Writ serves to preserve the entrusted good, and to bridge the separation of space and time between the early and the later church.

Of course, there are other humanistic arguments for the authority of the Bible. But the examples given are sufficient to show the sensitive perception and enlightening commentary that stand behind this kind of apologetics. Perhaps the formula, "Thus says the Lord," is explained away too easily by the humanist apologists, but they may have been listening more carefully than their orthodox opponents to the statements that follow it, as well as to all those passages in which no claim is made for divine authorship. Both the strengths and weaknesses of the humanistic arguments demand careful consideration.

The Ministry of Poetry

The psychological, aesthetic, and sociological presentation of the authority of Scripture is grounded in the understanding of the Bible as a work of lyric poetry. Since it gives eloquent expression to human need and the answer to need given by the experience of love, acceptance, and understanding; since it achieves an artistic formulation of the highest and deepest emotions that man can feel; since it speaks of and to the people with a voice more compelling than that of bare facts or rational argument, the lyric character of the Bible may be the key to the real nature of its power. This may be illustrated by a brief discussion of the ways in which poetry occurs in Scripture.[65]

Among both the older and more recent elements incorporated in the Bible there are verses, couplets, ballads, and songs, used on the most diverse occasions. "Arise, O Lord, and let thy enemies be scattered," is the shout that goes up before battle. After victory, comes the song, "I will sing unto the Lord, for he has triumphed gloriously. . . . Saul has slain his thousands, and David his ten thousands. . . . This is the Lord's doing; it is marvelous in our eyes. This is the day which the Lord has made." After defeat, "Thy glory, O Israel, is slain. . . . Tell it not. . . . How lonely sits the city that was full of people! How like a widow has she become. . . . I am the man who has seen affliction. . . . I have been hunted like a bird." Over the death of a child, "O my son Absalom, my son, my son Absalom! Would I had died instead of you!" In captivity, "We must pay for the water we drink. . . . By the waters of Babylon, there we sat down and wept." When standing guard, "Watchman, what of the night?" When angry, "I have slain a man for wounding me. . . . If Cain is avenged sevenfold, truly Lamech seventy-sevenfold!" When digging a well, "Spring up, O well—sing to it" (Num 10:35; Ps 68:1; Ex 15:1 ff.; 1 Sam 18:7; Ps 118:23–25; 2 Sam 1:19 ff.; Lam 1:1; 3:1, 52; 5:4; 2 Sam 18:33; Ps 137:1 ff.; Is 21:11; Gen 4:24; Num 21:17). Poetry accompanies and vocalizes war and politics, love and hatred. Abounding joy takes turns with heartbreaking lamentation. One man moans, "Out of the depths I cry to thee, O Lord"; another meditates on the vanity of vanities, man's life; a third dances without restraint or propriety before the Lord. A queen warns her son not to drink wine, but encourages the poor and bitterly distressed to "drink and forget"; an angry and deeply hurt man expresses his resentment that he was ever born, made, as he is, of clay, poured out "like milk" and curdled "like cheese"; "a man who drinks iniquity like water" (Ps 130; Eccles; 2 Sam 6:14–23; Prov 31:1–7; Job 3; 10:9–10; 15:16).

It is not only isolated lines, verses, chapters, or books of the Bible that are lyrical in character. The so-called mythical elements of the Bible (e.g., Gen 1–11; Is 11; 14), the work of historiographers (among whom the author of 1 Sam and Lk are outstanding), the collections of legends (stories of the patriarchs and David, in the Gospels and Acts), of popular or wise men's aphorisms (Proverbs; the Letter of James), of parables, examples, riddles—all these elements of the Bible contribute, each in its own way, to enliven prosaic texts.[66] Even the visions recorded by classic and apocalyptic authors may be considered lyrics in a wider sense. The authors of the Books of Chronicles, Ezra, and Nehemiah, may seem to be genealogists and ecclesiastics; but since some of their lists and conclusions may be imaginary rather than factual, even they may have to be called poets.

The reader of the Old Testament is confronted with the surprising fact that although prose predominates throughout the Bible, the things that are most important are said in poetic language. Relevant utterances are never made in poor style. Blessings and curses, oracles and prayers, recitals of the beginnings, accounts of ancient events, and promises concerning the last things—the joy of life and the horror of death—are all in verse, or expressed in metaphors, parables, and symbols, or told in artful prose.

The New Testament seems to offer a different picture. The language in which its seventy-seven books are written is a late, somehow degenerated or artificially revived form of Greek. Jesus' nativity story (as told in Lk 1–2), certain parables, and outstanding parts of sermons or treatises (for example, Mt 5:3–10; 1 Cor 13; Jn 1:1–18) are highly poetic in character and diction. Revelation is dramatically structured, and contains many moving hymns and acclamations. But since the bulk of the New Testament is narrative and didactic, lyricism is not its main form of expression. However, one feature calls for attention: throughout the New Testament, decisive statements about Jesus Christ[67] are made in the form of verses. These verses have confessional, though not individual or personal character; they were probably composed and used long before the New Testament books were written, and they appear to constitute the core of the written message.

Since poetry plays such an outstanding part in the Bible, those scholars who have concerned themselves with its lyric character have made an important contribution to our understanding. But certain objections must be made to the way in which they use their insight to defend the Bible's authority.

The Misery of Lyricism

It is obvious that neither the general yearning of mankind for an authority that lies beyond the bounds of pure reason, nor the experience of heartwarming encounters with superrational forces prove the unique authority of the Bible. Religious experience may be nothing but voluntary or involuntary submission to suggestive power. Errors and crimes may be the result of blind acceptance of authority, as well as true insight and good deeds. Human finitude and need alone cannot, therefore, demonstrate why the words of the Bible are to be trusted and obeyed. Everything that makes an impression on man is not necessarily true and relevant, even if it is expressed in the finest poetic style.

Despite the great aesthetic and educational value of many biblical passages, it is clear that the Bible as a whole is not a work of and for spiritual aristocrats. It also contains—perhaps to its credit—prosaic, pedestrian, and plebeian elements. Other books consistently maintain a higher aesthetic or symbolic level. Why should the Chronicles be read, if Thomas a Kempis' *Imitatio Christi,* Luther's *Magnificat,* or Bunyan's *Pilgrim's Progress* are at hand; or if Sophocles' *Antigone,* Michelangelo's *David* and Mozart's *Don Juan* are of higher aesthetic and symbolic force? Any great work of art may, indeed, express both the human condition and the highest human yearning at least as eloquently as the Bible. Although an allegorical interpretation, such as Philo's, can find a sublime religious and moral value in each letter and on each page of the Bible, a similar approach has actually led to comparable claims for Homer, and can transform any Western movie into a morality play.

The sociological argument that the Bible gives voice to the heartbeat of the religious community may well be the most impressive among the anthropological reasons for the Bible's authority. In such an approach, there is fortunately some interest, affection, and humor left for the baser passages of Scripture. This argument may explain why the Bible must have some authority in the church, if the church is to preserve its identity. But it contains little to prove the universal authority of the Bible. Although it illustrates why all the great religions of the world possess one or several holy books,[68] it does not tell us why each ethnic or religious group should not be entitled to ascribe to its own holy books the same authority as that ascribed to the Bible. The many holy books that exist—the Egyptian Book of the Dead in its many forms, the myths of Mesopotamia, the Sibylline Oracles, the Avesta, the Tripitaka, the Koran, the Vedas, the Upanishads—have all expressed the religious life of a community. And if the esteem in which a book is held decided a religion's value, Mohammedanism would have to be considered superior to both Judaism and Christianity.

In sum, the presence of religious need; the impact of great religious men and inspiring leaders; the voice of tradition, liturgy, and hope—all these elements may call fine words and traditions into being, yet fail to demonstrate that the true God is present and revealed in the testimony of the Bible. Lyricism alone does not prove that the Holy Spirit is at work. According to 1 Kings 22:22–23, a lying spirit was accepted by both religious specialists and by the masses of the people. God himself had to intervene in order to reveal the truth. The friends of Job argued religious questions expertly, but God turned against them. After Jesus' resurrection, two of his disciples were engaged in a discussion which reveals a sense of tragedy and the disenchantment with human existence characteristic of a post-Christian age: "We had hoped that he was the one to redeem Israel" (Lk 24:21). The risen Jesus had to interfere in person. Only he could lead them beyond tragedy and self-pity. He did so by teaching them to understand the Scriptures, to recognize who had been with them, and to enjoy the work of the Spirit (Lk 24:13–49). In no case was human need, human religious feeling, or the word of human experts enough to establish the truth. Poetry by itself, however deep and sincere, cannot solve the problems of the human predicament.

The Bible is the record of God's interference on behalf of man. The conversation that takes place and is heard by the reader of the Bible is neither a soliloquy nor a debate between the higher and baser self (e.g., the spirit and the body), nor a mere exchange of words between man and man. God is the main partner in the biblical dialogue. Before man asks about God, God himself speaks and asks Adam, "Where are you?" (Gen 3:9) God calls man by his name and sets him apart for his service (1 Sam 3:4; Amos 7:14–15; Mk 1:17; 2:14; Acts 9:4; Is 43:1; Ex 3:4). Even those who are in a position to rule and judge others (e.g., by rightly condemning them as thieves) cannot escape God's interference. Of all people, the judges among men have to accept God's judgment. For God says, "You are the man!" (2 Sam 12:7) Not only individuals, but a whole people may be addressed by God in a manner no man would have chosen for himself. It is said precisely of God's chosen people, "Your father was an Amorite . . . you were cast out on the open field . . . you were naked and bare . . . you trusted in your beauty and played the harlot" (Ezek 16; cf. Hos 1). Corresponding to God's surprising address is man's response. Israel is told to acknowledge its election without any display of pride: "You shall make response before the Lord your God, 'A wandering Aramean was my father . . .' " (Deut 26:5 ff.). God's conversation with man does not contain only disclosures and charges in regard to man's existence. By addressing himself to man, God overwhelms him with the revelation of this goodness and the promise of blessing. "The Lord, the Lord, a God merciful and gracious, slow to anger, and abounding in steadfast love and faithfulness . . . forgiving iniquity and transgression and sin. . . . I will bless you, and make your name great, so that you will be a blessing. I will bless those who bless you . . . by you all the families of the earth shall bless themselves. . . . Before they call I will answer. . . . The words that I have spoken to you are spirit and life. . . . [Lord] you have words of eternal life. . . . You shall be my witnesses. . . . Lo, I am with you always" (Ex 34:6; Gen 12:2–3; Is 65:24; Jn 6:63, 68; Acts 1:8; Mt 28:20). In the dialogues between God and man, "there is only one lawgiver and judge; he who is able to save and to destroy" (Jas 4:12). If man "takes upon himself to speak to the Lord," it befits him to confess that he is "but dust and ashes" (Gen 18:27).

The same is true of the Bible. All its poetry is but dust and ashes unless God himself recognizes it as prayer, response, or witness to himself. The humanistic apologetics of the Bible was based upon a doubt similar to the one uttered by the serpent in paradise: "Did God say . . . ?" (Gen 3:1) It seemed so obvious to enlightened readers that no one but man spoke in the Bible! Less and less was man understood as the living God's chosen partner, created and redeemed to respond to him. More often, God was taken for a human idea, and religion was seen as the sum of man's intuition and experience of a higher being. Whether man was understood to be the maker or the victim of his religion, that religion became largely a matter of feeling. The spirit to which reference was still made[69] was now identified with the spirit of religion. And the *homo religiosus* was left alone in the company of that spirit, the religious community, and the heroes of religion. Man was thus led to believe that he must ultimately live in solitude and loneliness. The pronouncement made by F. Nietzsche and his imitators that "God is dead" was a necessary consequence of this kind of biblical apologetics.

The result of the anthropological defense of the Bible's authority is thus widely different from the legalism of the theological defenders. But lyricism cannot claim to lead to any better appreciation of the Bible's authority. Legalism at least recognized a partner: God the Lawgiver. Lyricism leaves man alone with himself, in a hell from which there is "no exit."

Since the Bible presents a mystery that transcends the rigor of Law as well as the pulse of human need, great art, and religious folklore, its defenders were forced to seek still another way of demonstrating its authority.

CHAPTER V

A CHRISTOLOGICAL ANALOGY FOR TWO NATURES[70]

Chalcedon Applied

1 *Reality and Desirability of a Third Way*

In the preceding two sections some of the theological and anthropological arguments that have been used to explain the authority of the Bible were presented. In one case its divinity, in the other its humanity was the basis of pleading the cause of the Bible. If conservatives asserted that the Bible is the very "word of God" because it frequently says so, humanists maintained that the Bible is spoken and written by men and is, therefore, "word of man." Both camps may continue to war against each other;[71] or they may meet on the basis of compromise formulae.[72]

Whether they decide for war or for peace, for a mutually exclusive or a complementary attitude and solution, they may be suffering from a common weakness. Both argue from real or alleged evidence regarding *those who speak* in the Bible. Both show a tendency to relegate *what is said* to a position of secondary importance. Yet, if it could be shown that, not only material introduced by formulae such as "God said," "I [Paul] speak," or "the fool says in his heart," but the entire contents of the Bible defines and manifests the Bible's authority, then a radically new approach would lie open to both conservative and liberal apologists.

On given occasions a voice that possesses no formal authority may be heeded, even when the speaker is unknown. A New Testament writer once introduces an Old Testament text with the surprising words, "Somebody says somewhere [It has been testified somewhere]" (Heb 2:6). He does not feel it is necessary to refer to the divine or inspired speaker; the words speak for themselves. Calvin's maxim, *Summa Scripturae probatio passim a Dei loquentis persona sumitur* ("the proof of the Bible's authority is derived from the person of God who is speaking"),[73] obviously does not apply to the quotation formula used in Hebrews 2:6. The same may well be true of large parts of the Bible. They need not be spoken by a previously known speaker in order to be valid. The human author of many biblical books is not known to us, though they bear the name of a prophet or an apostle. But if they speak of somebody or something that possesses authority beyond comparison, they may partake of the authority of that which is attested by them. As we have shown earlier,[74] the books of the Bible are signs, pointing to a mysteriously powerful center. Like the spokes of a wheel, their usefulness depends upon the hub and axle which hold them together and give them their function.

The center of the New Testament is the person and work of Jesus Christ. In the service of this center the historic, didactic, and eschatological pages of this part of the Bible were written. In New Testament writings it is explicitly asserted that the same Jesus Christ is also the focus of the Old Testament. Who Jesus is, what he suffers, what he effects, is called the fulfillment of all that, "according to the Scriptures" (i.e., the Old Testament), was promised or commanded by God, or expected by God's servants and God's people (Mt 5:17–19; 1 Cor 15:3–4; Rom 3:21; Lk 24:27; Acts 3:21; Heb 1:1 ff., etc.) Jesus Christ alone is the cornerstone or capstone of the building whose foundations are the prophets and the apostles (Eph 2:20).

Obviously, not every student of the Bible is willing to state that the Old and New Testaments have their center in Jesus Christ. Jewish interpreters may readily admit that the New Testament is a culmination of essential elements of the Old Testament; many of them are willing to count Jesus of Nazareth among the prophets of Israel. But they do not believe that all Scripture bears witness to Jesus Christ; that Moses and the prophets wrote about him; that through the prophets, the "Spirit of Christ" made known the suffering and glory that were to come to Christ; or that in Psalm 16 David "foresaw and spoke of the resurrection of the Christ" (Jn 1:45; 5:39, 46; 1 Pet 1:11; Acts 2:31). The Jew Trypho, against whom Justin the Martyr argued in the second century, is one among many protesting Jewish voices. But opponents to a Christological interpretation of the Old Testament are found among Christians as well. Since the time when Justin's contemporary, Marcion, denied the identity of the Father of Jesus Christ and the God of Abraham, Isaac, Jacob, and Israel, the question of the Old Testament's witness to Jesus Christ has been raised even in Christian congregations. Some of the most outspoken early opponents of direct relationship between Jesus Christ and the Old Testament were considered heretics by the Church. But some of the more recent skeptics have been eminent Protestant scholars in the field of Old Testament studies. That Jesus Christ is the focus of both Testaments is thus not an undisputed fact. Still, there is a Roman Catholic consensus, in which the Eastern Orthodox and a great number of Protestants join, that the two Testaments have their common focus in Jesus Christ.

Once this premise is accepted, it is possible to demonstrate the Bible's authority in a third way. The Christological approach differs from both the theological and the anthropological arguments we have considered previously. Its presupposition is the "orthodox" profession that Jesus Christ, the center of the whole Bible, is neither God only nor man only, but both true God and true man, in an inseparable, personal, "hypostatic" union. In the synodal decrees of Ephesus (431) and Chalcedon (451), this union was solemnly affirmed. In Orthodox, Roman Catholic, and Protestant Statements of Faith, the same union was reaffirmed again and again. Why should what is confessed true of Jesus Christ not be true of the Bible as well? The Bible's power may be due precisely to the mysterious union of true deity and true humanity to which the book itself bears testimony. To anyone willing to exploit the logical potential of the principle of analogy, biblical Christology—the derivation of the authority of the biblical words from Jesus Christ himself—offers a promising approach.

II *The Leadership of Origen*

Origen of Alexandria (d. 254) was the first Christian thinker to realize what conclusions might be drawn from an analogy between Christ and the Bible. It is impossible to exhaust the richness and variety of Origen's biblical hermeneutics with a few slogans, but Christology is surely one of the keys to his respect for the authority of the Bible, his concern for its literary and historical form, and his doctrine and practice of spiritual interpretation.

Several second-century documents, e.g., the Epistle of Barnabas, the writings of Justin the Martyr, and treatises of Clement of Alexandria—each in its own way—had emphasized that Jesus Christ, the Word, was speaking, and had already been described in the Old Testament. Finally, Irenaeus of Lyon (d. *ca.* 200)[75] summarized the relationship of Christ to the Scriptures in the following sentence: "Everywhere in Moses' Scriptures the Son of

God is inseminated." It is unlikely that "inseminated" is used here in other than a metaphorical sense, for there is no evidence that Irenaeus wanted to say the logos was incarnated in that body which is called the Old Testament. He used a metaphor but did not make an ontological statement. In some of Origen's books, on the other hand, the metaphorical speech becomes an ontological affirmation.[76]

Origen teaches that as the untouchable and invisible spoken word "becomes, as it were, flesh" when it is written in a book, so also the Word of God assumes flesh when it is written in the Bible. Since the Word and the Son of God, Jesus Christ, are one and the same (Jn 1:1), it may be said that Jesus Christ becomes, "as it were," flesh when *He* is written in the Bible! Alluding to Matthew 1:1, Origen calls the Bible the book of the birth (*genesis*) of Jesus Christ. There is not only one advent of Jesus Christ—his birth in a stable. There are three advents to be discovered: one in the time of the Old Testament, another in the time of the New Testament, the third in the present, whenever Christ comes to dwell among men. "The Word becomes continually flesh in the Scriptures in order to tabernacle among us." The Scriptures are to be understood "as one perfect body of the Word." For "as the Word of God is there [i.e., in the person of Jesus] clothed by the veil of the flesh, so it is here clothed by the veil of the letter."[77]

Distinguished recent interpreters conclude that Origen considered the Bible an incarnation of the Word. H. U. v. Balthasar writes, "In the Scripture a genuine incarnation occurs. . . . This incarnation of the Word in the body of the Scripture is at the same time more universal and more spiritual than the incarnation in the fleshly body of Jesus Christ."[78] H. de Lubac connects Origen's view of the Bible with his doctrine of the Sacrament and of the Church; for Origen there are three forms of incorporation of the logos—in the Bible, in the Eucharist, and in the community of God's people. But de Lubac distinguishes these incorporations from the one incarnation, and he assumes that Origen intends no more than to make a comparison between them.[79] R. P. C. Hanson, finally, interprets Origen as the initiator or promoter of "the startling doctrine of the Bible as the extension of the Incarnation."[80]

However, Origen wrote only of an embodiment, "as it were," of the Word in a book.[81] Once he says explicitly that the logos came to Moses, Jeremiah, and Isaiah, "not bodily."[82] The text quoted above, concerning the continued incarnation of the Word in the Scriptures,[83] may not have been written by Origen. It is therefore not necessary, and perhaps not fair, to attribute to him the doctrine of a second or extended incarnation which takes place in the Scriptures and which comes near to making the Bible a second Jesus Christ. It is more than doubtful that Origen considered the Bible a "second Christ."

However literally or spiritually Origen is interpreted, his intention is clearly to say that the same Word which was incarnate in Jesus Christ was also heard by Moses and Jeremiah when the "Word of God came to them"; it is also to be heard by the enlightened Bible reader today. What Paul had said of Jesus Christ—that he knew him no longer according to the flesh and that he is the Spirit (i.e., the Lord whom the Jews could not see; 2 Cor 3:14–17; 5:16)—became for Origen a key to interpretation.[84] The comparison of the Bible with a person's body, soul, and spirit and, even more, the comparison between the lower and higher senses of the Bible and the fleshly and the exalted Christ served to invite the Bible student to find the divine Word, the Son of God, in the Bible. Origen's adoption of a Christological interpretation led him on the way chosen almost two hundred years earlier by Philo. And he went beyond Philo. In his comparison of Scripture with a person, Philo distinguished between the body and the soul of a text; he urged the student to ascend to the perception of the text's hidden, higher meaning.[85] Origen, however, asserted that Christ's body and spirit were represented by the Scriptures, and that the ascent from the fleshly to the spiritual meaning of a text would lead to an encounter, not with some ideal spiritual truth or with an absolute being, as in Philo's case, but with the person of Jesus Christ. By progressing from the literal to the spiritual sense, from knowledge of Christ according to the flesh to the eternal logos, the student submits himself to the mysterious nature of the Bible itself. Its humanity is to be transcended; the perfect reader is to discover and to behold the divinity of the Word.

But there remains at least one unsolved problem. Did Origen, or did he not, treat the humanity of Christ and the literal character and meaning of the Bible as merely steppingstones to be left behind after they have served their purpose? "Even though we once regarded Christ from a human point of view, we regard him thus no longer" (2 Cor 5:16). This cryptic statement of Paul's, combined with 2 Corinthians 3:4–18, could lead to a somewhat haughty attitude to the humanity of Christ and the literal character of the Bible. Does Origen believe that only the highest sense of Scripture, the sense reserved for the perfect, possesses the authority of the Word? For J. Daniélou, "It is necessary to go beyond the humanity of Christ in order to attain the hidden divinity."[86] R. P. C. Hanson indicts Origen for underestimating the incarnation of the logos and the literal and historical sense of the Bible.[87] H. de Lubac[88] follows H. U. v. Balthasar's interpretation:[89] in the process of spiritualization the flesh does not cease to be true flesh. What is fleshly is abrogated, and simultaneously lifted up to a higher level. It is not relinquished or annihilated, but *aufgehoben,* i.e., terminated, absorbed, and consummated by the divine. Origen himself states, "We affirm that the mortal body and the human soul in him [Jesus] received the greatest elevation not only by communion but by union and intermingling, so that by sharing in divinity he was transformed into God."[90] The biblical union of fleshly letter and divine Word, the eucharistic union of bread and the body of Christ, and the mystic union of the church—which is both an assembly of mortal men and the body of the risen Christ—all follow this pattern of the assumption of the lower into the higher.

The principle of incarnation, understood as the double movement of the Word's descent into the realm of flesh and the flesh's elevation into unity with the Word, becomes the basis of all theological thought. This principle can be called Christological, incarnational, or sacramental. According to Balthasar, not only God's plan of salvation, but the whole universe, and being itself, rest upon one common "quasi-sacramental structure. . . . For Origen, the Church is the great universal sacrament which continues the Sacrament of the body of Christ; the Sacrament of his body contains in itself the Sacrament of the scriptural word, and enacts the Sacraments of Baptism, Eucharist, Confession, and Matrimony."[91]

While the incarnational understanding of the church and the sacraments was to be strengthened and utilized by later scholars, Origen's Christological doctrine of the Bible had a less successful history. As de Lubac shows,[92] some echoes of Origen's doctrine are to be found in the Eastern theologian, Maximus Confessor (d. *ca.* 622),[93] in Ambrose of Milan (d. 397),[94] in Augustine,[95] and in later medieval writings. But apparently the most daring features of Origen's hermeneutics were taken up neither by the great scholastic divines nor by the Reformers. That both the Old and the New Testaments bear witness to the one Word incarnated in Jesus Christ was not questioned; but the Bible was not seen as an embodiment of that Word. Luther called the Bible the swaddling clothes of God's Son,[96] but the employment of this beautiful metaphor does not prove Origen's powerful idea. When, in the centuries following the Reformation, Lutheran and Calvinist "orthodox" scholars and official documents enumerate the Bible's "perfections, affections, criteria," and defend its authority and inspiration,[97] no reference is made to an analogy between the union of the two natures of Christ and the presence of both Word of God and word of man in the Bible.

III *Neo-Origenism*

Many modern theologians are making a passionate attempt to reinstate the Christological thinking characteristic of church fathers like Irenaeus, Origen, Athanasius, or Augustine. Several among them show an inclination to illustrate the essence and role of the Bible by references to the two natures of Jesus Christ. D. F. Schleiermacher declares that the "natural standard [of the Bible's inspiration] . . . is the analogy of the doctrine of Christ's Person."[98] He holds that the activity of the Holy Spirit is related to the life, the works, and the writings of the apostles in a fashion similar "to the person-forming union of the Divine Essence with human nature which constituted the Person of Christ (this without prejudice to the specific differences that obtain between the two modes of union)." E. Brunner moves in the same direction when he asserts, "Inspiration is . . . the incarnation in written form of the living personal revelation. . . . The Church must develop its doctrine of the Scriptures on the same lines as the doctrine of the two natures. The Bible shares in the glory of the divinity of Christ and in the lowliness of his humanity."[99]

At one place in his *Kirchliche Dogmatik*,[100] Karl Barth affirms the existence of a connection between the Trinity and the unity of the revealed, written, and proclaimed forms of the Word. "The doctrine of the Word of God in its threefold form is the only analogy . . . to the doctrine of the three-in-oneness of God." God the Father and revelation, God the Son and the Scriptures, God the Spirit and the continuing proclamation of the good news may be considered interchangeable, since the interrelation of Father, Son, and Spirit resembles the relation between revelation, Scripture, and proclamation. This trinitarian analogy is matched by a

Christological one: "In the relationship between Jesus Christ and the apostles, there is therefore repeated and reflected in some degree the economy of the incarnation of the Word. . . . In its own way and in its own degree, it [Holy Scripture] is, like Jesus Christ himself, very God and very man, i.e., a witness of revelation which itself belongs to revelation, and also historically a very human literary document."[101]

To this we would add but one Anglican, one Roman Catholic, and one Presbyterian voice. L. S. Thornton writes, "Scripture as a whole is that Whole with which Revelation is to be identified. But if we say that Revelation has identity with the vessel in which it is conveyed to us, it is at once obvious that this is that kind of identity which involves distinction, like the identity of the divine and the human in the person of Christ."[102] K. Rahner refers, in passing, to "the well-known analogy between incarnation in the flesh and incarnation in the word."[103] T. F. Torrance affirms, "I do not believe we can state an adequate doctrine of the Bible in terms of the third article (i.e., of the doctrine of the Holy Spirit) . . . I believe that our common understanding of the doctrine of Scripture requires thinking it out in the terms of the Word made flesh and of his atoning work, and on that ground in relation to the Spirit. I am sure this can be done and must be done."[104]

None of the authors just cited, however, has actually developed a full doctrine of the Scriptures on the basis of the analogy between the two natures of Christ and of the Bible. The tentativeness of their statements is striking. Only L. S. Thornton speaks of an "extension of the incarnation."[105] Karl Barth goes so far as to say, "The uniqueness and at the same time general relevance of its [the Word's] becoming flesh necessarily involved its becoming Scripture. The divine Word became the word of the prophets and apostles by becoming flesh."[106] But in the same context he states, "In contrast to the humanity of Jesus Christ, there is no unity of person between God and the humanity of the prophets and apostles. . . . It is not taken up into the glory of God. . . . That the Word has become Scripture is not the same as its becoming flesh. . . . The Bible is not the Word of God upon earth in the same way as Jesus Christ, very God and very man, is that Word in heaven."[107] Such sentences argue against a direct identification of revelation and inspiration, or of Jesus Christ's humanity and glorification with the lowliness and glory of the Bible. Although some Fundamentalists appear guilty of equating the rank of the Bible with that of Jesus Christ, one of their distinguished protagonists, B. B. Warfield, fights the notion of a hypostatic union between the divine and the human elements of Scripture as energetically as Karl Barth: "We cannot parallel the 'inscripturation' of the Holy Spirit and the incarnation of the Son of God."[108]

In two recent books on the Bible it is suggested that the doctrine of the Scriptures held by Luther and Calvin rested upon the belief in an analogy between Christ and the Bible. J. K. S. Reid believes "Luther would fully agree"[109] with the contents of the Brunner statement cited above. R. S. Wallace holds that Calvin considered word and sacrament "the form of abasement which Christ the mediator today assumes," for they are the "flesh" or "form" in which Christ "appears" before man. He also suggests that when Calvin formulated his doctrine of the Scriptures, he had in mind the two natures of Christ, the Chalcedonian formula for the relation of the two natures ("unmixed, unchanged, undivided, inseparable"), and the "mystery of sacramental union."[110] Actually, Luther's poetical comparisons of the Bible with Jesus Christ do not serve to revive Origen's concept of multiple incorporations of the Word; and Calvin[111] called the mystery of the two natures of Christ "incomparable." Speculation about an "extended incarnation," whether it draws on Origen consciously or unconsciously, seems far from the thought and intention of the Reformers.[112]

A distinction must be made between Origen's Christological interpretation of Scripture and more recent ways of connecting

Christ and the Bible. Origen believed he was following Paul (2 Cor 5:16) when he found the Word of God in and through the Bible, *although* this Word was hidden in a fleshly form. Luther's concept of the *larvae* in which God conceals himself,[113] and Karl Barth's early understanding of the incarnation as God hiding his majesty,[114] may correspond to Origen's concept of "revelation despite humanity." However, in the later volumes of Karl Barth's *Dogmatics,*[115] and in recent Catholic, Anglican, and Presbyterian literature, a different accent is put upon the humanity of Christ. It is now being emphasized that it is not despite, but because of the Word's incarnation, that the glory of God's Word was seen. Biblical texts such as John 1:14; 1 Timothy 3:16; and Hebrews 2:7–9 appear to offer strong support for this. Similarly, the human, documentary, literal character of the Bible is no longer considered a steppingstone to be relinquished by the pursuer of higher truth who masters the art of pneumatical interpretation. Rather it is held that the human character of the Bible reflects God's revelation in his Son. L. S. Thornton, an Anglican, says, "The imperfections of the earthen vessel in which the divine treasure is conveyed are themselves integral to the very nature of revelation itself."[116] And J. Barr, a Presbyterian Scotsman, adds, "It needs to be said emphatically—the *human* character is the bearer of revelation, the *human* word is the word that has authority. . . . It is paradoxically the humanity of the Bible which leads us to restate a view of inspiration."[117]

How can something imperfect be granted so much authority? It is being argued that just as Jesus Christ the man was resurrected and ascended into heaven, so the human elements in the Bible have been taken up into glory and covered with glory. Some consider this process of *Aufhebung* so complete that no stain is left on the Bible's human words. There are Fundamentalists who, in harmony with Roman Catholic statements, establish a logical connection between the sinlessness of Jesus' human nature and the inerrancy of the Scriptures. They argue that just as the flesh of Jesus was kept free from sin by its assumption into unity with the Son of God, so the words of the Bible are infallible by reason of their union with the Word.[118] He who dares deny the infallibility of the Bible thus becomes guilty of insinuating that Jesus could or did sin. When the presence of minor deficiencies in the Bible is acknowledged, they are ascribed to a corruption of the original script by copyists; or to the misunderstandings of interpreters; or to implicit quotations made by God of fallible human statements; or to folkloristic sidelights, or *obiter dicta,* to which, for example, the description of the hare as a ruminant (Lev 11:6; Deut 14:7) may belong. Such arguments are intended to prove that the Bible contains no error at all. Just as the Roman Catholic and the Eastern Orthodox churches teach that the church—because it is the body of Christ and holy—cannot err and cannot sin, the attribute of inerrancy is transferred to the Bible. Only when the Bible is considered a further embodiment of the same Word who was incarnated in Jesus of Nazareth, can this transfer of attributes be considered more than a logical fallacy built upon a clever way of changing the subject. In sum, supposing that the Christological analogy is valid, the Bible must be said to be a transformed, transfigured, glorified book of human letters. He who handles this book is then handling the very Word and revelation of God, just as the disciples and the captors of Jesus had in their midst the very Son of God. Thus the Bible comes near to being a second Christ. Although in its outward appearance it resembles other books, in reality it is as different from them as Jesus Christ is from other men, as the church is from other societies, or as the eucharistic host is from other bread.

The shortest way to describe the Bible, in its double relationship to the creative and gracious deity and to created, historical humanity, is to call it a sacrament. No other term seems to comprehend as fully and deeply the mystery of incarnation and of

God's presence in the church and in the world of all ages. What looks, at the beginning, like farfetched Christological speculation may thus become a reality to be experienced like any other sacrament. When, in Orthodox, Catholic, and Protestant churches, the Bible is placed in an elevated spot; when candles or other lights draw attention to it; when it is carried in solemn procession, and kissed or opened with ceremonial decorum; when public oaths are sworn upon it and scholarly debates are settled by quotation from it—then the Bible is given the honors of a sacrament. Whether or not Christological and analogical arguments are known or used in defense of such rites, the Bible has acquired the dignity of an object of worship. The honorable place given to the Tablets of the Law in the Old Testament Ark of the Covenant, or to the Torah scrolls in a synagogue may serve as examples. While it cannot be doubted that Christians display great speculative power and sacramental devotion whenever they depict and celebrate an analogy between the two natures of the Bible and Jesus Christ, it remains to be carefully examined whether the Bible itself encourages readers to think along these lines.

The Miracle of Discipleship

According to the testimony of the Bible, Jesus Christ is the Word of God, and all testimonies of God and to God find their verification and fulfillment in Jesus Christ alone. Had the words spoken by God's witnesses had nothing at all in common with the Word of God, they could not be testimonies for him and would not deserve to be heeded. The questions now to be answered are: What does the Bible say about the union of the witnesses' word with the Word of God? Is there reason to say that a "hypostatic union" between God's Word and man's word resembles the union of God and man in Jesus Christ, as described at Chalcedon? How far does the Bible itself go in pointing to an analogy between Christ and the testimony to Christ? It is obvious that the New, rather than the Old Testament has to provide the answers to these questions in which the mystery of Christ's person is so deeply involved.

The Bible tells us that as there is but one Jesus Christ, there is but one "Gospel of Jesus Christ"; yet there are four Gospels, to which may be added what Paul calls "my Gospel" (Mk 1:1; Rom 1:1; 2:16). "Word of God, that lasts in eternity" is used for the oracle proclaimed by a prophet, the preaching of Jesus Christ, and the apostolic message proclaimed across Asia Minor (Is 40:8; Mk 13:31; 1 Pet 1:25). The same Spirit who rests upon Jesus Christ moved the Old Testament men of God; he continues to inspire the apostles and other disciples of Christ, and he breathes in the Scriptures (Jn 1:23–24; Lk 4:18; Acts 16:38; 1 Pet 1:11; 2 Pet 1:21; 1 Cor 7:40; Rev 1:10; 2 Tim 3:16). Jesus Christ holds, for all men, the keys of death and hell; and to Peter and the disciples, the keys of the kingdom, the authority to bind and to loose, are given (Rev 1:18; Jn 20:23; Mt 16:19; 18:19). A far-reaching analogy is implied when Jesus states, "He who receives you receives me. . . . As thou [the Father] didst send me into the world, so I have sent them into the world. . . . Lo, I am with you always, to the close of the age" (Mt 10:40; 28:20; Jn 17:18). "In the name of the Lord Jesus" these men preach, heal, baptize, suffer, and pray (Acts). They have the promise that their confession to him will be matched by his confession to them (Mt 10:32). With him the Christians die and rise; they carry his death "in the body . . . so that the life of Jesus may also be manifested in [their] bodies." They "have this treasure in earthen vessels . . . becoming like him in his death that, if possible, [they] may attain the resurrection" (Rom 6:5; 1 Tim 2:11–12; 2 Cor 4:7–11; Phil 3:10–11). Found worthy of participating in his suffering, they are assured they will also participate in his glory (1 Pet; Acts).

In each case analogies are made between Christ and the life, work, and ministry of his people. Salvation is in Christ alone; it is also through the Gospel alone—for all who believe; finally, as Paul states, it is only through that Gospel which Paul preaches (Acts 4:12; Rom 1:16; Jas 1:21; 1 Pet 1:23–24; Gal 1:6–9). Jesus Christ is the only sure foundation, but Paul has also laid a foundation, and the prophets and apostles are the church's foundation (1 Cor 3:10–11; Eph 2:20; Rev 21:14). Life is in Jesus Christ; his words are spirit and life; and the Scriptures are searched by people who are convinced that life is in them (Jn 1:4; 5:39; 6:62).

Different groups of analogies may be distinguished. Some, like the corresponding function of Jesus Christ's and Peter's keys, may not have been created or proclaimed consciously. Matthew and the author of Revelation probably did not know of each other when they wrote, and they may have used their metaphors in different senses.

Other analogical statements distinguish sharply between the action of the master and that of the disciple. What the witnesses of Christ do is called a following after Christ, a walking in his footsteps, an imitation. Their status as servants is emphasized. "Where I am, there shall my servant be also" (Jn 12:26). The master-servant relationship implies that there exists an irreversible order of rank and quality. The Christians may be called to act, to die, to rise with or like Christ; but they are never said to become (another) Christ. The imitation is never confused with the original, and it cannot substitute for it.

There are even passages in which the analogy between Christ and the Christian is expressed in terms of contrast or paradox rather than similarity. "He was rich, yet for your sake he became poor, so that by his poverty you might become rich. . . . For our sake [God] made him be sin who knew no sin, so that in him we might become righteous after God's standard [the righteousness of God]" (2 Cor 8:9; 5:21). Such reverse analogies preclude the idea that Christians may be like Christ in all respects.

Most important, however, are those statements which clearly indicate that Jesus Christ is not far removed, but present (Mt 18:20; 28:20), active (2 Cor 3:18; 4:11), taking form in—and delighting in—the life and witness of the community of Christians (Gal 4:19; Jn 17:6–26; Mt 10:32; 11:25; 25:21, 23). It is impossible adequately to praise the miracle by which the master, who is to be followed and imitated, acts in and through the servants. The Almighty does not suppress but strengthens the weak. Since the Christians were sometimes called the body of Christ (1 Cor 12:27; Eph 1:22), many interpreters like to speak of an incorporation of Christ in his followers. But when the church is described as the body of Christ, Christ is sometimes described as the head (Eph; Col), and sometimes reference is made to the lifegiving Spirit (of God, or of Christ) and his gifts (1 Cor 12; Rom 12:3 ff.). Incorporation, therefore, is hardly a fitting term, for neither head nor spirit is "incorporated" in the body. It is characteristic of those texts containing the strongest expressions of the identification of Christ with his witnesses that they neither obfuscate nor deny the distinction between Lord and servant, head and body, lifegiver and recipient of life.

All Christians, and the apostolic witnesses as the first among them, are called to the imitation of Christ, to the participation in his lowliness and his exaltation, and, finally, to a service which he will bless and reward. But the authority which they are given does not make them the equals of Jesus Christ, a second Christ, or objects of worship beside Christ. Because of the manifold ways in which the New Testament describes the relationship between Christ and his witnesses, a blunt analogy between the two natures of Christ and the Bible should not be accepted too hurriedly.

There are three specific reasons for caution. First, the intimate relationship between Jesus Christ and his witnesses is due to a gracious, ever-new act of identification, which God alone can bring about and make known. Theologians must not transform this unilateral, gracious act of God's condescension into a human claim, boasting identity of man and God. Jesus Christ is called the life of his body, the church (Col 3:4; Phil 1:21; Gal 2:20), but this does not mean that the church or the apostles can possess the attribute of Christlikeness. The two sides of a mathematical or logical equation may be interchangeable. But biblical language and the Bible's logic do not invite such a comparison. The analogies by which Christ and the Christians are bound together express dynamic action, a gracious event, a marvelous announcement; they do not represent a static balance. Jesus Christ can and does identify himself with the persecuted congregation; he stops the persecutor by saying, "Saul, why do you persecute *me*?" (Acts 9:4) Yet from this, one must not derive the conclusion that a church, whether faithful or not, possesses the attribute or quality of being Jesus Christ himself. The same applies to the apostolic confession and witness. Jesus Christ has promised to bless it by his confession before the Father and by the gift of the Spirit. It is still not automatically a "power of salvation," or a "fragrance from life to life." Unless God himself works from day to day in those preaching and hearing the Gospel, it is (as Paul observes in 2 Cor 2:14–16) "a fragrance from death to death."

Second, in order to fulfill his ministry, Jesus Christ had to be abased, then to be exalted by God; he had to die and to rise again. What was confessed at Chalcedon concerning his two natures served to proclaim both the servant ministry and the majesty of Jesus Christ. The Ecumenical Councils' decrees were directed against heretics who believed themselves to be saved either by a human Jesus Christ who was richly endowed and exalted by God without having descended from on high, or by a divine Jesus Christ who was only seemingly humiliated and for that reason never truly exalted. The orthodox fathers wanted to confess the reality, necessity, and fittingness of Christ's twofold commission and work, his humble obedience and sovereign kingship. They called this twofold charge given to Christ his "two natures." Nineteenth- and twentieth-century concepts of "nature" differ widely, both among themselves and from the late Greek concepts to which the fathers alluded; these differences have led to misunderstandings and condemnations of the early church's Creeds. Actually, "modern man" has no reason to decry the way in which the Chalcedonian fathers endeavored to safeguard and to affirm the mystery of Jesus Christ.

But neither in the Bible nor in later church declarations is the service of the apostolic word described as twofold. It is God who has the right and power to abase and to exalt, to kill and to raise again. It was Christ's mission to go though the darkest death to the brightest glory. The Gospel preached by the apostles produces a twofold effect: to some it is a fragrance of life, to others of death (2 Cor 2:14–17). Some interpreters of the Gospel have split it into two parts, the Law and the Gospel, or judgment and grace. But the apostolic witness does not possess two "natures." It has only one intent, to serve as a signpost. Its purpose is to turn men toward the new covenant between God and man, to direct them out of darkness into light. Under no circumstances is the apostolic testimony meant to be anything but gospel. "Gospel," if we follow Paul, is not the announcement of two things in two forms, e.g., judgment and grace, but the proclamation of God's gracious judgment (Rom 1:16–17; 3:21–26).

Jesus Christ is praised only when he is recognized and celebrated as both God and man, as God's humiliated and rewarded servant. The Bible is not meant to bring death. The capacity of the letter to kill (mentioned in 2 Cor 3:6; cf. Rom 7:6) is not a second nature or function of the Bible. God's will is one only: to call sinners through the word of his witnesses to repentance, life, and joy. Those who consider the two natures of Christ an analogy to two natures of the Bible have, therefore, neglected the qualitative difference between Jesus Christ's twofold work and the Bible's single purpose.

Finally, concerning the great number of biblical statements that treat of an analogical relationship between Jesus Christ and the apostolic witness, it is obvious that these statements pertain to the life, the work, the suffering, and the glorification of *persons*. Persons who are witnesses become an analogy of him to whom they bear testimony. But the biblical utterances regarding persons do not automatically apply to the qualities of a book. In describing God's covenant with man, the Bible does not treat of a covenant of God with the Bible. Many things are said of the covenant partners that express the analogy between lord and servant, master and disciple. This analogy is based upon election, discipleship, or imitation. "God created man in his own image" (Gen 1:26–27). However, it cannot be said that the letter of Jeremiah to the captives in Babylonia, or Paul's letters to Corinth are in themselves an "image of God," or imitations of Christ. Only persons are called imitators of Christ or God (1 Cor 11:1; Eph 5:1). The privilege, temptation, or service attributed to a chosen partner of God is not conveyed to a thing, not even the Bible. There is no substitute for the service rendered by an elected person. True enough, when the servant of God is "corporally absent" from the congregation, the congregation need not be completely deprived of his service and presence. The written word—a letter, for example—may substitute for oral preaching or counseling. But if we follow Paul, the letter's writer is present "in spirit" (1 Cor 5:3; Col 2:5; 2 Cor 3:1–3). The church is built upon Jesus Christ and upon prophets and apostles, not upon a book (Eph 2:20).

It is impossible to speak of the two natures of the Bible and of their hypostatic union without transferring to a thing statements appropriate only to a person. Should Jesus Christ's twofold ministry be equated with two elements combined in a given piece of matter? Should the justification of sinners be commuted into a transsubstantiation of letters? Should a gracious event become a frigid quality? Should all that which has been received by faith, and may be received by faith alone, be delivered into the hands of analogical reasoning? If so, then the Christological analogy may be useful in demonstrating the Bible's authority, but such a demonstration, based as it is on attributing to the Bible qualities appropriate only to God, Jesus Christ, or the Spirit, is valueless. While the Bible gives testimony to the miracles of grace and discipleship, it is itself neither an image nor an imitation of God.

The Magic of Images

The question may be raised whether, by renouncing the Christological argument of Origen, Christians would give up the decisive element that distinguishes their doctrine of the Bible from the beliefs other religious men and groups hold about their holy books. The answer can be brief. It is precisely when Christians attempt to exploit Jesus Christ and the mystery of his person for apologetic purposes that they travel those roads which they intend to avoid.

Four illustrations can be given. First, analogies to the Christological argument concerning the Bible are found in several great religious systems. Early *Jewish* literature shows that some theologians attempted to identify Wisdom with the Torah. Of course, no dogma developed from this, but traces of such an identification have been collected.[119] If Wisdom is identical with the Torah, and the Torah is identified with the Pentateuch, then the books that are carefully guarded in the shrine, and even more carefully handled and read in divine service, are a sign and guarantee of Wisdom's presence in the congregation.

Should the Christians imitate this Jewish manner of devotion?

The Gospel of John does not deny that "the Law was given through Moses"; but it does not go on to say that the Gospels were the work of Jesus. Instead we read, "Grace and truth came through Jesus Christ" (Jn 1:17). It is possible that Matthew, in his report of the Sermon on the Mount (Mt 5–7), wanted to compare its setting and content with the legislation given on Mount Sinai. The Letters of John speak of a new commandment (1 Jn 2:7–8; 2 Jn 2:4, 6, etc.), and the Letter of James of a perfect and royal law (Jas 1:25; 2:8, 12). Finally, Paul compares his ministry with that of Moses (2 Cor 3:4–18), though he marks more differences than similarities. Still, none of the New Testament authors wanted to teach that the eternal Word, after its embodiment in the flesh, ultimately became both letter and law. Luther showed sensitivity to the difference between legalistic respect for a sacred book and the hearing of the Gospel brought by Jesus Christ when he said, "Properly speaking, the Gospel is oral proclamation."[120] It is the hearing of the Gospel, the trust in, and obedience to its message, rather than the preservation and veneration of a book, that ascertains the Word's presence in the congregation.

Second, there is as little reason for Christians to imitate the attitudes of non-Christians, whether Moslems or Gentiles, in respect to the mystery and value of their sacred writings as there is for them to emulate the most orthodox among the Jews who come close to venerating the holy scrolls. In one school of Moslem thought, a doctrine of the Koran's pre-existence and its divine and human nature was developed. The controversies among Islamic scholars in regard to the nature of the Koran have been considered "an exact parallel to the Christian disputes about the nature of Christ."[121] As for the Veda, the speculations of Indian sages reveal that they know more of incarnation and of multiple incarnations than Christians will ever know or be willing to accept. Hermetic literature is deeply influenced by at least three sources—ancient Egyptian belief in the divine origin of the art of writing and of specific books, teachings, and formulae; elements of Platonic philosophical thought; and finally, the liturgies of one or several of the mystery cults—each of which contributed to the high place given the *hieros logos,* i.e., to myths, cultic formulae, or holy books used in religious ceremonies and instruction. "The Gentiles of Alexandria identify wisdom with Hermes, therefore with the Logos."[122]

In short, the analogy employed by Origen and his followers between the Word's incarnation and its expression in Scripture does not represent an original method of demonstrating the authority of a holy book. Knowledge of Jesus Christ and faith in the triune God are obviously not prerequisites for the discovery of powers of salvation in Holy Writ. Though Origen's understanding of the Bible as an embodiment of the Word looked distinctly Christian and was buttressed by quotations from John and Paul, his way of glorifying the authority of Holy Writ is easily duplicated (and perhaps motivated, too) by non-Christian thinkers and communities. A more humble doctrine of the Bible, involving greater faithfulness to its contents, may well be the only appropriate way for Christians to meet the challenge of the world's religions. Those religions have been called "high" that possessed sacred books. The Christian should not imitate them by forming a book-belief after their pattern.

Third, the conviction that the word, along with the sign, serves a mediating function between the thing that makes itself known and man who yearns to know may well be Platonic in origin. Philo, Origen, and Augustine owe much of their education to Neoplatonism. It is difficult to determine how far their doctrine of the Bible was derived from their study of philosophy, and to what extent their theory was a reproduction or adaptation of Neoplatonic axioms, reinforced by some selected Mosaic, Johannine, or Pauline quotations. It was certainly the Bible that taught Philo of the election of Abraham and Israel, and of the covenant of

God, including his holy commandments. He followed the Bible when he considered the way opened by God the only route to enlightenment, salvation, and life. Equally, the Bible taught Origen and Augustine that the incarnate, crucified, and risen Jesus Christ is the one Word of God and the only sign given. Still, neither Philo, nor Origen, nor Augustine, proved able or willing, in their doctrine of the Bible, to dispense with arguments received from Platonism. They interpreted the authority of the Bible in terms of the philosophical quest of their contemporaries. They attributed to the words of the Bible a power which was open to misunderstanding. Those who identify Bible and revelation, who make the Bible a representation of Christ, or who ascribe to it the authority of Christ, succumb to a temptation into which Neoplatonic philosophical language easily leads. The Bible then becomes a mediating principle.

Finally, it appears to be a law observed by all religions that there can be no cultus or liturgy without an image. The image may have the form of an idol, or of a recital of traditions depicting the tribe's ideal relationship to its deity; it may involve a sacramental reenactment of the contents of a myth or a past event; or it may be a combination of these forms. The physical, verbal, or dramatic image is never an end in itself, nor is it simply identified with the deity or all its blessings. But by means of the image a re-presentation takes place. Pictures and pageants, stories and formulae, show the presence of the spiritual in the sphere of the fleshly. They show that the eternal, or divine order of the universe reaches into the present and sanctifies human undertakings.[123]

Since Jews and Christians meet for worship in sanctuaries, display symbols, recite holy legends and formulae, and celebrate sacred events in sacred actions, they appear to possess a religion not unlike others. It is doubtful whether they make a strong point when they call their own rites sacraments and call the Gentile cultus magic. Certainly the sacramental role given to the

Bible makes of the written word an image, or representation of God and his deeds. The more the Bible is declared to be an image of Christ, representing his two natures and their union in Chalcedonian terms, the more it assumes the role of a magic instrument of worship. Surely neither Jeremiah, nor Paul, nor the other biblical authors intended their writings to serve such a purpose. The Bible prohibits the making of images of God, for Jesus Christ alone is his image (Col 1:15), and the living man, not objects, or words, or books are created in God's image (Gen 1:26–27).

So much for what may be said on the basis of comparative religion. But at least two aspects of the church's history should also be mentioned in connection with a consideration of the Christological analogy.

First, even though Christians find God's authority represented by, and re-enacted in words, books, and sacred customs, the sacramental explanation of the Bible's character is not sufficient to establish its specific authority. As early as the second century, the authority of the *regula fidei* and the episcopal office was recognized, in addition to that of Scripture. For Origen, the incorporation of the Word in the Bible stood together with Christ's embodiment in the church and the sacraments. After Origen, belief in the Bible as an extension of the Word's incarnation was seldom expressed, but statements that church and sacraments are a continued or extended incarnation are all the more frequent. It is obvious that the doctrine of incorporation held by Origen and his followers does not answer, but rather poses the question: Which among the several incorporations of Christ possesses supreme authority over the others, and what role does the Bible play among them?

Roman Catholic, Eastern Orthodox, and Protestant Christians have answered differently, favoring either the sacraments, the church, or the Bible. But the lines that divide these different groups seem about to change. It might be expected that a Presbyterian like J. K. S. Reid would feel bound by Reformation tradition to decide in favor of the Bible; but he comes close to admitting that the authority of a living community—that is, the church—takes precedence over the dictates of dead, though perhaps infallible letters.[124] The works of Catholic theologians like G. Tavard and K. Rahner[125] present a different emphasis from that of older Roman anti-Reformation utterances which submitted the Bible to the church's authority and jurisdiction. A recently published book on the role of Holy Scripture in the Orthodox Church[126] seems to indicate that among Eastern Christians, too, the issue will be restudied. A. Sabatier,[127] L. S. Thornton,[128] S. Kierkegaard,[129] and many others are all tired of the unending fight between papal and Protestant claims. One theologian calls for a religion without external authority, that is, for the religion of the Spirit; another postulates a new Reformation that would remove the Bible as effectively as Luther removed the Pope; a third suggests that "revelatory capacity" or the "order of creation" be recognized as superior to both the church and the Bible. It is plain that Origen's arguments for a Christlike biblical authority have not settled the question. Just as a series of murderous and devastating wars was started to decide control of the empire among King Alexander's successors, so the defenders of various extensions of Christ have but succeeded in creating battlefields and ruins. It is hardly imaginable that support given to one or another of the pretenders to Christ's authority will help to terminate the war. As for Luther, he certainly did not struggle against the idea that the church is a second Christ, for the purpose of enthroning the Bible as another Christ. In Calvin's theology, respect for the role of the Spirit is too important to suggest that he considered the Bible an image of Jesus Christ. Those Protestants who today try to strengthen the doctrine of the Bible by using Christological, Chalcedonian terminology cannot claim that they are carrying out a program outlined by the Reformers.

Second, whenever it is held that the Bible possesses two natures whose combination resembles the hypostatic union of the two natures of Christ, two methods of Bible interpretation must necessarily be adopted—one concerned with the literal sense, the historic meaning, even the humanity of the Bible; the other with a spiritual, theological, timeless interpretation. The two methods will have to be kept distinct and "unmixed," and yet neither must pretend to exist without the other, for they have to be "inseparable." Now, different methods of exegesis have always coexisted. Something like the controversy of the early Alexandrian and Antiochian schools has always been inflaming scholars and creating divisions in the churches. Indeed, if the Bible itself has two natures, the two different methods of interpretation must survive to the end of the ages; for then they alone are entirely appropriate to revelation in the God-man Jesus Christ and the divine-human Bible. On the one side stands Origen's and Augustine's ascent from the lower to a higher sense of the Bible and the distinction—triumphant in both older and more recent allegorical interpretation—between different senses of the same biblical texts. On the other side, demanding literal interpretation, stand Paul of Samosata, Lucian and Diodore of Antioch, Theodor of Mopsuestia, Thomas Aquinas, Nicolaus of Lyra, Luther, Calvin, and the recent critical scholars. But is it really necessary that the war between flesh and spirit in each Christian (Rom 7:7–25) be duplicated in this conflict among exegetes? If it were, hermeneutics—the rules of interpretation of the Bible—would be different from the rules observed by readers and expositors of other documents. It would be necessary for the biblical scholar to master and apply two mutually exclusive methods. The result of such a demand could only be devastating. It would deliver the Bible and its interpretation into the hands of specialists presuming to do the impossible. Manipulations of this kind distinguish the magician, the pagan priest, or the hierophant, not the biblical scholar; they characterize Old Egyptian and

Delphic holy writings, not the Bible. Most of the Bible professes to be written for the benefit of *all* who read it—Jews and Gentiles, experts and laymen alike—and many of its documents are "letters to the congregation."

The argument built on the Christological analogy is perhaps one of the most resplendent attempts to prove the Bible's authority. Its content, development, and consequences had to be more extensively described and criticized than other apologetic procedures, for it looked superior to them and it appeared that it might solve their dilemmas. A full development of a strictly Chalcedonian argument is probably not yet to be found in theological literature.[130] But the more theological reflection and liturgical renewal move toward the center of the Bible—the mystery of Jesus Christ—the greater is the temptation to rationalize that mystery. The use of analogies is one of the temptations to which Christocentric thinkers and worshipers are exposed. Karl Barth warns us not to treat the incarnation or Christological formula as a principle from which the solution of urgent theological problems can be derived by a simple logical process.[131] Among many others, H. U. v. Balthasar,[132] W. Pannenberg,[133] and J. McIntyre[134] have submitted different concepts and uses of analogy to critical analysis. Despite their divergent positions, they agree that argument by analogy alone is not sufficient to prove questionable statements.

It is therefore unlikely that the use of Christological analogy will solve the problem of scriptural authority. This analogy is but another yoke fabricated by those who want to impose the Bible on its readers. To convert the Bible into a yoke of biblicism means, however—as we have attempted to show in the preceding chapters—to contradict the very content and intention of this book of dialogue between the free God and the man to be freed.

Probably no alternative can be found merely by elaborating yet another "doctrine of the Bible." In the following chapter, however, some observations will be made regarding the Bible's own utterances on authority and its recognition; on the basis of these observations, conclusions regarding a proper use of the Bible will be drawn.

CHAPTER VI

THE AUTHORITY OF A CHARTER OF LIBERTY

God's Authority and Man's Authorization

The Bible has as much authority as it receives from God. For the one authority to which all things and all men are subject is the authority of God the Father, the Son, and the Spirit. The Old Testament asserts that God is above all gods and lords (Dan 2:48); that his chosen king shall rule over God's people and its enemies (Ps 2; Is 11); that his Spirit's power is superior even to death (Ezek 37). In the light of Christ's birth, death, and resurrection, New Testament writers reaffirm and expand what Israel had professed. Now it is said, "Worthy art thou, our Lord and God, to receive glory and honor and power, for thou didst create all things, and by thy will they existed and were created" (Rev 4:11). The kingship of God is established and revealed especially on behalf of sinners who seem to be beyond its reach (Mt 5:3–12; Rom 5:12–

21). Jesus Christ is identified as the awaited son of David who was to exercise his might over all enemies, and his righteousness among the poor and needy. "All authority in heaven and on earth has been given to me" (Mt 28:18; 11:27; 1 Cor 15:24 ff.; Phil 2:10, 11; Col 1:13, 16, 20; 2:10, 15; Eph 1:20–23; Rev 5; Acts 13:22–23). And the Holy Spirit is either directly identified with God's power (as in Acts 1:8; 1 Cor 2:4–5), or clearly described as that agent by which God makes men bear testimony to others and pray to him; it is by the Spirit that men are led to live "in Christ"; it is by the Spirit that they are reborn, raised from death, and equipped to preach, give witness in court, and perform miracles. The same supreme and unique authority is manifested by God the Father, Son, and Spirit.

We must describe the mystery, the transfer, the purpose, the servants, and the recognition of this authority. If the authority of the Bible is to be discussed in the light of that supreme authority to which it bears testimony, it is indispensable that the features of the latter be carefully presented.

First, we observe that for God's authority, including its manifold past and future manifestations, no arguments and proofs are sought. It is simply presupposed, and professed as an undisputable fact. "I AM WHO I AM. . . . For thine is the kingdom and the power and the glory, for ever. Amen" (Ex 3:14; Mt 6:13). On what basis do the biblical writers make this presupposition? Are they unaware that all sorts of other authorities rule over history and in man's heart? Some of the biblical authors give an answer to this question, especially in their utterances about the Trinity. They do more than say, "We believe"; they state why they believe.

The authority of God is described as an authority manifested within God himself. Before man experiences it, and regardless of whether or not he likes it, it is recognized in God himself. The eternal Son obeys the Father (Phil 2:6–8); the eternal Spirit is at the disposition of the Father and the Son (Jn 15:26). This implies a first surprising feature of the biblical concept of authority: it is obviously considered as divine to obey as it is to command. The divine majesty and freedom of Christ and the Spirit are not impaired by their obedience to the Father. God's authority is eternally exerted both in command *and* in obedience, in promise *and* in trust.

We also note that God's authority can be imparted without any detriment to the honor of its origin. God's authority cannot be described without reference to its bestowal. It is given by the Father to the Son—to the glory of the Father (Mt 28:18; Phil 2:9–11). By giving the Spirit, God gives full power—as the baptism and resurrection of Jesus, and subsequent events show (Mk 1:9 ff.; Acts 2:33–35; Eph 1:19–23). While authority, like holiness, is and remains God's own, he manifests it by conveying it.

Second, God does not convey authority only within the Trinity but also to some of his creatures. Authority is given to John the Baptist; to the disciples and the apostle Paul; to Pilate and other officials of the Roman Empire; to Satan, the demons, and angels; and finally to all who believe (Mk 6:7; 1 Cor 9:4 ff.; Jn 19:11; Rom 13:1; Lk 4:6; Job 1–2; Rev 6:8; 14:18). "You shall be to him as God. . . . You are gods, sons of the Most High, all of you. . . . He appointed twelve . . . to have authority. . . . To all who received him, who believed in his name, he gave power to become children of God" (Ex 4:16; Ps 82:6; Mk 3:14–15; Jn 1:12; 10:34 ff.). God's authority does not need to be jealously guarded, for it is not a naked power or a liberty that God wants to keep for himself. God enjoys granting rights to his creatures; he is a liberal giver of that authority which makes its bearer free.

Third, the authority granted by God is not an authorization to do whatever one likes. It involves a specific charge and calls for the fulfillment of a specific ministry. Authorization by God is always limited—if not by space and time, then by the giver and the purpose for which it is to be used. The priests Eli and Samuel, the kings Saul and David, the apostles Peter and Paul, all undergo tests and trials. As God's chosen servants, they are charged to be examples of that faith and obedience expected from all those to whom they are sent.

The Bible leaves no doubt that the imparted authority is exposed to misuse (Lk 4:6; 1 Cor 6:2; 8:9; 10:23). Those sometimes called "gods" in the Old Testament and "authorities" in the New Testament, are expected to manifest their divine commission; but actually they often behave as rebels, rising against the purpose of the commission and the one who gave it. Nevertheless, the Bible emphasizes that all authority is from God, under God, and judged by God (Ps 2; 82:1–3; 110; Rom 13:1–4; Heb 1:5–13). God has addressed those to whom his authority is given, and by word and deed they have to respond to him. Authority given by God makes its bearer a servant of God for the good of many—even when it involves the punishment of an evildoer or the testing of a righteous man (Rom 13:4; Jer 29:7; Job 1 ff.). It calls for respect and obedience. Misused authority—Saul's persecution of David, Rome's persecution of Christians, the Corinthians' libertinism (1 Sam 18 ff.; Rev 13; 1 Cor 6:12; 10:23)—is met not with contempt but with amazing patience or passionate reproof.

A fourth consideration concerns the purpose for which God grants authority to chosen men. The many stories that treat of God's appointment of servants seem to have a common denominator: all are instances of appointment to a service in the cause of redemption. Noah's righteousness before God results in his building of the ark by which he and his kin are to be saved from the flood. Abraham makes use of the privilege of speaking to God by pleading for the inhabitants of sinful Sodom and Gomorrah. Joseph becomes the savior of Egypt and also rescues his people from famine. Moses is appointed to lead Israel out of captivity. The prophets have to warn the kings and the people of the snares of dynastic power politics, of false religions, and of sanctimonious misuse of God's promises and sanctuaries. The priests are assigned to serve God and the people by teaching the law and by interceding and sacrificing for forgiveness of sin. Ezra and Nehemiah intend to restore and protect the independence of God's people from foreign customs. Jesus is described as the one who, by his teaching, healing, and dying frees man from disease, sin, and the misapplication of the law. The disciples are empowered to make known Christ's ministry to all men. Paul defends the origin and purpose of his apostolate as the proclamation of the freedom of the children of God, against both a new legalism and a frantic libertinism. Even the pagan officials of the Roman Empire are given the sword and the right to levy taxes—in order to procure a quiet and peaceable life for all people (Rom 13:1–7; 1 Tim 2:1–4).

All these servants of God owe their appointment and ministry to his authority. They are to minister to God, who will procure freedom for many. If they use their authority to enslave others, or to make themselves equal to the one who gave them their commission, they are as much rebels against God's authority as Satan himself. Unless the use they make of their authority reveals that they serve the liberation of the many, they are denying the very nature of the authorization which they claim to possess.

Fifth, what does the Bible tell us of the mode of authorization and the recognition of imparted authority? The right to exert authority and the wisdom to discern its implications are frequently ascribed to the Holy Spirit, but the Bible does not state that every commission is due to the Spirit. Satan is granted considerable authority (Rev 13), but his only concern with the work of God's Spirit is to fight it (Mk 1:10–13; Acts 8:19–23).

On the other hand, the presence of the Spirit does not necessarily imply inspiration. While the Old Testament distinctly refers to the power of God's Spirit over the waters, over all nature, and even over the dead (Gen 1:2; Ps 104:30; Ezek 37:1–14), it does not explicitly speak of the waters' or of nature's inspiration. The Old Testament knows of no other inspiration than that of persons. Joshua, the Judges, Saul, David, the prophets, and others among God's people are described as inspired or are promised inspiration (Gen 41:38; Ex 31:3; Num 11:17, 25, 29; 14:2; Deut 14:9; Judg 3:10, etc.; 1 Sam 10:6; 16:23; 1 Kings 3:28; Hos 9:7; Mic 3:8; Is 11:2; 42:1; 61:1; Zech 7:12; Joel 2:28–29; Ezek 36:25–27; cf. 2 Pet 1:21).

Even more abundant are New Testament statements about the gift of the Spirit to men. The Pauline and Johannine writings, the Gospel and the Acts of Luke, frequently refer to the demonstration of God's presence, and to his giving authority through his Spirit. Neither Jesus, nor the apostles, nor the Christian congregation could stand in God's service unless they were equipped by the Spirit with knowledge, power, and courage. Each man is urged to ask for the promised Spirit (Lk 11:9–13; Acts 2:38; 19:2–6) and nothing less than a new birth, a new creation, and resurrection are expected from receiving the Spirit (Jn 3:5–8; 2 Cor 5:1–5; 1 Cor 15:44). According to the New Testament, the "power to become children of God" is conveyed, and the appropriate conduct among fellow men assured by no other means (Jn 1:12; 3:1 ff.; 20:11–13; Rom 8:9–17; Gal 5:16–26). "Filled with the Holy Spirit," the men of God do their work (Acts 4:8, 31; 6:3, 5; 7:55; 11:24).

Sixth, the New Testament teaches that the authority conveyed by the Spirit can be recognized only by those given the same Spirit. John the Baptist professes that Jesus is the lamb and son of God because he saw "the Spirit descend as a dove from heaven" (Jn 1:31–34). When Peter addresses Jesus with the majestic title "Messiah," "flesh and blood has not revealed this to you, but my Father who is in heaven" (Mt 16:17). The disciples are promised the Spirit to be led to the complete truth regarding the person, words, and deeds of Jesus (Jn 14:17, 26; 15:26; 16:13–14). Paul does not carry letters proving his authorization for the apostolic ministry, for the only convincing evidence of his commission is the congregation in which the Spirit is clearly at work (1 Cor 2:4; 9:1–2; 12; 2 Cor 3:2–3). He will exert disciplinary authority only "when you are assembled, and my spirit is present, with the power of our Lord Jesus" (1 Cor 5:4–5). Those who have been anointed by the Spirit are called upon to test pseudo prophets (1 Jn 2:20, 27; 4:1). According to Acts, the only ones who believed the apostles' message were those added by the Lord to the congregation (2:47)—that is, whose heart God opened (16:14) by the gift of the Spirit (10:44, etc.). The gift of the Spirit to Gentiles proves that preaching to them and communion with them are authorized by the Lord himself (Gal 3:2–3; 4:6).

Other events are sometimes mentioned as authenticating a servant of God. Moses and Paul were enabled to perform miracles before the eyes of unbelievers and believers (Ex 4:2; Acts 28:3–6; 2 Cor 12:12); the miraculous deeds of Peter and John draw as much attention as Jesus had gained through his teaching and healing (Acts 3–5; Mt 5:28–29; Mk 1:27; Jn 5:9). But miracles may be ascribed to Satan or copied by magicians (Mk 3:22; 13:22; Ex 7:11, 22; 2 Cor 11:13–14; Rev 13:13). Without the "demonstration of the Spirit and power" (1 Cor 2:4), the God-given authority of a servant of God cannot be verified.

If the authorization of a servant of God can be recognized only by the Spirit, then it is God alone who makes sure that it is recognized and respected. The same Spirit with which he endowed his servant is given a second time—to those to whom the servant ministers. Apart from this second gift of the Spirit, it is impossible to expect that anyone would recognize the authority given by God. Authority, in the biblical sense, is real and beneficial when a meeting of at least two inspired persons takes place. Spiritual things must be discerned spiritually; spiritual men are understood only by spiritual men. Paul says this most explicitly:

What no eye has seen, nor ear heard, nor the heart of man conceived, what God has prepared for those who love him, God has revealed to us through the Spirit. For the Spirit searches everything, even the depths of God. For what person knows the things concerning man except the spirit of the man which is in him? So also no one comprehends the things concerning God except the Spirit of God.

Now we have received not the spirit of the world, but the Spirit which is from God, that we might understand the gifts bestowed on us by God.

And we impart this in words not taught by human wisdom but taught by the Spirit, interpreting spiritual truths to those who possess the Spirit.

The unspiritual man does not receive the gifts of the Spirit of God, for they are folly to him, and he is not able to understand them because they are spiritually discerned. The spiritual man judges all things, but is himself to be judged by no one (1 Cor 2:9–15).

The first paragraph of this statement shows that the Spirit of God alone knows the mysteries and depths of God; the second affirms that He brings man to know of God's gifts; the third states that the same Spirit makes chosen men (like Isaiah and Paul) witnesses to God's mysteries; and according to the last paragraph, the Spirit causes other men to receive (and to discern) this testimony. In this text, Paul distinguishes not only a twofold, but a fourfold work of the Spirit! In the light of this passage, inspiration is not exhausted in a *past* influence of God upon his witnesses; it is rather a self-manifestation of God which continues even today in the hearer or reader of the prophetic and apostolic testimony. Unless the Spirit is living, he is not the Holy Spirit. The authority of God's inspired witnesses can only be recognized by people who themselves prove to be inspired.

We referred earlier to the saying that man must possess a sunlike eye if he is to perceive the sun at all. But man's eye is not by nature capable of seeing God. His sight is not merely gravely impaired; he is actually blind. As Paul put it, "The natural man does not receive the things . . . of God," (1 Cor 2). Paul is sent to "open their eyes, that they may turn from darkness to light" (Acts 26:16–18). God has his own way of making sure that his revelation reaches man. He himself opens the eyes of the blind and enables them to see. This miraculous opening of man's eyes to spiritual things is the "gift of the Spirit." Thanks to God's interference, the witness of the apostles did not—and will not—fail. "While Peter was still saying this, the Holy Spirit fell on all who heard the word" (Acts 10:44). Luke knows very well that every apostolic speech is not as obviously blessed by God as this one, which was delivered by Peter in a devout Gentile's house. The intention of his report, however, is that the Gospel can be enjoyed, knowledge and faith can grow, and the Christian congregation can expand only when God, after giving the Spirit to his witnesses, also gives it to those listening to them. The servant of God may have to wait a long time for the Spirit to come over those he serves. He is as dependent on God's blessing as the farmer is on rain. It is not inherent in his labor; he can only trust that it will come. And finally, one day, it rains and the Spirit is poured forth.

Seventh, if only inspired men can recognize the authority of the Spirit, the act of recognition will itself bear distinctive marks. An unconcerned bystander does not honor the authority granted by God, nor can this authority be forced by one man on another. It is never recognized against a man's better judgment, or with a merely intellectual assent, without existential involvement. God's authority is properly acknowledged when a man bows before it and is lifted up by it. Its nature demands that it be obeyed by action. The authority to which the Bible bears testimony can be demonstrated and accepted only by means of the recurrence of ever-new faith, obedience, and witness. We remember that Jesus said, "My teaching is not mine, but his who sent me; if any man's will is to do his will, he shall know whether the teaching is from

God or whether I am speaking on my own authority. . . . When you continue in my word, you are truly my disciples, and you will know the truth, and the truth will make you free" (Jn 7:16–17; 8:31–32). If these words are true of Jesus Christ the Lord, how much more do they apply to the witness and ministry of his servants!

Eighth, it may be asked whether such recognition of spiritual authority can still take place today—even in an age far removed from apostolic times. Each biblical passage which promises the gift of the Spirit or encourages its readers to pray for it contains an answer: "I will pour out my Spirit upon all flesh" (Acts 2:17); "The heavenly Father [will] give the Holy Spirit to those who ask him" (Lk 11:13). If God had exhausted his power and authority in biblical times, and if, after inspiring chosen men to write down the biblical testimony, he was no longer present among men, then after the death of the last prophet and apostle there would be no way for man to hear God's voice. In the Old Testament this fearful "postprophetic" situation is depicted more than once (see 1 Sam 3:1; Amos 8:11; Ps 74:9). The New Testament, however, affirms that God *is* Spirit; the promise of the outpouring of the Spirit is still being fulfilled. The manifold gifts of the Spirit prevent the children of God who are living in the era after Jesus Christ's death and resurrection from becoming orphans (Joel 3:15; Acts 2:17 ff.; 1 Cor 12:14; Jn 14:15–18). Luke misses no chance to point out the unique position of the first eyewitnesses (Acts 1:22; 2:32; 3:15; 4:33; 5:32; 10:41; 13:31). But he also reports Peter as saying that Gentile latecomers to faith "received the Holy Spirit just as we did. . . . God gave the same gift to them as to us. . . . God bore testimony to them by giving them the Holy Spirit just as to us" (Acts 10:47; 11:17; 15:8). The whole book of Acts may be considered an account of the operation of the Spirit after Jesus Christ's death and resurrection. Inspiration is designated as a miracle that belongs not only to the church's past but to its present and future as well. Because of the Spirit, there is hope that God's authority, and the authorized testimony to him, will also be heeded in the future. According to Paul, there is no life in faith except "in the Spirit" (Rom 8; Gal 4 and 5; 2 Cor 3).

Ninth, those who recognize the authority attested by prophets and apostles are promised great rewards. It is not enough to speak of the joy of enlightenment. Paul speaks of a transformation of man analogous to creation. This transformation is the result of seeing "with unveiled face" (2 Cor 3:18–4:6). The Book of Acts describes the apostles' willingness to go through suffering to glory with Jesus Christ. According to the Gospels, Christ accepted Moses, the prophets, and the Psalms as witnesses to his ministry of serving, suffering, and dying; his knowledge of Scripture helped him to "fulfill all righteousness." Matthew and the author of Hebrews were convinced that only through listening to the testimony of the Old Testament witnesses could they and their readers understand who and what Jesus is: the Lord, the Son of God, the true reconciliation of God and man. Therefore, the criterion and reward for recognizing the Bible's authority are the discernment of God's will, the renewal of man, and the joyful readiness to fulfill the commission given by God.

It is obvious that the man living under God's authority is privileged and happy. The truth *does* make him free (Jn 8:32)—free to know and love God and to "go on his way rejoicing" (cf. Acts 8:27–39). Since it was God's intention to make men free, God's authority means man's salvation and is fully recognized when men enjoy the freedom granted them. Its internal essence is the power of God to evoke the faith and obedience appropriate to a child and to a covenant partner. Its external form is the exclusiveness, the patience, and the passion with which God is faithful to his plan.

The point has been reached at which the specific authority of the Bible can be described. This authority will be as inferior to God's as a testimony is inferior to the subject attested. But it can in no way contradict the character, purpose, and effect of God's authority and remain legitimate authority derived from God.

Inspiration and the Bible

At first sight the Bible may look like no more than a record of words concerning God that were spoken to men and by men and that deserves as much or as little respect as other records. But the fact that the Scriptures also contain accounts of the deeds and events initiated by these words cannot be overlooked. Indeed, the Bible has proved to be much more than a record of specific experiences, words, and events. It has imposed itself upon many, and has been treated by many, as if it were a living person charged with the task of leading to God those who heed its contents. Jews and Christians who declare, "The Bible speaks to me. . . . We believe in the Bible. . . . We must follow the Bible," obviously recognize in it features that distinguish it from other books. That which speaks and is believed and followed must possess the qualities of a person rather than of a thing. Thus the Bible is accepted as possessing the dignity and authority that distinguishes a friend or master. The Bible becomes a servant of God and helper of man.

Is it the mystery of the Bible that it represents God's own authority as directly and strongly today as did Moses, Jeremiah, Peter, and Paul in their time? Was the authority given the prophets, apostles, and other servants of God simply transferred to the Bible?

The Bible's own answer to these questions appears to be affirmative. What "God said" in the Old Testament is sometimes introduced in the New Testament with the words, "The scripture says" (e.g., Ex 9:16 in Rom 9:17; Gen 18:18 in Gal 3:8). Scripture is heard speaking as if it were a person—and no less a person than God himself! What the author of a psalm said centuries ago is boldly quoted as still being spoken by the Spirit (Ps 95:7–11 in Heb 3:7 ff.). We are forced to the conclusion that the Scriptures say what God says, and God says what the Scriptures say.

But by what miracle does this identification take place? The biblical passages most often referred to when this question is asked are those that deal with "inspiration." Inspiration is the gift of God's Spirit to selected men, by which they are enabled to be, to do, and to say what God wants of them. *Words*—preaching, admonishing, praying—play an important part in what God's inspired servants are meant to do. They are to be witnesses through their oral testimony. But the biblical concept of the "gift of the Spirit" covers much more than authorization to convey oral messages. For the fruits of the Spirit are mighty deeds and a life lived in love, joy, and peace. Wisdom, rebirth, purification, resurrection are some of the marvelous effects of the Spirit. Whenever the charge and the capacity to be a witness by the speaking of words is in the foreground, then by inspiration a man becomes a speaker in God's name, a prophet. In postexilic times, references to the Spirit became somehow reduced to this one function: Spirit came to mean primarily, though not exclusively, the spirit of prophecy. In the New Testament, for example in Acts 2, the act of inspiration culminates in the gift of tongues that speak to men and to God (cf. Mt 10:32; 1 Cor 2:13, 14; Rom 8:15) and in the gift of hearing the witness to God which is delivered in many languages. It is necessary, then, to consider specifically the function of inspired words.

God manifests his authority by speaking words. By words he appoints his servants. When he appears to make a man his servant he is not always seen, but he speaks (e.g., Gen 12:1–3; Ex 3:1 ff.; Josh 1; Is 6; Mt 3:13–17; Jn 20–21; Rev 1). Again, the authority which God conveys on these occasions is demonstrated by words. All specifically appointed witnesses of God are witnesses by their verbal testimony. They may also bear testimony by performing miracles, by suffering, or (as the Letter to Timothy and Titus most incisively points out) by leading a normal, quiet life. But oral testimony is still their main charge, and without it, even a martyr's death like Stephen's (Acts 7) might be testimony to a strongly held conviction, not to God.

By the use of words the witnesses of God set in motion those things that God wants to do through them. Their words are instruments of authority. "I say to one, 'Go,' and he goes; and to another, 'Come,' and he comes; and to my slave, 'Do this,' and he does it" (Mt 8:9)—with these words a Gentile has fittingly described his own and Jesus Christ's authority. A similar charge is given to Jesus' disciples. By words they shall bind and loose (Mt 16:19; 18:19). Those who believe in God are not only encouraged to use certain words in prayer and proclamation; they are also forbidden to misuse them. For by words they touch upon God's own authority. Indeed, what the Bible says about the character and power of blessing and curse is so strong that it may seem closely related to the belief in a magic power exerted by words or names themselves (Gen 12:2–3; Ex 20:7; Num 22–24; Joel 2:32; Mt 8:8–9; Mk 7:34; Acts 3:6; Jas 2:7).

But even if authority is manifested in words, it is still not naturally or magically inherent in them. A prophet may begin, "Thus saith the Lord," and still speak lies. A king may consider himself as wise as a god; he may say, "I am a god," yet he is still a man doomed to die. Inspired enthusiasts may speak in many tongues and yet be lacking the authentication consisting in love alone. Words may be food, joy, a burning fire, the heart's delight, or the very life of man; the Gospel may be called the power of salvation, or the word and wisdom of God; its effect may be as purifying as the pruning of a vine or the washing of a bride, or as joyful as the release of captives (Deut 8:3; Jer 15:16; 23:31–32; Ezek 2:8; 3:3; 28:2–10; Lk 4:18; Jn 6:35 ff., 63; 15:3; Rom 1:16; 1 Cor 1:24; 13:1–2; Eph 5:26; 1 Thess 2:13; Jas 1:21; Rev 10:8), but it is God's power in the word and not the power of the word itself to which these praises are due. The Bible records that it pleases God to use his servants' words, but they do not themselves possess the power, authority, and effectiveness which are God's alone. The words are but tools; they are not an authority.

We may compare their usefulness to that of the Sabbath. "The sabbath was made for man, not man for the sabbath" (Mk 2:27). It does not make sense to speak of the authority of the Sabbath and to ask man to submit to it. The authority to which man is submitted by the Sabbath laws, and the authority whose recognition of the Bible invites is God's. For this reason the words "authority of the Bible" may be misleading. The authority of God has been manifested *through* words—such words as are contained in the Bible. Still, it is not inherent in words. The hammer of God does not become a blacksmith. The sword of God is not transmuted into an heroic fighter. The tool does not become the master.

Nevertheless, there is one New Testament passage in which much of what has just been said appears to be contradicted. Paul (or someone writing in his name) writes to the Bishop of Ephesus, "All scripture is inspired by God" (2 Tim 3:16). This is the only biblical text in which words, not persons, written words, not preaching or praying, are called inspired. Here, too, inspiration appears to be understood as a past event. It is on this passage that the Roman Catholic and Fundamentalist doctrine of the Scriptures has been built.

It seems that for the author, for Timothy, and for all who believe in God, the books of Scripture stand as equals *beside* the persons of the inspired prophets and of the inspired people. Qualities proper to personal servants of God are also attributed to the words of those servants in some other biblical passages. In the New

Testament the preached word of biblical witness grows, speeds on, is glorified, dwells, is not bound (Acts 19:20; 2 Thess 3:1, etc.). Among the Old Testament books, Deuteronomy and Jeremiah are outstanding for their hypostatization, or personification, of the word. The words spoken by God or his witnesses seem to participate in the glory due to God alone and the authority granted his servants. He who "hears" what the Scriptures say, "has Moses and the prophets"; he who "believes the writings of Moses" is said to "believe Moses." True faith in Moses and the prophets is daringly connected with faith in God, or is equated with faith in Jesus Christ (Lk 16:29; Ex 14:31; 19:9; Jn 5:46–47).

It has been said that in the Bible itself there is a "certain confusion in casual speech between Scripture and God."[135] The story is told that when Rabbi Chananja was wrapped in a Torah scroll and burned alive, he saw the letters of the Law fly to heaven.[136] In this vision the very letters of the Bible repeat the ascent into heaven of Enoch, Elijah, Jesus. Again, Origen spoke of the body, soul, and spirit of a given scriptural text.[137] The elevation of the Bible to the rank of a person, even of God, may express the high esteem in which the Bible is held. But does the quotation from 2 Timothy 3:16 attribute to the Bible the same dignity and commission as to a servant of the Lord? Does it state that the Bible ultimately has no less authority than God himself?

The statement, "All scripture is inspired by God," is to be understood in the context in which it appears in the Bible. In contrast to evil men and impostors who make progress from bad to worse, cheating and cheated as they are, the "man of God" is to "continue in what you have learned and have firmly believed, knowing from whom you learned it and how from childhood you have been acquainted with the sacred writings which are able to instruct you for salvation through faith in Christ Jesus. All scripture is inspired by God and profitable for teaching, for reproof, for correction, and for training in righteousness, that the man of God may be complete, equipped for every good work" (2 Tim 3:14–17).

This passage contains some philological and grammatical problems which still defy solution. The source "from whom" Timothy has "learned" may be his teachers, or the writings used for teaching and study. The studying done in early childhood to which he refers may or may not include the learning of the alphabet. The syntax does not permit a final judgment on whether the writings are "able to instruct . . . for salvation" by faith in Christ alone, or whether, even before there is faith in the student, the writings are capable of instructing for *that* salvation which is *through* faith in Jesus Christ. It is possible that the beginning of the last sentence contains but one statement, namely, that the inspired Scripture is useful for teaching, reproof, correction, and training in righteousness. In this case Timothy's belief in inspiration is presupposed by the letter's author. But it is also grammatically possible to understand that two statements are made: (a) "Each holy book is inspired," and (b) "as such it is useful for . . ." In this case Timothy is instructed to believe in inspiration. Further, the Scriptures as a whole, or each book of Scripture, may be in the author's and reader's mind when the term "all scripture" is used. The term *theopneustos,* which is used as an attribute or predicate of all Scripture, may mean either "inspired," or "inspiring," or both together.[138] The righteousness referred to may be either God's way of righting wrong (as described in Rom 1–5; 9–11), or a way of right living which was also sought by moral philosophers.

Beside these as yet insoluble riddles stand other problems, the solution of which appears less difficult, though it is still anything but certain. The last sentence of the quoted text (verses 16–17) is phrased in a didactic, dogmatic manner, unlike the intimate tone of the preceding references to Timothy's youth, his teachers, and his study. The last sentence may thus be a quotation from a catechism, confession, or systematic treatise. The sacred writings mentioned in verse 15 are probably identical with "all scripture." "All scripture," in turn, probably means some or all of the Old Testament books, rather than apostolic writings, possibly including one or more of the Gospels of New Testament times. The codices and scrolls mentioned in 2 Timothy 4:13 offer no certain clue; but it is likely that in 2 Timothy 3:15, 16 and 4:13 the author refers to writings accepted as sacred by the teachers of Timothy, by Paul, and by Timothy himself. These generally accepted writings can hardly be anything but Old Testament books.

Insight into the meaning of the statement, "sacred writings . . . are able to instruct you," and illustrations of the usefulness of the Scriptures as tools for instruction in righteousness, may be gained from different sources. One may study the role of the Scriptures in the writings of Matthew, Luke, and Paul, in 1 Peter and the Letter to the Hebrews. Also to be examined is a special kind of "Scripture-gnosis" (that is, a gnosticizing interpretation of the Bible reserved for the "perfect" among God's servants) as it is displayed by Philo of Alexandria, the Epistle of Barnabas, and the writings of Justin the Martyr, not to speak of the Christian Alexandrian scholars. Despite the mention of "what is falsely called knowledge [so-called gnosis]" in 1 Timothy 6:20, it is unlikely that 2 Timothy should have to be dated so late as to possibly include a reference to Gnostic or anti-Gnostic hermeneutics.

Several features stand in clear contrast to those ambiguous elements of the text that still escape final elucidation. Timothy is told to hold fast to what he has learned and what has proved true. His steadfastness will be the greater the more he remembers the sources of his instruction. It was believed by teachers and pupil alike that canonical books are good textbooks, and that they are good because they do not only convey knowledge but also make a man wise in the way of salvation. The wisdom to be gained from Bible study stands neither above nor beside faith in Jesus

Christ; but there is no wisdom and no salvation apart from faith. The Old Testament points to salvation by Christ or confirms it. Timothy is not to benefit from the Bible for the sake of his own salvation alone. The Bible is to be received and is useful among the people entrusted to Timothy's care in the same way it was received and used by Timothy and his teachers. The Spirit, who was at work when the holy books were written, is the living Spirit of the living God. His operation is not a thing of the past. Therefore, what was experienced when the Bible was used for Timothy's instruction will be experienced again. Only as a learner and teacher of the Scriptures can Timothy be a true bishop. He is not asked for his opinion about the function of the Scriptures. He is reminded of his own experience, of the purpose of the inspiring Spirit, and of his responsibility to his flock. These last considerations constitute a command to let the specific usefulness of the Bible have its way.

The verses quoted from 2 Timothy do not intend to define the essence of the Bible, or to establish a doctrine of the Bible. Their purpose is the admonition of a bishop, and the bishop is an example of a "man of God." These verses do not stipulate that no voice other than that of the Bible was heard or is to be heeded by either the bishop or his congregation. Timothy received the Bible and biblical instruction from teachers (among whom not only professional teachers like Paul but also his grandmother Lois and his mother Eunice are outstanding), and he is to instruct others (2 Tim 1:5–7). In one form or another, it is within the framework of the church that the Bible was and is to be used. The reference to the Spirit is not an historical reference. It is not said that the Bible *was* inspired, but that the Spirit of God stands in a present, living, continued relationship to the testimony he has provoked and which is now found in writing. The unique power and the specific usefulness of the Bible are explained not as a paradox, but as something that has occurred and will occur whenever a man lives and behaves as a member of the congregation. The author of this passage speaks of Timothy's past and present conversation with the Bible, and of the relevance which this conversation has for his ministry and his personal conduct. The Bible is mentioned as a tool that was used and is to be used for a specific purpose. Its goodness and relevance are described only by reference to its usefulness. For the author of 2 Timothy, the Bible lives neither in a shrine nor on a dusty shelf. It is a tool that was used by God and is still to be used by man. Its relation to God's Spirit is inseparable from its actual employment in learning and teaching.

This does not mean that either the person and ministry of a bishop, or the tradition of teaching, or the characteristics of a worshiping community are permitted to compete with the power and use of the Scriptures. Two Timothy 3:14–17 is an affirmation of the unique and incontestable place of the Bible. Just as Timothy would not be a Christian without having received biblical instruction, neither can he remain a Christian, or be a servant to other men, unless he continues to be a student of the Bible. The instruction he has received and is to transmit is not the only authority. But it is the only standard of his knowledge of God and of his service to both God and man. The affirmation, *sola Scriptura,* is thus an appropriate interpretation of this passage.

Finally, in this passage neither Timothy nor anyone else is told that he *must* heed the Bible. Instead, he is reminded of the privilege he enjoyed when he received biblical instruction, and of the tool he possesses for teaching what is right. The very existence of the Bible is a call to gratitude. The gift of God's grace is dishonored when the Bible is used like a lawbook or imposed upon any man by force.

This passage from 2 Timothy, therefore, is itself "useful" in clarifying the character and place of the Bible. It does not say that words or books rather than persons are inspired by God's Spirit.

It does not assert that a certain belief concerning the Bible must precede and dominate the actual teaching and faith imparted by its contents. Nor does it affirm that God stopped inspiring men after the completion of the Bible.[139] It does not encourage worship of the Bible, but rather a happy, thankful remembrance of the things learned from it. Timothy is to serve God and the congregation, not the Bible.

If this key text fails to establish an authoritarian role for the Bible, is it wise to speak at all of the "authority of the Bible"?

The Freedom Letters

The classic attempts to demonstrate biblical authority have never been fully convincing. The biblical concepts of authority and inspiration support neither legalistic nor poetical interpretations of authority, and the biblical message of Christ defies the creation of a second Christ. It may thus be necessary to find new words to describe the character, rank, and power of the Bible.

Before an attempt is made to summarize what has been said so far, three concepts of authority that are definitely inapplicable should be mentioned.

First, any authority inherent in the Bible, or manifested by it, is different from the authority of a dictator, a general, or a specialist. Such authority is basically external and leaves little, if any, freedom of choice or decision. The authority of someone who holds a higher rank may be legitimate and his deeds praiseworthy. Still, authority that derives only from an external, superior position is a precarious thing. The essence of a given authority will always be recognized by the effect it produces and the response for which it calls. A tyrant will be fawned upon; a sergeant may make his soldiers move like marionettes; a great teacher's doctrines will be memorized; an outstanding surgeon will be permitted to operate on a king.

Neither God nor any of his authorized servants asks for this sort of recognition, but instead for the response of love, the enjoyment of partnership in God's covenant, and a life lived in freedom.

Second, if there is any authority proper to the Bible, it will speak for itself. True authority is not dependent on being demonstrated by self-appointed attorneys. Every defense of a given authority will have to use a definition of the authority to be defended. To "define" is to limit. A definition of authority is thus a limitation and restriction of authority. The authority granted to inferiors may appropriately be delimited, but the attempt to define a higher authority comes close to rebellion.

A man who lives under a true authority will bear witness to this authority, not by argument but by obedience and trust. The more sophisticated his arguments, the more dubious he will appear. Jews and Christians have always borne better witness to their respect for the Bible by quiet confidence, brave and unselfish deeds, and patient suffering than by apologetics. Their witness is convincing in the same measure as their attitude proves them free and happy men who live courageously and voluntarily under the authority they recognize. The authority of God is such that by it, men are saved from slavery and granted freedom. Obedience rendered voluntarily, and freedom displayed in the acceptance of God's order are the only means of indicating respect for the Bible. The authors of the Bible show by their own example how their witness may most appropriately be received. As Karl Barth put it, "Why and in what respect does the Biblical witness possess authority?—In that it claims no authority whatsoever for itself, in that its witness amounts to letting the Something else [i.e., God's revelation] be the authority, itself and by its own agency."[140]

Third, the authority of the Bible cannot be the same as that exerted by palpable things or social institutions. The Roman lictor's bundle and the policeman's badge, any good or widely read book, an academy of art or a university, tradition and public opinion, all have an authority that cannot be left unheeded, for they are indicative of a power that is greater than that possessed by individuals. Biblical authority must be essentially different, or it will be doomed to disappear among the host of transitory competitors.

In itself, a thing, an institution, or an abstract concept, cannot be a living example of God's will. Unless a temple is used by living people for acceptable worship, unless a holy tradition is kept alive by living faith, unless holy words and names are used in honor of the living God, they possess neither holiness nor authority. We must therefore conclude that it makes no sense to ascribe to holy Scripture an inherent, undestructible, unquestionable authority. The Bible, as much as any instrument of worship, needs to be proved holy in action. God's authority is manifested by the use of the Bible on those occasions when it pleases God to make himself known. From day to day man depends upon grace alone to perceive and know that authority to which the Bible bears testimony.

By the act of canonization, authority was neither given to the Bible nor acknowledged as inherent in it. Rather, the collection of the biblical books served to state the conviction that God himself had manifestly spoken to the authors of the Bible—and through their words to all the faithful—and that he would continue to do so. Canonization is an act of trust in God's past and future self-manifestation. It should not be understood as an act of inauguration by which authority is established. Three positive statements may indicate how to recognize the unique character and place, power and use, of the Bible.

The Bible is a Magna Charta of Liberation. The Bible bears testimony to that authority whose aim is to grant freedom to all mankind so that they may live as covenant partners of the one, true God. The words of prophets and apostles were put into writing and collected to remind Israel, the church, all nations, and each man that the "King of Kings" had redeemed a great and ever-growing people in order to give them freedom and to make them enjoy both his love and mutual love. This freedom is forced upon no one, but is freely given by God, and is to be enjoyed voluntarily by man. The Bible is a record of the covenant of the free. It is in no way similar to a *lettre de cachet.*

The biblical words and events possess the validity of precedents. The many stories describing God's dealings with man and man's various responses to God are powerful demonstrations of the identity of God, the character of man, and the history of the covenant made and upheld by God. The sequences of promise and fulfillment, of announcement by God and response in human prayer, of detailed law and authentic obedience, show that God has engaged himself in a conversation with man which culminates in the communion of Father and child, of Friend and friend, of the Helper and the helped.

While the biblical records do not claim to give exhaustive information (except perhaps in Rev 22:18–19), they have clearly been proved to contain sufficient clarity, poignancy, and exemplification to instruct one generation after another in all that pertains to the communion between God and man. The church had ample reason to recognize that this book is unique because of its unique relationship to the incarnation and resurrection of God's Son. Here the only trustworthy testimony of the eyewitnesses of God's full revelation is set down in writing. The Bible treats of the love of God poured out into the hearts of men, and it shows how, before and during and after God's full revelation, men have responded to God. It cannot therefore be used as a timetable of future events, a book of rules for behavior, or a source of easy answers. It will be heard as an invitation to such worship as is encouraged and directed by God's presence among men, and by experiences gained by earlier generations of God's servants.

The voice heard in the Bible calls for response and action from free and happy men. The God of whom the biblical witnesses speak is the living God, whose voice is still resounding. The Bible itself has proved useful in preparing men to hear and respond. It serves as a tool for God's own address and as an encouragement for men to reply with their own voices and in their own manner. The Bible's value is realized when, in fear and trembling, but also with courage and joy, its readers partake in the conversation between God and man. It is misused when it is employed to suppress the freedom and responsibility of man.

The gist of this chapter is that the final proof of the esteem in which the Bible is held is given by the use made of it. Only by showing how he hears, reads, understands, and applies the words of the Bible can a man confess his respect for the authority to which it bears testimony.

This observation leads to the question: What interpretation of the Bible was and is most appropriate to its contents? This question, which is identical with the search for a faithful interpretation, will be extensively discussed in the remaining chapters.

PART THREE

THE INTERPRETATION OF THE BIBLE

CHAPTER VII

FREEDOM EXEMPLIFIED: THE USE OF THE OLD TESTAMENT IN HEBREWS[141]

Interpretation of the Bible is best, if not exclusively, learned by actual engagement in the interpretation of specific texts. Laws have to be understood legally, lyrics lyrically, and editorials as editorials. The same hermeneutical principle applies to scientific, journalistic, humanistic, and biblical texts. Faithfulness to the author's viewpoint, language, and intention will always be the standard of true interpretation.

The Letter to the Hebrews is an appropriate subject for a case study of biblical interpretation. Its intention is to describe the special authority of Jesus Christ; its method is to a large extent exegetical; to achieve his purpose, the letter's author refers more extensively and intensively to his Bible (i.e., the Old Testament) than most New Testament authors.

A full commentary on this epistle cannot be offered here. Instead, after sketching briefly the historical background and the structure of the letter, we shall attempt to answer only one question: How does the author understand and fulfill the task of interpreting Scripture?

Characteristics of Hebrews

The author of Hebrews calls his work a "word of exhortation" (13:22). Therefore, his document is to be understood not primarily as a treatise but rather as a sermon or homily of the type delivered in Jewish synagogues or Christian meetings (cf. Acts 13:15). The name of the author is not known. Origen himself tried to identify him, and reached the conclusion that "God only knows."[142] Since many allusions are made to beliefs and themes that played a major role among the Qumran community, which flourished near the Dead Sea until its destruction between A.D. 66 and 70 during the Judaean War, it is possible that the author was a Palestinian who had once belonged to that priestly sect, or that he addressed members of it.[143] He was certainly a well-educated Jew; perhaps he was trained in Alexandria, in Egypt. He may have been a scribe; he was a teacher in a Christian congregation, and he may also have been a pupil or companion of Paul. Apostasy from Christ, relapse into Judaism, and victimization by "strange doctrines" appear to have been the major temptations of those addressed (2:1; 3:12–14; 6:4 ff.; 10:25; 12:3, 12–13). Since apostasy from Christ for the sake of participation in Jewish festivals and sacrifices could hardly have been an urgent problem after A.D. 70 (i.e., after the destruction of the temple and city of Jerusalem), the Letter to the Hebrews may have been written before this date. On the other hand, it may have originated in Rome in the period between A.D. 80 and 90. For the author is a third-generation Christian (2:3); many of the issues faced by Paul in the middle of the first century are not mentioned because they may no longer have been important; great persecution has been endured, and threatens again (10:34; 12:4); and finally, the text is first quoted in a letter from Rome dated *ca.* A.D. 95.

The structure of the Letter corresponds roughly to the treatment of three topics, although none of the main themes is found only in one part.

In the first part, covering the first four chapters, Jesus Christ is introduced as Son of God, the final shepherd, helper, leader, and king who has been sent, equipped, and vindicated by God himself. This Son is said to be superior to any other angelic or human mediator or steward. It is surprising to learn that it is not in spite of his lowliness but because he has been humiliated to the lowest form of human existence that he is exalted by God (2:5 to 3:6 especially).

In the second part (Chapters 5 to 10), the same Jesus Christ is described as a priest after God's heart. This priest is not exposed to the prophetic battle cry, "To obey is better than sacrifice" (cf. 1 Sam 15:22; Amos; Mic; Hos; Jer 7:22–23; Ps 40:6–7). For he is obedient (5:7–10; 10:5–10) in the midst of all those who stand impure and sinful before God, and he offers his life as an acceptable sacrifice on their behalf. Thus obedience and sacrifice are not only joined but identified. To intercede was the duty of the priest, but lasting atonement could not be gained by any Old Testament sacrifice. As a priest of royal dignity, Jesus Christ, with one sacrifice, interceded for sinners in such a way that their purification from sin need not be repeated, but only revealed and celebrated. They now have free access to God, and they are admonished not to waver on the way opened to them.

In the final part (Chapters 11 to 13), the people of God are described. Christians may learn from the example of the patriarchs: They were pilgrims who looked forward, not backward; they suffered and were ready to receive more chastisement from the hand of the Father; they walked by faith, not by sight. Christians know where to gather and what to celebrate: they assemble around the one altar of Jesus Christ—that is, under the cross found outside the gates of traditional religious sanctuaries. Hence their worship is not something for a few hours or days. Their treatment of one another, and their suffering among the Gentiles is as much part of their worship as their inner conviction, their steadfast fidelity, and their attendance at meetings for preaching and prayer. May they be patient! Just as the high priest is hidden behind a curtain during the ceremony of the Day of Atonement, Jesus Christ, too, is hidden for a time with God. But he will appear in might to justify the trust set upon him and to confound his enemies (9:26–28; 10:36–38; 12:14–29).

The Letter to the Hebrews is a sermon encouraging God's people to trust the authorized guidance and accepted intercession of Jesus Christ. Though Chapter 13 may not have been part of the original text, the whole Letter forms a homiletic unit. In order to support his historical, doctrinal, and ethical points, the author refers to the Old Testament throughout.

Four sorts of references may be distinguished: (a) direct quotations (as in 1:5 and about thirty other cases);[144] (b) indirect quotations or allusions (as in 11:5 and between forty and eighty other cases); (c) summaries, or reflections on the Old Testament (as in 1:1; 10:1–4); and (d) Old Testament names ("Jesus," "Christ") and topics ("people," "rest," "priest," "blood"). Implicit references to the Old Testament are so evenly spread over the Letter that the whole of Hebrews, and not only the comments made on Old Testament texts, is relevant to a description of the author's hermeneutics.

The references are made to texts contained in an Old Testament canon that was similar to the post-Jamnia Jewish canon which became the first part of the Christians' canon.[145] Some of those Hagiographas whose canonicity was contested among Jews even after the end of the first century A.D. (as Koheleth, Song of Songs,

Esther, and perhaps also Ezekiel) are not referred to. On the other hand, allusions to apocryphal writings—for example, to certain parts of Enoch, to 1 and 2 Maccabees, and to the Ascension of Isaiah—have been discovered in Hebrews 5:8 and 11:34–37. In 7:14, one finds a statement directly opposing the doctrine of a messiah arising from the tribe of Levi which is found in the Testaments of the Twelve Patriarchs, in the Damascus Covenant, and in other sectarian documents related to the group of Qumran. But explicit citations of noncanonical texts (as found in 1 Cor 2:9; Jn 7:38, etc.) are absent.

Among the books of the Old Testament to which the author refers, the Pentateuch and the Psalms play a major role. Among the prophets, considerable space is given to Jeremiah (in Heb. 8:8–21; 10:16–17), while Isaiah (in 2:13) and Deutero-Isaiah (in 9:28) are quoted much less than in Matthew, Paul, and 1 Peter. In view of the cultic and eschatological interest of the author, the omission of any reference to Chronicles, Malachi, and Ezekiel (Heb. 13:21 may contain an allusion to Ezek 37:26) is astonishing. In these books, the covenant with Levi and the honor of the Levites—especially of the sons of Zadok—play an outstanding and eschatological role to which the author does not allude.

Like any great Bible interpreter, he works with a "canon within the canon." He repeats some texts (Ps 110:4 about ten times); others he never mentions. Utterances about the Son (that is, king) and the Priest, obedience and sacrifice, the people and the representative Man, sanctification and rest, and faith and suffering are more frequent than references to prophet or judge, righteousness and freedom, the soul and the family. Despite his great concern for the priestly cult, the writer by no means neglects the prophetic call to total obedience (10:5–7; cf. 11–13). From what does he derive this concern? What is the special character of his interpretation?

Exegesis—A Necessity

In all his dealings with the Bible, the author of Hebrews looks deeply into the history of Israel. He studies the mighty promises of God (1:3), and the obedience, faith, and praise which are accepted by God (3:7 ff.; 11; 12:15; 13:21, etc.). But it should not be assumed that he looks into the texts alone. For he also looks for and at something other than words, stories, or cultic practices. Neither literature and history, nor values and principles, nor institutions and personalities are the focus of his interest. Whether or not he knows Paul, he follows a method described by him. According to Paul, the reader of the Old Testament sees only ink until he turns to the Lord (2 Cor 3:7–18). He considers all revelations of the Spirit unintelligible, unless "spiritually discerned" (1 Cor 2:13–15).

Now, the author of Hebrews speaks less frequently than Paul of the Spirit. But he does what the Apostle says: When he studies the Bible he looks at the Lord. He seeks him. We cannot say that he presupposes unshakable faith, either in himself or in his hearers, when he reads, reflects, and lets the Old Testament speak. But he searches for faith. "I believe, help my unbelief!" (Mk 9:24)—this might be his own confession, and it is with this attitude that he undertakes to speak to his brethren and to exhort them to strengthen one another (3:13; 12:12). But God alone can accomplish such a task (13:20–23). The author observes that in the Old Testament, God gives witness to faith (11:5, 39), and he therefore looks for God's testimony in the Scriptures. He wants to find out what is said about Jesus Christ, the leader and perfector of faith (12:2). According to John 5:39 (cf. Lk 24:27; 1 Pet 1:11; Acts 26:22–23, etc.), Jesus himself affirmed that the Scriptures bear witness to him. "If you believed Moses, you would believe me" (Jn 5:46).

No student of the Bible should assume that he reads this book without prejudice and purpose. Even the most open-minded reader is subject, for better or worse, to some preconceived ideas that are foreign to the book and will hamper his understanding. In order to be an empathic interpreter he ought to be motivated by concerns closely related to the content of the texts he studies. All too often a decision is made even before the actual study of a text is begun; for much Bible study is done for the purpose of confirming one's notions of facts, values, or literary and historical evolution. In this case the curiosity and willingness to look for faith and for the Lord himself will take a secondary rank. The author of Hebrews searches for what is said about Jesus, the final spokesman of God (1:2), the Son and Priest and Shepherd of his people. He does not ask for definitions (except in 11:1, 6). What is attempted is a description of how Jesus Christ is God's image (1:3)—that is, how he establishes justice (1:8 ff.), proclaims God's name (2:12), governs God's house (3:6), leads to a final rest (4:8 ff.), and opens access to God himself (4:14–16; 6:20; 10:19–22) by virtue of his eternal intercession (5:7–9; 7:25). He intends to show that He who has come is still coming "to help in time of need" (10:35–39; 4:16; 2:18). The author has a "canon within the canon." He collects utterances about the righteous, faithful, merciful, eternal, coming helper (Jesus) who is appointed and equipped by God himself (Christ). *That* Jesus Christ has come, and that God has spoken through the Son (1:2; 7:14), he knows from a source outside the Bible. He has been told by informants whom he trusts (2:3–4), and he is convinced of it. But *who* exactly the One who has come is, and what he is before God and means for man—this he learns from the history of Israel as it speaks from the Old Testament.

The promise and the fulfillment of the promise of the Lord's coming into the world—this is his canon within the canon. The author is confronted with urgent reasons for recognizing and acknowledging this canon. He is surrounded by those who live in great danger of unbelief, apostasy (3:12; 6:4 ff.), tiredness (12:3, 12), heresy (10:26; 13:9), persecution (12:4), forgetfulness (12:5), dullness (5:11; 6:12), and death (3:17; 6:8). He does not consider scriptural interpretation an end in itself. It is a brotherly service to a congregation that is exposed to actual temptation. What has he to say to his brethren?

He answers with the Letter to the Hebrews. Jesus Christ is sent by God and comes into the world as one who is humiliated below the level of sinful mankind. He comes in order to participate in their flesh and blood—even in their fear of death—and he leads them to their rest. They need never again worship according to laws that fail to establish peace with God and fellow man. The Hebrews are like pilgrims whose procession is guarded both before and behind by Christ. Even while they wait and march, suffer and hope, in the wilderness of temptations and trials, they belong to the assembly of God's people. They are not only instructed but equipped to live as men who have free access to God.

No other book of the New Testament (except the Fourth Gospel) puts the divinity and humanity of Jesus Christ so clearly side by side. Because Jesus Christ is both so high and so low, his compassion for man is convincing. The Christological interest of the writer does not lead to a Bible interpretation without practical application to daily life. For the author of Hebrews, exegetical theology is practical theology.

In conclusion, exegesis is first of all the endeavor to tell people in need of help what the Bible says of their shepherd and helper, Jesus Christ. Since it is undertaken to meet and overcome fear, and danger, and flagrant weakness of faith, it is a necessary enterprise, not a luxurious pastime.

We now ask, How does such exegesis come into being? How does it happen that the author's search is not in vain?

Exegesis as Listening

An external, and seemingly unimportant feature of the Letter to the Hebrews contains a clue to an essential element of the author's hermeneutics.[146] The quotation formulae "it is written" and "according to the Scriptures," and explicit references to "Scripture" or "letters" are conspicuously absent from Hebrews. There is one exception. The One coming into the world says, "I have come to do thy will, O God, as it is written of me in the roll of the book" (10:7; Ps 40:7). It is Jesus Christ alone who is thus explicitly submitting himself to the contents of a book. But that book may well be something similar to the impalpable "book of God" or the "book of life" (Ex 32:32–33; Ps 69:28; 139:16; Rev 3:5; 5:1–9; 20:12, 15). Man has no power over it. The author of Hebrews does not ask his hearers to become slaves to things written by men. Instead, when he introduces a quotation he employs words expressing speech. He refers to what "he says," is "saying," "said," or to what "is said" (1:6; 2:12; 1:5; 3:15, etc.); and he uses the verbs "testify," "swear," "reveal," "blame," "converse," "command," "promise" (2:6; 10:15; 7:5, 8; 12:5, 20, 26). The present tense is preferred to the past, and active forms to passive.

Since the context (except 2:6) usually makes it clear who is speaking, the phrase "he says" should not be translated "it says" (i.e., the book, the law says) and must not be considered a reference to the "heavenly voice" of rabbinical literature.[147] On the other hand, since it is sometimes God (1:5), sometimes the Son (2:12–13), sometimes the Spirit (3:7 and 10:15 only; cf. 9:8), sometimes a known or unknown speaker (2:6; 9:20; 12:21; 13:6) who is cited, it is not the authority of the speaker's person or rank alone, but also the importance of *what* is said that makes a passage worthy of quotation. What "has been testified somewhere"

(2:6) is no less to be heeded than what "[God's] voice" says "today" (3:7, etc.).

Hearing, coupled with obedience and "mixed with faith [united in faith]" (4:2), is the only way to receive the words spoken. To quote from the Bible means to extend an invitation to hear, to listen, to trust, and to act. "Today, when you hear his voice, do not harden your hearts. . . . The word of God is living. . . . [He] converses with you as with children [addresses you as sons]" (3:7, 15; 4:7, 12; 12:5)—this is the author's opinion of the words found in the Bible, and he attempts to make his hearers realize that the ongoing "conversation" concerns them. Their life depends upon hearing and obeying that living voice.

Not only the author of Hebrews, but the rabbis, Philo, and the early fathers, preferred to speak of what God, the Scriptures, the book, or the law "says." Only a minority of their Scripture quotations is introduced by reference to what "is written." But the author of Hebrews is consistent in avoiding any reference to written words and Scripture. What differences exist between the two manners of quoting?

First, emphasis on the written word often has a legalistic or polemical character. In the Old Testament, laws rather than promises are written down, deposited ceremoniously, and quoted in legal decisions. The writing down of law appears as part of a covenant ceremonial in Exodus 24:4, 12; 34:27, and in Hebrews 9:19.[148] In Greece the phrase "it is written" can be traced back only as far as the fifth century B.C. It apparently originated in courts of law and found its way from there into priestly language. The judge refers to the written law when he proclaims a verdict. In Matthew 4:1–10, Jesus fights the devil with quotations. When the devil, in turn, also quotes Scripture, the greater weight of a Torah text is used to confound a quotation from the Psalms. Paul, Matthew, and John often refer to what "is written" in the course of heated debates. According to Deuteronomy 31:24–27, the book, both while stored away and when read publicly, is a witness against a rebellious people.

But the author of Hebrews does not use the Bible as a handy legal reference book with which to overcome enemies. Though he once scolds them passionately (see 5:11 ff.), the "Hebrews" he addresses are not treated as adversaries in court, whom he intends to convict. To him the Old Testament, including the laws contained in it, is basically promise. His only concern is that God's voice be heard and heeded by the congregation today (3:7 to 4:13)—for their own "benefit" (4:2) and "salvation" (2:1–4).

Second, emphasis on written dicta and statutes leads to the question of interpretation: which among several possible interpretations of a quoted text is to be preferred or is applicable today?[149] The author of Hebrews, however, does not consider the Old Testament texts ambiguous. For him there is only one meaning of a statement. When the living God's voice is actually heard "today," a discussion of different meanings is impossible. How often is such a discussion only a way of avoiding immediate obedience! If the word of command, promise, or oath is really heard, then obedience and trust, not discussion, is the appropriate response. The literal and historical meaning is the only meaning with which the author is concerned. For him it is literal and present historical truth that God calls his people through the Son, and that he cares for them. And it is literary and grammatical fact that "Melchizedek, king of Salem" means "king of righteousness" and "king of peace," and that the bearer of this name is in many respects (in himself, in history, and in the Bible; not as the result of interpretation) similar to the Son of God, Jesus Christ (7:1–3).

Third, the writing down of spoken words is not merely a gain for the words. Its maximal advantage was, perhaps, envisioned by Origen when he compared the writing down of words to the incarnation of the eternal Word in Jesus of Nazareth. Other less mysterious gains are obvious: by being written, an occasional verdict may become the law of the land, time-bound sermons may become canonical prophetic books, whispered utterances may become testaments affecting the life and property of many. Once words are written down they can be heard and heeded in distant places and at other times. So much can all be for the good. But the fixing of speech in writing may also cause a petrification or an actual murder of speech. Sometimes the Bible itself calls the letter something dead, old, or killing, that stands opposed to matters of the heart, a fresh spirit, a living voice. In Romans 2:29; 7:6, and in 2 Corinthians 3:6, Paul refers to the "oldness" of the law and to the killing power of the letter.

The history of the Church is full of attempts to meet the problem of the age and apparent ossification of the Bible. By a process of elimination and emendation, or by ever-new reinterpretation, theologians of all periods have attempted to resuscitate the written word, to resist legalistic and literalistic narrowness, and to make a living challenge out of the dead letter. What is written seems always in need of a creative interpreter.[150] According to Matthew 5 to 7, Jesus Christ was such an interpreter: "I have come not to abolish them [the law and the prophets] but to fulfill them."

Since for the author of Hebrews the Old Testament is a living voice to be heard today, he is free from the temptation to magnify or to belittle the written word. He is convinced that what *has* been said in the Bible is also *being* said; the "living word" of the "living God" sounds from the Bible (3:7; 4:12). This may be why he prefers to speak in the present tense of what the Bible "says," and why he never uses the word "fulfill" in relation to the Old Testament texts he quotes. He does not consider the Bible a record, a *corpus juris,* or an empty will or promise whose contents need implementation, canonization, or specification—or whatever the meanings of the word "fulfill" may seem to require. For the author of Hebrews, the Bible is sometimes the voice of God and sometimes the response given by men to God. In its twofold capacity, the Bible is and remains a spoken word that demands to be heard and honored, trusted and acted upon. As an interpreter of the Bible, the author does not try to make the Bible say something. He does not attempt to give it actuality, because for him it is actual, and he hopes to point out to his hearers and readers why it is a living voice.

Exegesis, then, for the author of Hebrews, is the willingness to listen to what God is saying to the fathers as well as to the present generation. God's voice is good to hear; it is gospel for all who hear it; it is the word of salvation; in it God's power is felt. Exegesis is joyful appreciation of the Gospel's power.

Now, the perception and appreciation of the voice and words of God may require a special way of listening. The manner in which the author of Hebrews listens has therefore to be discussed next.

Exegesis with Discernment

Since, in the Old Testament, God speaks "in many and various ways" (1:1), how and to what shall man listen? According to Hebrews, the Old Testament sets down what God says to the Son (1:5–13; 5:5 ff.), to an individual (11:18), to angels (1:5, 13–14), and to "us" (13:5). But the Son also speaks to God. He speaks of his obedience and faith (2:12–13; 10:7; cf. 12:2); he prays, and he is heard (5:7). And he promises God that he will speak of God to man: "I will proclaim thy name to my brethren, in the midst of the congregation I will praise thee" (2:12). Finally, at a given time (cf. 9:8 and 4:7) the Spirit speaks to the congregation: "Today, when you hear his voice . . ." (3:7). On another occasion, the Spirit "bears witness to us," saying, "This is the covenant that I will make . . . says the Lord" (10:15–16). As the Son's words to God and to the congregation express submission to God, so the Spirit acts as a servant who draws attention to the revelation and the words of God. Hebrews contains no passages in which God or the Son speak to the Spirit; nor does the Spirit speak to the Father or to the Son, but only of God.

In consequence, listening to the Bible means listening to a dialogue between God the Father and the Son. It is a privilege to be given this opportunity. For the Father and the Son speak about what they are doing and will do for men. Man depends on hearing God's own voice. For by what other means could a son and priest—a royal high priest resembling Melchizedek—be acceptable to God and "appointed to act on behalf of men in relation to God," except by God's election and calling (5:1–5)? If he is to be legitimately appointed, then God must appoint him. The great royal psalms of the Old Testament all refer to "oracles" of God by which he elects, appoints, and confirms the king (Ps 2; 89; 110; 132; cf. 2 Sam 7). Similarly, the author of Hebrews refers to things said by God. To listen to God's words of inauguration means to participate in the revelation of a mystery of God. Even what God says to himself, the Father to the Son, shall not be hidden from man.[151]

But the Old Testament does not bring to man's ears merely an intertrinitarian conversation. The Son does not address himself to the Father alone, but brings the name of God to the public. And the Spirit does not rest until the hearts of the people are ready to listen, to trust, and to obey. The Old Testament shows what happens inside the Trinity; but it also reveals the triune God's concern for man. God is his own witness, and man knows of him only because the Trinity discloses him.

This may be the reason why the term "to testify" is used primarily of God himself (2:4; 7:8, 17; 10:15; 11:2, 4, 5, 39). But as this God speaks "by the prophets," "through David," "by Moses" (1:1; 4:7; 9:19), the role of a witness is occasionally also attributed to men (12:1; 3:6; cf. 10:28). In other books of the New Testament, the Scriptures, John the Baptist, and the Apostles are called "witnesses"; an event or act is sometimes called "testimony" (Mt 8:4; 24:14; 1 Tim 2:6). This terminology ascribes a quasi-legal function to persons and historical events; the world in which the mission work goes on is identified with a vast courtroom (especially in Acts), and the Scriptures are called to the witness stand to serve as a sort of legal evidence. How far the author of Hebrews is from using the Bible in this way was shown earlier.

In Hebrews, the words spoken by God, and the acts performed by God are God's testimonies. God is his own witness. His word is not one among many reasons but the only means to the Son's enthronement and kingship. Human witnesses do not contribute to the judgment. The word of God alone is the judgment of man. "The word of God is living and active, sharper than any two-edged sword, piercing to the division of soul and spirit, of joints and marrow, and discerning the thoughts and intentions of the heart. And before him no creature is hidden, but all are open and laid bare to the eyes of him with whom we have to do" (4:12–13).[152] The student of the Old Testament who hears God speak in his various ways has always to do with the mighty, majestic, living God himself.

It is not only the words spoken *by* God that are heard in the Bible but also the words spoken *to* God. The Bible does not represent the monologue of a lawgiver but the dialogue of God with his children. The Old Testament is thus a book of man's response to God, of which Israel's rebellion and Abraham's "reckoning" in faith form the two extremes (3:13 ff.; 11:19). Moses' confession at God's appearance, "I tremble with fear," and our reply to the promise of God's presence and assistance, in which "we can confidently say: 'The Lord is my helper, I will not be afraid,'" also show the breadth of human response (12:21; 13:6). It is characteristic of Hebrews that the same Jesus Christ through whom God says his final word (1:2) and who proclaims God's name and salvation *to men,* is also the One great high priest (4:14) and eternal speaker for mankind *before God* (7:25). He alone offers, "through the eternal Spirit," that obedience which men failed to offer (9:14; 10:5–7). He experiences fear of death, "like his brethren," and salvation from death, to become the cause of their salvation (2:14–17; 5:7–10).

Because Jesus Christ, the Son of God, is not only God's spokesman to men, but also man's spokesman before God, there is good reason not to call only the promises and commandments of God "word of God." For by a specific event the words of human reply to God and the confessions of faith God made before men have become word of God. If the Son of God takes man's words into his mouth, they become words of God. What God the Son says to God the Father, or to a congregation, is as much the word of God as what the Father says to the Son, or the Spirit to Israel. It is because of Jesus Christ that the whole of the Old Testament, including the human voices of God's chosen people, may be called "Word of God." God's conversation with man would not be a dialogue (12:5) if it did not also contain man's response to God. The voices of both partners are heard in the Bible. The human partner chosen by God is given the privilege of hearing human words spoken by Jesus Christ to the Father. Bible interpretation means listening to all conversing partners. It means respecting the fact that, according to the Bible, diverse kinds of human speech were fully understood, completely embraced, daringly taken to God the Father by God the Son. They must no longer be despised or ignored. The interpreter who seeks faith in Jesus Christ will also seek to understand the words of men as Word of God the Son.

For the author of Hebrews, exegesis is overhearing the dialogue that goes on within God, and between God and man—a dialogue which contains and honors human words, whether of trembling or trust, of begging or praise. Man and his word are taken up, assumed into unity with God through the Son, when God's word is heard. God's word cannot be attended to unless attention is also given to man's word, spoken to God, or delivered in God's name or delivered to other men.

In practice this means that whenever the one word of God is to be heard, different speakers have to be listened to. Indeed, whenever he refers to the Old Testament, the author gives his attention to different texts, events, and persons (see especially 3:7 to 4:11). His argument is consistently based on more than one statement, and the various texts are chosen, as far as possible, from different parts of the Old Testament. In this way he deviates from the *Pesher* method of those Qumranite documents that like to identify the contents of one ancient Bible verse with a later current event or contemporary person. His method is closer to the *haraz* ("string of pearls") method of the rabbis, which in turn seems to be reflected among the Qumranites by the collection of *testimonia*.[153] A *haraz* is the artful combination of at least three statements chosen from the three parts of the Old Testament for proving one specific point. Just as the testimony of two or three witnesses prevails over the claims of a single individual, listening to several Old Testament utterances is better than relying on only one verse.

As a result of these observations we come to the conclusion that exegesis is participation in the dialogue of the Bible. It means listening to, and enjoying, the great variety of ways in which the Word is being spoken. The Old Testament interpretation of Hebrews is basically neither typological, nor allegorical, nor is it a search for a "fuller sense."[154] To the dialogue of the Bible only what may be called "dialogical interpretation" is appropriate.

We can now ask: What happens to and in the man who listens to the dialogue which is carried on within God and between God and man?

Exegesis by Decision

Participation in the biblical dialogue is neither passive nor detached. According to Hebrews, the crucial question is whether the participant will recognize Jesus Christ as the authorized, competent, merciful helper, and give him due honor and obedience. Risk is involved in such recognition because man's life is at stake (3:7 ff.). Those who hear what the Old Testament says are urged to discriminate and decide between different statements that are unequal in weight.

According to Hebrews, not all that is being said in the Old Testament has the same importance, for not all is said with the same tone of finality. A distinction is made between promise and oath—but both co-operate to confirm "the unchangeable character of [God's] purpose" (6:13–18). On the other hand, even an oath of God, sworn to "in wrath," may be qualified by an interpretation given by God himself at a later time (3:18 to 4:9). Law and oath are distinguished (7:5, 11, 18–21, 28), and are treated as opposite and antagonistic modes of speech. A "legal requirement concerning bodily descent" stands against the "power of an indestructible life" (7:16). The law is "set aside" by the substance of the oath, and its "weakness and uselessness" become apparent. It "made nothing perfect" (7:18–19). The author dares to say such things even though he knows that God "will put [his] laws into [men's] minds" (8:10; 10:16), and that, provided sufficient witnesses are present, capital punishment follows violation of the law of Moses (10:28).

He is bold enough to state that some things said in the Old Testament are "better" than others, though both come from God, and both are spoken through men. He has a sharp eye for the different, if not contradictory, statements contained in the Bible. He considers the new covenant mentioned in Jeremiah 31:31–34 "better" than the first, which is "becoming obsolete and growing old," is "ready to vanish away," and was never "faultless" (7:22; 8:6–7, 13; 9:15). Different promises are given by God. Some of them are "better," or constitute the basis for a better legislation (8:6). Different hopes are "introduced"; one of them is "better" than the others (7:19). The Old Testament gives hints of a tabernacle "greater and more perfect" than the earthly "tent" (9:11; 8:2–7; 10:1). The division between Holy and Holiest in the ancient sanctuary points to the preliminary character of the sacrifices made in the "Holy Place" (9:2–10). The difference between Day of Atonement and daily or occasional sacrifices is pointed out (9:6–7, 13, etc.). As there are "better sacrifices," so a "better homeland" and even a "better resurrection" are already envisaged in the Old Testament statutes and stories (9:23; 11:16, 35). Thus the author of Hebrews distinguishes qualitatively among different elements of the Old Testament; only the better things attested are immediate references to Jesus Christ.

But he is not solely concerned with differences in quality. The Old Testament speaks separately about priests and kings; they are different persons and fulfill different ministries (Lev; Deut; Ps); and yet, both originally and finally (Gen 14:18–20; Ps 110:4), a priestly king is to be met. The Old Testament says that God himself rested after the work of creation; it speaks of the rest withheld from those who died before Joshua entered the promised land; it implies that Joshua failed to grant rest to the people; and it contains the promise of a last, final rest (3:7 to 4:11). It speaks of the one and the many (2:6 to 3:6). It deals with sacrifices that call sin to remembrance (10:3), and of days when God "will remember their sins no more" (8:8–12; 10:16–17). The number of allusions made in Hebrews to apparently conflicting Old Testament statements is very great. To interpret the Old Testament means to notice them and take them seriously, rather than to overlook them, whether negligently or magnanimously.

A number of observations should be made concerning the way in which the author of Hebrews treats such conflicts.

First, he uses no simple key to decide what is "better." Sometimes he seems convinced that "the old is better." Jesus himself—perhaps with a twinkle in his eye—had already mentioned this axiom of connoisseurs (Lk 5:39). According to Mark 10:5–6, Jesus appealed to an order that had existed "from the beginning of creation" when he wanted to show the limitations of a statute written by Moses. In the same way, Paul referred to the promise given to Abraham, in order to refute those boasting of Moses' Law or Abraham's circumcision (Gal 3; Rom 4). The author of Hebrews is convinced that at the end of time the original will be triumphant over all that "came between." Thus he points to the archetype of tabernacle and liturgy, which were made by God himself. Israel's cultus is something secondary. It followed the original, but it is later and only a copy. Human hands could do no better than to form an antitype; worshipers on earth saw but a shadow or figure (Heb 8:5, 23; 10:1; 11:19) of the original and final things. The archetypes are valid in heaven; they alone will prove to be triumphant and lasting.[155] Some of this sounds like Platonism—if not like Plato's own teaching, then like a daring hybrid of biblical and Platonic elements. But the first impression is misleading. For the author of Hebrews is too passionately concerned with specific events and persons, and with the final eschatological goal to which all revelation leads, to submit to metaphysical or religious dualism. Platonism is not built upon such burning interest in history as is displayed in Hebrews.[156]

On the other hand, the author of Hebrews does not adhere rigidly to the rule that the old is better. In 4:7; 8:8–12; 10:15, he introduces Old Testament texts by saying that the new covenant promised for the last days and the words spoken "so long afterward" are the norm by which preceding things are to be measured. As a result of that covenant and those words, the antiquity of some utterances, institutions, and persons seems more like obsolescence or senility (8:13). Similarly in the Synoptic Gospels, the words spoken at Jesus' last Passover declare that the old Passover celebration is terminated in favor of ("remembering," Lk 22:19) the lamb whose flesh is now given and whose blood is now poured out (Mk 14:22–24). The new covenant, promised in the Old Testament and concluded through the sacrifice of Jesus Christ, replaces the first. According to Hebrews 10:9, the very distinction made in Psalm 40:6–8 between the bringing of offerings and the doing of God's will, reveals that He who comes into the world, Jesus Christ, "abolishes the first in order to establish the second." It should be noted that the new things ushered in by Jesus Christ are not abstract truths, values, or principles, but a specific order of life which is at least as concrete as its Old Testament foreshadowings. The author does not support sheer spiritualization. But he teaches that through Jesus Christ all tears, all sweat and blood, all obedience and pain—everything characteristic of life on earth—are brought before God and accepted by the grace of the Eternal.

Consequently it cannot be held that the author's exegesis is inspired by a belief in progressive revelation and spiritualization, in the higher development of institutions, morals, and general enlightenment.[157] Nor is he convinced that all phenomenal occurrences on earth and in history are by nature and definition inferior to an ideal truth or to God's true will. Neither does he suggest a successive pejoration of Israel's worship and faith. The discipline of God, which he mentions in 12:5–6, and which is reflected in the excursus concerning maturity and stability (5:11 to 6:12), is not to be identified with what is advertised today as progressive religious education or the growth of personality. For the heart of God's discipline or pedagogy lies not in the idea of evolution or development, but in God's faithful presence with his people wherever and however they are. The education given by

God is reflected in acts of faith performed throughout Israel's long history—from the days of Noah to the time of the Maccabees.

The author's value judgments and decisions concerning what are "archetype," "better," "lasting," and what "shadow," "senile," "disappearing," are thus ultimately based neither upon the antiquity nor upon the modernity of given elements of the Old Testament. He uses other criteria altogether. He is convinced that God's promise was always there and that there were always men living in faith. God himself, as he was revealed by his words and acts of promise, and as he was obeyed in faith, is the standard by which all times and all Scripture are judged.

Second, the author does not use distinctions similar to those Luther derived from Galatians as criteria. He does not divide the Bible into Gospel and Law, and then give the crown to the evangelical elements. Among the different elements of the Old Testament, not only promise and hope but the legal will of God (his "covenant," 9:15–16), the firm order ("of Melchizedek," 7:11, etc.), and strict obedience ("by faith Abraham obeyed," 11:8), are upheld and considered eternal "types." On the other hand, not all that is promise and hope is said to be lasting. For, as we have shown before, the author distinguishes between different hopes (7:19), different promises (8:6), and different covenants (8:13; 12:24, etc.). He does not say that faith is essential to a child of God, but that strict obedience is fitting only in a slave. For faithfulness in this epistle is the attitude of a "servant" like Moses; obedience is "learned" by the Son (5:8). As disbelief and disobedience are the same (3:12, 18, 19), so faith and obedience are identified (cf. Rom 1:5). Correspondingly, the author is far from playing the Prophets and Psalms against the Pentateuch. In almost all of the three parts of the Old Testament, and not only in some so-called messianic passages or in prophetic predictions and visions, he finds utterances regarding that which is true and lasting.

Finally, the author follows those Old Testament prophets and writers who, long before his time, discerned analogies between certain past, present, and future acts and words of God. The restoration of paradise and the coming again of David; the reconstruction of Jerusalem and the temple; a return to the first love shown in the wilderness; a "new creation" and "a prophet like Moses" were all promised by the prophets.[158] Not cyclic recurrences, but the faithfulness of God to his eternal plan and the miraculous power of his grace were thus proclaimed. The patriarch legends, the Exodus from Egypt, and the stories of the judges and kings, as well as the miracles of creation were remembered, narrated, celebrated, and put into writing in order to encourage Israel to live in hope, trust, and obedience, and to endure the many periods of oppression and despair suffered at home or abroad (Deut 26:5–19; 29:2–29; Josh 24:2–27; Ps 74:12 ff.; 77:16 ff.; 89; Is 44:24; 51:9). It is not the New Testament or Hebrews that makes a type out of this or that event recorded in the Old Testament. Long before Jesus Christ, the events of ancient times were related and written down to serve as types of God's election. The author of Hebrews does not add to the Old Testament records a meaning which is entirely strange to them, but he discovers and unveils a direction, a thrust, an applicability that corresponds to their very nature. To give an example, the Old Testament legends dealing with the tent of meeting and the ark of covenant, and the stories and statutes concerning the priestly service of the Levites, of Zadok, or of Aaron were probably told and written down in order to give impetus or distinction to a reform or rebuilding of a temple, to explain the liturgy, or to keep the longing for proper order and worship alive among an exiled people. "Now these things happened to them in a typical way [as a warning], but they were written down for our instruction" (1 Cor 10:11). The Israelites of the monarchic and postexilic periods had already adopted this view of the relation between history and Scripture; it was not a view held only by Paul and Christians of his own and later times.

Thus, when the author of Hebrews directs attention to archetypes and antitypes found in the Old Testament itself, he does not trespass beyond the intention of the texts he quotes. Compared with the ocean of analogies between archetypes and antitypes, he might have chosen (and from which later Christian writers, such as Barnabas, Justin the Martyr, Origen, and Tertullian drank abundantly), the selection he makes is a limited and careful one.

What, then, is his mode of interpretation? For him, exegesis means making careful, yet bold moves forward and backward, downward and upward across the landscape of the Bible. It means perceiving diverse, if not conflicting elements and the tension between type and antitype. Just hearing the many voices sounding from the Old Testament is obviously not enough. The exegete compares, weighs, and evaluates them and makes decisions after long and careful study. To study the Bible means to face and collate parallel and divergent passages, earlier and later texts, and to think deeply about directions and warnings, and the contexts in which they appear. It is likely that the author (no less than Matthew, Paul, and the writer of 1 Pet) had gained much from an exegetical and theological education of either priestly, or rabbinical, or Qumranite character; that he made some use of contemporary paraphrases and comments on the Old Testament; that he knew more than one of the apocryphal books; that he stood in a relation of brotherly consultation and exchange with fellow Christian teachers. Therefore, not all his exegesis need be his own. In many places he may reproduce teachings of an exegetical school which present-day scholars cannot yet identify. But above all, he was searching—searching for the humiliated and glorified Jesus Christ, the helper (2:18; 4:16; 13:6, etc.), who is appointed by God for a people in need. What the Old Testament says about him, the author gladly hears, receives, and elaborates. Jesus Christ himself is the spiritual criterion of the author's spirited interpretation. Thus the author fulfills, in his own way, what Paul called discerning spiritual things spiritually (1 Cor 2:14).

This does not imply that the author finds whatever he wants to find in the Old Testament. He is looking only for the Lord. And he makes it very plain that not everything said in the Old Testament directly concerns the Son, Priest, mediator, and shepherd. But—probably to his own and his hearers' amazement and joy—he discovers in the Torah, in the Prophets, and in the Writings, not only preliminary, ambiguous, easily obliterated words, but also statements of an enduring and eschatological character. These statements show the pledged fidelity of God, the one perfect mediator, the unique and eternally valid sacrifice for sinners.

Further, it does not look as if, in the course of his Scripture study, the author merely found support for a preconceived Christology, soteriology, and eschatology. The uniqueness, the pointedness, and the daring application of his main teachings are considerably different from other (third generation, see 2:3) teachers of the second half of the first century. After learning, from those who heard Jesus Christ, that he had brought not only the message of salvation but salvation itself (2:3), the author was ready to learn even more. Should he now look into his own soul? Should he consult outstanding Christian teachers? Should he try to establish what was believed by, or acceptable to, the various Christian majorities and minorities? He chose instead to search the Old Testament. He expected this book to help him know and understand who and what Jesus Christ is, in his relation both to God and to man. The voices heard in the Old Testament assured him and his readers that the One who was coming into the world would come surely and without delay (10:37) in order to appear "a second time" (9:28).

In sum, when the author studies the Old Testament, he distinguishes sharply between different or conflicting events, institutions, accounts, promises, and persons in Israel's history. He does justice to the "historical" character of the Old Testament, and he reads "critically." And while he reads, before he speaks or writes, he meditates. All the subtle or surprising tensions and conflicts between God's eternal, universal will and the same God's preliminary, intervening, or transitory arrangements, are carefully considered before he points them out to his hearers. That which is said to be immovable and which remains the same yesterday, today, and into the ages—this, he says, is but one person, Jesus Christ himself (13:8).

Briefly, the exegesis of the author of Hebrews is critical research done in the history and literature of Israel, with the purpose of learning more about the helper of man anointed by God. It is the attempt to spell out the meaning of "Jesus" ("helper") and "Messiah" ("anointed") from the only textbook available. The textbook is the living God's ongoing conversation with Israel, of which man gains knowledge through the living voices heard from the Old Testament. Exegesis involves the risk of trusting in God's way to Israel, and of associating oneself with Israel's ways of praising God.

This leads to a last observation.

Exegesis for Worship

The author's study of the Old Testament is not purely intellectual or academic. As we have stated before, pastoral responsibility and concern play no small part in his mode of interpretation. Thus we have finally to ask what role the life of God's people plays in the hermeneutics employed in Hebrews?

The author exhibits an unmistakable interest in the festivals, the holy assemblies, the symbolic acts, and the institutions of God's people. This concern is shown when he says, "You have come to

Mount Zion and to the city of the living God, the heavenly Jerusalem, and to innumerable angels in festal gathering, and to the assembly of the first-born . . . not neglecting to meet together, as is the habit of some" (12:22–23; 10:25). The same interest makes him speak of "God's house" (3:6; 10:21, etc.), "the people of God" (4:9; 8:10; 11:25, etc.), the "congregation" (2:12), the service of the one high priest for the many who approach God's throne of grace (2:10–18; 4:14–16; 5:1–10; 10:19–22).

According to the Fourth Gospel, Jesus Christ preferred to make himself known on the occasion of great Jewish festivals, or at places of celebration (Jn 2:1 ff.) or symbolic significance (Jn 4:5 ff.). Similarly, in Hebrews frequent references are made to Jewish festivals, their solemn rites, and the Scripture readings used in the liturgy. The author's notion of the festivals provides the framework and the imagery for explaining Jesus Christ's unique work and its consequences. Each cluster of quotations and allusions (Chapters 1-2; 3–4; 5–10; 11; 12–13) appears to refer to a specific festival or feature of Israel's worship. If the "Hebrews" addressed in this epistle were Qumranites or a related group, or if they behaved like Peter and Paul who took pains, even as Christians, to participate in temple festivals (Acts)—then a connection between Jesus Christ's person and work, on the one hand, and central features of Jewish festivals, on the other, does not seem artificial or superfluous.[159] But which festivals are these?

It is obvious that those passages (especially in Chapters 5–10), dealing with the high priestly office of Jesus Christ reach their climax in the discussion of the Day of Atonement in Chapter 9. As in Leviticus 16 and the Mishnah tract, *Yoma,* the references are not exactly a flawless record of what went on in the temple before the catastrophe of A.D. 70. Hebrews contains a partly scriptural, partly factual, partly ideal or fictitious description of certain liturgical features. In discussing what is present and what is wanting on Yom Kippur, the author proclaims the completeness and finality of Jesus Christ's priesthood and sacrifice. Since this is generally accepted, we turn at once to another, less frequently noted festival reference in Hebrews.

A King's Festival (perhaps the Feast of Tabernacles) seen in the same perspective in which the author sees Yom Kippur may well stand behind most, if not all, Old Testament references and the concomitant reflections made in Hebrews 1 to 2:6.[160] In the quotations found in Chapter 1, the Son is successively addressed as "Son of God," "God," and "Lord," and the works attributed to him are the establishment of righteousness, creation, universal victory (1:5, 8, 10, 13). With hardly an exception, these texts are chosen from Old Testament royal or "enthronement" psalms. Hymns such as those from Psalms 2, 45, 97, 102, and 110 (cf. 2 Sam 7), quoted in Hebrews 1, were composed for, and probably used on a day of specific celebration of the kingship of God and of his Anointed One. The oracles of God concerning the king he had chosen to be his vizier on earth apparently belong to this celebration. But the reference made in Hebrews 2 to Psalms 8 and 22 (and to Is 8) may also have to do with a ceremonial act concerning the king; for as was stated earlier, the "man," the "son of man," the "child" (or "servant" of the Lord) described and epitomized in Psalms 8, 22, etc., may be the same representative person who is addressed in the royal psalms.[161] References to the role of the Servant and the Son in and over "God's house" (Heb 3:1–6) are well suited to an allusion to a festival.

At any rate, it is unlikely that the author was the first to select and draw together the statements about the Son and his God-given honor and ministry that appear in Hebrews 1:5 to 3:6. Psalms 2, 45, 89, 110, and especially 132, contain "oracles" about the king; these oracles were obviously collected and cherished before the author's time. A recent commentator believes that the writer of Hebrews used a *testimonia* book[162] for his quotations, and did not look up the Old Testament texts in their original context. This theory accounts for the inaccuracies which occur in the quotations. But the existence of a psalm like Psalm 132 makes it more likely that a liturgy, an order of worship, or a collection of hymns used before or in the author's time stand behind the collection of texts presented in Hebrews 1 to 3.[163] It would seem that the liturgy, or festival acclamations, of a certain day of joy (1:9; cf. Ps 118:15, 25) forms the background, and the author need no longer be slandered or pitied as a fabricator of artificial and meaningless "proof texts."[164] He stands on solid theological and homiletical ground when, by reference to the texts read and sung in Israel's worship, he proclaims that a faithful man appointed by God is the nucleus of all worship. He is the priest without whom nothing makes sense. He has good reason for saying that the oracles about the king of Israel would be blunt overstatements or sheer pagan mythology unless they referred to the true Messiah, Jesus.[165]

The Old Testament texts quoted in Hebrews 1 to 3:6 may indeed have to be understood as a call to worship. If they are, then the author of Hebrews recalled them not for academic purposes but with a practical intention. The Hebrews were to hear the familiar words as a call to participate truly and faithfully in the worship of God. True worship is offered by the Son; in their own way, angels participate in it, and it takes place among many brethren (1:6, 14; 2:6, 10, 12–13; 10:5–7). The Hebrews cannot but adhere to their confession (4:14; cf. 3:14; 10:23; 13:15), and "share in a heavenly call" (3:1) when they hear the call to worship extended in the Old Testament, as it resounds even "today" (3:7 ff.).

Other allusions to the worship of Israel are found in 3:7 to 4:13. In this passage the author presents an eschatological interpretation of "sabbath rest" (4:9). The legalistic observance of the Sabbath is radically challenged. Together with the Tabernacle and Atonement festivals, the celebration of the Sabbath is now seen as the imperfect placed in judgment by the appearance of the perfect.

The emphasis laid upon pilgrimage and alienation in Hebrews 11 stands shoulder to shoulder with that kind of polemics against the temple which was characteristic of some Jewish sects and which is also documented in the Hellenist Stephen's speech (Acts 7).[166] Nevertheless, Hebrews 11 is not against liturgical symbolism. The author mentions with sympathy the faith shown in "bowing in worship over the head of [Jacob's] staff" (11:21). And unlike Stephen (Acts 7:42), he does not cry out against all sacrifices, but cherishes those brought in faith by Abel, Abraham, and Moses (11:4, 17, 28). It is not in order to advertise individual or exclusively moral piety, but to invite his hearers and readers to participate in the acts of faith of the whole community of Israel, that Hebrews 11 is placed at the head of the ethical chapters. The Fourth Gospel calls true service, "worship . . . in spirit and truth" (Jn 4:23–24). Similarly, the author of Hebrews says that the Holy Spirit calls to worship today (3:7), and that "through the eternal Spirit" the true offering is brought (9:14; cf. 9:8; 2:4; 6:4; 10:29).

The final two chapters of Hebrews make allusions to the day on which the Law was given to Israel. Whether this event was celebrated in the first century A.D. during the Tabernacle days in the fall, or, as later, on Pentecost (the Festival of Weeks) in late spring, is a controversial question. But it is certain that a cultic vocabulary is as frequently used in Hebrews 12–13 as in earlier chapters. The author explains certain basic features of the Christian congregation's life by appealing to that knowledge of the service due to God and to one another which the Hebrews received earlier from the Old Testament. The path of the congregation includes both an approach to God (12:22–24), and a going forth "outside the camp" which is comparable to certain features of sacrificial worship and to Christ's suffering "outside the gate" (13:11–14). The references to Old Testament and Jewish worship are an invitation to join in true worship—that is, in such service as is offered both in the communal festival meetings and on the long, steep pilgrim's way followed by God's witnesses. All worship is centered in the sacrifice of Christ. It is not an institutional matter of given places, hours, or days. Ever-new obedience to God's call is as much a part of it as the singing of hymns; both are called "sacrifices" pleasing to God (13:15–16). In his applications of Old Testament texts, the author shows concern, not for a narrow concept of liturgy and worship, but for brotherly love and brave testimony in a hostile environment.

So much for the cultic framework and liturgical connotations of the author's use of Old Testament quotations and of his allusions to, and reflections on the Old Testament.[167]

Clearly, the author does not wish to exclude from his concern all that the people of God actually receive or fail to receive in the service of God. He considers the Bible a book for people—however and whoever they are. And he understands the different parts of the Bible as calls to service, and reports on service to God. That the Old Testament is neither historiography of the nineteenth-century kind, nor a collection of thoughts, ideas, or principles, nor an analytical work, but a collection of legends and stories, challenges, instructions, hymns, and orders and promises intended for use in worship—this is today widely recognized.[168] The Old Testament is a testimony from faith to faith. In it the living God's faithfulness calls for a faithful people. The author of Hebrews recognizes this call and passes it on to those listening to him. In so doing he acknowledges the authentic, literal, and historical purpose of the Old Testament. He uses the Bible in a manner true to the intention of the community and the individuals who contributed to its composition. They collected all the words found in today's Bible for the benefit of, and as a warning to their contemporaries and to future generations. What is written "was written for our sake . . . for our instruction" (Rom 4:24; 1 Cor 9:10; 10:11).

Approached in this way, the usefulness of the Bible resides in the fact that in this book God invites men to serve him, freely, joyfully, and faithfully. Exegesis is the act of hearing the Bible as a call to worship God in truth, together with the people who were gathered to serve him, the people of the Jews. Only in solidarity with Israel, never in anti-Semitic division, can that worship be offered to which the Bible invites and urges its readers and interpreters. Exegesis is the acceptance of that call and obedience to it.

It is also the act of passing on the call to contemporaries who are living, suffering, and dying. It continues the urgent invitation of prophet and priest to worship God faithfully in the face of apostasy and error; joyfully, even in persecution; hopefully, though the time seems long. Consequently, exegesis is not only a prerequisite of preaching, it is in itself a prayerful proclamatory and exhortatory act. Without prayer and public witness, no true exegesis of biblical texts is possible.

Hebrews and Its Critics

Among the New Testament authors who make most extensive and frequent reference to the Old Testament, the author of Hebrews is a relatively lonely figure. He frequently selects other texts than they do, and quotes from different versions, traditions, or liturgies. His typology is different from Matthew's, his allegory from Paul's, his imagery from that of Revelation. It was stated before that the prose and the hymnic sections of Deutero-Isaiah (Is 40 ff.), which play a major role in almost all early Christian writings, are hardly touched upon. Whenever attempts at analyzing and describing the hermeneutics of other New Testament authors are made, the results look decidedly different. Is this the reason Hebrews is often treated as a stepchild in the family of the other canonized early Christian writings?

The answer must be negative, both in regard to the early

church and to those scholars who are distinguished by their love for patristic studies. It has to be affirmative when it is asked of modern critical biblical scholarship.

The distinctive method of interpretation used in Hebrews does not appear to have been a major reason for its neglect by early Christians. While Eastern churches and theologians have treated it as canonical since Clement of Alexandria, doubts about whether the Letter was written by Paul were upheld in the West. And there were also dogmatic and pastoral objections to the exclusion of a second repentance (cf. Heb 6:1–8; 10:26–27, 32; 12:15–17). The Letter's dubious authorship and the harsh treatment of defectors played an important part in the reluctance to recognize its canonical rank. But Western theologians and the Roman Church found ways to meet these objections. Paul was officially declared the author, and the Letter was interpreted as merely prohibiting a second baptism. Emphasis on the precedents set by the Jewish liturgy and hierarchy was welcomed as a support of the development which cultus and church government had taken. In addition, the evangelistic message of Hebrews was heard again and again, and by A.D. 400 it is found in both Eastern and Western lists of canonical books. We must now ask to what extent its exegesis was imitated after it became one of the readily quoted books of the orthodox majority of Christians.

A hermeneutics which is reported to resemble that of Hebrews had been flourishing in Alexandria since Philo's time. However, the combination of Christological, liturgical, and pastoral concern which distinguishes Hebrews has hardly ever been matched. Alexandrian hermeneutics thrived on the different "senses" of the Bible; in Hebrews, such a distinction is not made. Its hermeneutics did not become the program or ideal of a school of exegesis. It was tolerated rather than emulated within the church.

Critical Protestant exegesis of the last two centuries has often questioned the exactness, reliability, and exemplary character of the hermeneutics employed in Hebrews. Many commentators feel obliged to mark the exegetical slips, improprieties, or distortions they observe. They indict an author who uses a Greek text of the Old Testament rather than the Hebrew Masoretic text; who does not quote exactly; who combines different texts into one citation; who uses statements out of context; who attempts to make points by means of etymology, if not allegory; who uses arguments from silence as evidence; who selects seemingly apocryphal and superstitious elements incorporated in Old Testament and Israelite tradition—"mythical" statements about the king, and "primitive" notions concerning the effect of sacrificial blood. The author of Hebrews is found guilty of all these sins, and more, and he is seriously rebuked by liberal and conservative critics alike. To most modern scholars it appears that the author of Hebrews is too middle-Platonic, or Philonic, in his philosophy and hermeneutics; that his doctrine of inspiration is more rigid than it need be; that, despite his polemics against temple ceremonies, he trusts too much in arguments based on the Jewish hierarchy and liturgy; and that his concepts of faith and sin do not have the depth of Paul's.

Be that as it may, until clearly defined alternatives have proved their superiority over the method chosen by the author of Hebrews, modern criticism will remain ineffective. If the results of Hebrews' hermeneutics are not only tolerable but are important contributions to the knowledge of Christ and the consolation of many, then its exegetical method remains a challenge to all who, despite their improved methods, did not attain comparable results. Ever-changing "modern" critics come and go. The Letter itself is still a living, unique, and indispensable voice that draws attention to Israel and the Old Testament. It conveys knowledge and understanding of who the King of the Jews and the priest of the weak is. It proclaims Jesus Christ to suffering men by saying words of comfort, guidance, and encouragement. So far, the witness borne to Christ by Hebrews is clearer and stronger than that of its critics.

Still, the exegetical contributions of recent scholarship will have to be considered in their own right. But before we turn to modern exegesis, three decisive and inseparable features of the hermeneutics of Hebrews should be recalled.

1) Interpretation of the Bible is careful, critical listening to the dialogue between God and man.

2) It is not a quest for rocks to be stored in museums, for an evolution comparable to that of organisms, or for timeless principles or laws, but for the mystery of the person and work, faithfulness and mercy, majesty and lowliness, uniqueness and universal rule, of Jesus Christ.

3) Interpretation is a communication of the results of this quest. It urges people exposed to the world's temptations to participate trustingly, obediently, and joyfully in the life and service of God's people.

Such exegesis is essentially dialogical, Christological, and pastoral. It is obviously always unfinished. New situations in which God's people and the world find themselves will have to be met with fresh interpretation.

The author of Hebrews used the Bible as a free man should. He sought both information about Christ and words of comfort. He followed the Scriptures when he extended the call to true worship. Bound to the Scriptures, he is yet an original thinker who used imagination well. In his expository argument and in his daring application of his findings, he does not want to impose a law upon anyone. The freedom of the Hebrews to approach God under the leadership of Jesus Christ is his main concern. The best and most faithful pupil of the author of Hebrews will be one who uses his own capacities to participate freely and responsibly in the biblical dialogue, in the witness to Christ, and in the service of God's people.

CHAPTER VIII

THE BURDEN OF FREEDOM

The Bible itself indicates that there are many ways in which it can be understood.[169] The prophets and the authors of the great historical works found in the Old Testament interpreted the tradition of God's people in various ways. New Testament authors make different use of the Old Testament writings. The interrelationships among the several New Testament writers and writings reveal, again, a variety of mutual understandings—and perhaps of misunderstandings.[170] The purpose of this present chapter is not to linger on different methods of interpretation represented in the Old and New Testaments, but to focus upon essential features of the interpretation of both Testaments by postbiblical writers. Of course, a complete view of the approaches chosen in different periods by different schools and scholars cannot be given, but some examples from the last two centuries may be sufficient to indicate the issues raised, the methods employed, and the results achieved by academic interpreters of the Bible.

Every Bible reader is in his own way an interpreter. Novelists and playwrights, painters and sculptors, composers and musicians, philosophers and historians, may have contributed more to the understanding of the Bible—both quantitatively and qualitatively—than professors of the Old and New Testaments. Nevertheless, the search for exact interpretation, which has been going on in seminaries and universities, may serve as an illustration of the problems facing all who attempt to understand the Bible's contents.

What happens when this document of the freedom granted to man by God is interpreted? A Roman Catholic writer has recently observed, "After all, in the Scriptures we are in the Father's house where the children are permitted to play."[171] Such a deflation of professorial pride is extremely wholesome, for before God, the greatest Bible scholars are, at best, children. In the eyes of many Jews and Christians—not to speak of non-Christians—professional Bible interpreters have fallen into disrepute, partly because their fights among one another display not merely passion but a sort of rabidity. But if interpreters may be likened to children, their labors and achievements may be permitted to be both childlike and childish. There will be amazing constructions; there will be joy and delight. But there will also be noise and fighting enough to drive many to despair. The Bible teaches that God bears with his children; he forgives, and they are led to forgive each other. The interpretation of the Bible can live only in the forgiveness its well-trained and its freewheeling interpreters receive. It is the burden of freedom that not only free children, but all free men, both use and misuse the freedom given to them. No wise man will conclude from this that freedom should therefore be suppressed. Even fighting scholars remain a species of ***homo ludens.***

What has been achieved in the last two hundred years by those concerned with the interpretation of the Bible?

Triumphant New Methods

Since the Enlightenment, three methods of interpretation have become triumphant. If their application to biblical research was not a complete innovation, it was nonetheless only during the Age of Rationalism that it began to lead to conspicuous results.[172]

1 *Textual Criticism and Philological Research*

While the Reformers believed that in their Hebrew and Greek editions of the Bible they possessed a reliable tool for discovering the word of God, and while Roman Catholics of the Counter Reformation considered themselves able to restore a foolproof Latin text of the Bible, critical research found reason to question the accuracy of all the biblical texts used by the churches. Variant readings were found in Hebrew and Greek manuscripts, as well as in ancient and medieval versions of the Bible. None of the extant manuscripts or fragments of manuscripts of the Old Testament are older than the first century B.C.; none of the available New Testament majuscules and minuscules were written before *ca.* A.D. 135. The oldest complete Hebrew Old Testament text is medieval; the oldest complete Greek New Testament manuscript still in existence is from the fourth century. Now, by comparison of the various manuscripts available today; by drawing on Latin, Egyptian, Syriac, and other versions of the Bible; by observing the use of biblical quotations in early liturgies and theological treatises; and finally, by applying common sense, conjectural imagination, and theological judgment to the processes of comparison and correlation, important results have been and are being achieved. After additions or corruptions have been discovered and eliminated, a form can be restored that will presumably be nearer the text dictated by a prophet (e.g., Jer 36) or written by an apostle

(Gal 6:11) than the texts used during different phases of church history.

The necessity for this sort of scrutiny is undisputed. Origen employed it. Most of the manuscripts with which textual critics are working today (e.g., the codices of the Alexandrian, Antiochian, and Caesarean "families") have turned out to be themselves the result of critical emendation. Modern scholarship is constantly evolving improved methods of reproducing the original wording, and critical, annotated editions of the Bible that contain the most important variant readings of the text are the palpable result of this research.

But textual criticism poses spiritual problems as well. When Fundamentalists and Catholics affirm the Bible's infallibility, they no longer claim that one or another edition is free from error. Infallibility is ascribed only to the autographs of the biblical books,[173] which are, however, admittedly lost. It is sometimes argued that God would not have left his people with copies that were so full of errors that it was impossible to discern his will. But, whatever the argument, one result of the continuing critical search for the exact wording of the Bible is obvious. Possession of the Bible does not in itself guarantee the knowledge of truth. For the true word of God to man and the faithful witness to God, the Bible reader can but search, labor, and pray. The text of the Bible which is in the reader's and interpreter's hands is a useful tool in the search for the Bible's original wording, but it is not truth in a final written form.

The consequences of philological research are similar. Only a small minority of readers submits to the labor, and enjoys the privilege, of reading the Bible in its original languages; the majority is bound to use translations. Now, a translation can never pretend to be equal to the original, and in most, if not all cases, it will be inferior.[174] Every hearer and reader of the Bible, and therefore every translator, unwittingly makes selections, accommodations, and applications in which his own weakness and strength, his prejudice and devotion, his doubts, his certainty, and his own particular responsiveness play a major role. A translation of the Bible is thus always an interpretation which contains additions or omissions; and the opinions of the interpreter may sometimes be mistaken for the word of God.

During the last few centuries, more and more Near Eastern texts have been discovered and deciphered, and great progress has been made in understanding the languages, and penetrating the thought patterns of the different nations, groups, and individuals concerned. Archaeology, ethnology, and historiography are flourishing. Such progress has made it necessary for Bible translations to be submitted to one revision after another. The meaning of a great number of hitherto unknown words is now established with such certainty that it is no longer a matter of conjecture. References to passing through the needle's eye or to faith moving mountains have been recognized as idiomatic. If the literal meaning of "to pull one's leg" is "to tease somebody," then the literal meaning of the idioms used in the Bible could also be expected to be metaphorical. That apocalyptic language (as used in Zech 1–8; Dan 7–12; Rev) has a form, grammar, and a quality of its own has also been ascertained. Many philological mysteries, however, remained unsolved. No foolproof method has yet been developed to determine, for instance, whether a biblical sentence that resembles another in form or content is prior to, or dependent on, its "parallel." Since the meaning of key words such as "righteousness" and "spirit" changes not only from one period to another during the eighteen centuries of biblical history but sometimes also within the writings of the same prophet or apostle, and since the biblical writers make both obscure and transparent allusions to events and opinions contemporary to them, the task of translating their words is inseparable from continuing historical research. It is clear, however, that it is not only the results of research into ancient history and languages that make it necessary to revise and replace even the most excellent earlier Bible translations, but also the changes of vocabulary, grammar, meaning, and taste that occur continually in modern languages.

The introduction of new translations, based on new critical editions of the biblical text, deprives devoted Bible readers of the comfort and beauty of earlier translations, and is sometimes, therefore, greeted in a less than friendly fashion. Conservative clergymen and laymen alike have expressed the fear that, together with the wording to which they were accustomed, the content and authority of the Scriptures might suffer.

Actually, the critical work performed by those who labor to restore the text and produce the most accurate translation possible is not criticism of the Bible. It does, however, contain a necessary and edifying criticism of the synagogue, the churches, the schools, the scholars, and the copyists who transmitted the Bible from one generation to another and who interpreted it within the limits of their capacities.

As long as synagogue and church are ready to listen, to trust, and to obey the voice speaking through the Bible, they are bound to ask what that voice is really saying. If they trust the providence of the living God they are bound to believe that this providence has not exhausted itself with one of the earlier editions and translations of the Bible.

However, there is another sort of Bible criticism which has met with much stronger objections.

II *Literary Criticism*

When, during the Enlightenment, the Bible's relationship to the achievements of "modern" science became a matter of primary concern, an easy solution seemed to recommend itself. Rationalists felt entitled to consider the Bible a book like others; its authority was not held to be higher than any fallible human authority. In opposition to the belief in a divine author, the exact identity of the human authors was to be established. Perhaps a misunderstanding of the ancient church's references to God, the *auctor* (creator, founder, guarantor, or witness) of the two Testaments, and a mechanical interpretation of inspiration contributed to the interest with which the human authors of the Bible were studied. It was assumed that careful research into the style, the origins, and the content of biblical literature could deal a fatal blow to the belief that God was the author of the Bible. It was demonstrated that not one but many authors had written the Bible, and that various and contradictory human traditions and ideas were expressed.

Careful readers observed that, in the first books of the Bible, God is now called Elohim, now Yahweh; that in the New Testament, Jesus is called here the Son of Man, and there Lord; or that Jerusalem is spelled differently within the Book of Acts. What started with the observation of apparent trivialities led to the discovery that different nomenclatures represented different authors' special interests and emphases, the different times in which they lived, various traditions which they represented, and their varied theological outlooks. Images of a Yahwist and an Elohist narrator, of this or that priestly or prophetic writer of Israel's early history, and of Palestinian or Hellenist recorders of Jesus' sayings, miracles, and passion began to take shape. It was assumed that most of the narratives, hymns, and doctrines compiled in the Bible had originally existed in separate scripts; these reconstructed documents were now called the "sources" of the books of the Bible. Whenever possible, a name, place, date, and purpose were established for each of the sources' authors. Differences between the historical and religious value of the sources were enumerated. The final, present form of the biblical writings was, in most cases, ascribed to compilers or redactors. By drawing on their several "sources," and adding something of their own, they became the compositors of the Pentateuch, the Gospel of Matthew, Acts, Letters to Timothy, and the Revelation to John. The first six books of the Old, and the first five of the New Testament, proved to be most rewarding material for this sort of research. Among others, Luke (1:1–4), the Books of the Kings, and Chronicles refer explicitly to sources used.

This method of reconstructing the origin and composition of the Bible has been dubbed the "scissors-and-paste method." The biblical books were first cut into pieces so that their supposedly basic elements were clearly separated, and then the fragments were reassembled into new units that were deemed more reliable. The ancient collectors and redactors of the biblical material were sometimes made to look rather foolish. For the biblical scholars were convinced they had achieved two important results. First, by penetrating behind the redactors' work to the sources, they believed they had obtained more objective accounts of the actual events of the lives of the patriarchs, Israel, Jesus, and the apostles. In most cases it was simply assumed that the older source would be the more accurate. Second, by distinguishing individual traits of the biblical sources, authors, and redactors, scholars felt enabled to penetrate to the roots of various religious experiences and the idiosyncracies of religious personalities—just as in one recent school of nonbiblical literary criticism, the study of each author's life appeared to contain clues for understanding the sense of his writings.

The authors of most biblical sources, not to speak of the redactors of the source material, were at times submitted to severe criticism. Doubts were raised as to the exactness of their historiography, the trustworthiness of their belief that they spoke in God's name, and the obligation of later generations to endorse their viewpoint. As early as the second century A.D., Marcion and Gnostic groups had operated on similar assumptions. Only Paul, or John, at times together with selected apocryphal writings, were considered sacred. Even today, Protestant Bible interpreters reveal a preference for Old Testament prophetic, and New Testament Pauline writings. Because of their spiritual, ethical, ametaphysical, antisacerdotal character, these writings became, for many, the canon within the canon. But even among the Prophets and Pauline Epistles, distinctions were made. Whenever Jewish "legalism" or Roman Catholic "traditionalism" seemed to find support, it was assumed that one was dealing with a degenerate prophetism or a deutero-Pauline text. It seemed impossible that the same authors could have written both the spirited passages considered authentic and the more pedestrian passages that also bear their names. The Roman Catholic Church reacted against this tendency of Protestant interpretation by stating officially that Paul's authority is subject to that of Peter.[175] The Gospel of Matthew, especially the passage dealing with Peter's institution as the rock on which Christ's church is to be built (16:18), serves as a proof text for this dogma. The first Gospel, and the words of Jesus contained in it, were considered the oldest source of information.

Thanks to the work of the school of literary criticism, the humanity, the beauty, the individuality, and the history of the books of the Bible were discovered. In Chapter IV, the contribution made by representatives of this school to the discussion of the Bible's authority was considered. They also realized how difficult it is to apply all that the Bible says to modern thought and life. They tried to decide between a respectful and a contemptuous attitude toward the Bible by making sharp distinctions between its higher and lower elements.

Perhaps the inventors and promoters of literary criticism were too convinced that the origin, composition, and tendency of the biblical books resemble those of a dissertation or an historical, doctrinal, or confessional book. They have certainly succeeded in dividing the Bible into what now appears to be nothing more than a conglomerate of diverse literary units and fragments, histories and biographies, ideas and values. In any case, this sort of Bible criticism was bound to be criticized itself, not only by conservatives, but by other schools of critical research.

III *Historical Criticism*

There are at least three schools of historical critics. They are differentiated by the methods they use, and by the different goals they have set themselves. But they are all asking the same question: What actually happened? Which historical events are described in the Bible or provide the background necessary to understand the witness of this book? At first sight, they seem to have in common only the employment of methods and standards derived from the nontheological sciences. But they also share a spiritual concern which they may or may not make explicit.

While they do not repudiate the methods and results of literary criticism, they are not content to stop when the composite character of the Bible has been established and when a more or less arbitrary evaluation of the sources, their authors, and their value has been made. After all, the Bible is not merely a literary product determined by the faith or fancy of its authors. It is a book which originated in certain events that are more important than the collection and edition of literary sources. It claims that, through certain events that took place in history, God manifested himself as the God who is different from the deities of the religions of the world. Historical criticism sets itself the task of ascertaining and describing just those events. The history of Israel and of the earliest churches, the history of Moses and David, the life of the historical Jesus and of Paul have therefore been scrutinized, described, and revised again and again.

1) *The archaeological school* uses the tools of biblical research mentioned before, and also the spade, the magnifying glass, and, in recent years, the radioactive carbon test provided by modern

physics. It has obtained surprising results. It has been established, for instance, that there was a flood similar to the one described in Genesis. There were also not one but several towers of Babel. There were treaties made in and around Palestine and Asia Minor of the kind recorded in the Abraham and Sinai stories. Nomads did invade Egypt. They became settlers or were subjugated, and some of them eventually left again. Cities and holy sites of the Israelite amphictyony, referred to in Joshua and Judges, have been located. The pool and the water conduit mentioned in 2 Kings 20:20, and the pool of Bethesda mentioned in John 5, have been uncovered. The presence of Sargon, the king of Assyria, in Ashdod (Is 20:1) has been verified. A church constitution like that described in Acts 2 to 6 appears historically possible now that it has been established that an analogous constitutional pattern was adopted by the pre-Christian Qumran community.

Such examples might be multiplied almost ad infinitum, and much that has for centuries been considered legend or myth now has to be accepted as historically certain. Archaeology, used as an aid to the better understanding and appreciation of the Bible, rather than for cheap apologetics, proves to be a method of interpretation which is sober and exciting at the same time. It gives a necessary warning to all who would prefer to penetrate to the truth on the basis of speculation or the reconstruction of ideas alone.

2) *The history of religion school* takes as its beginning the observation that both Israel and the church, throughout their history, have not only fought the ideas and customs characteristic of the religious life of their neighbors but have also—for better or for worse—been influenced by both the forms and the content of those religions. Creation stories and enthronement rituals, descriptions of past disasters and future saviors, prayers and the healing of the sick, the seeking and interpretation of oracles, and the ministry of lawgivers and of court prophets are all found there. In

the light of comparative studies, allusions made by the prophets, in the Psalms, in the sayings of sages, and in the liturgies of festivals became not only less obscure but distinctly meaningful. But when the temporal priority of a non-Israelite myth or liturgy was established beyond doubt, it became necessary to ask whether the temporal posteriority of the occurrence of a similar idea or ceremony in Israel proved that it was taken over from the outside.

Whenever it appeared certain that the content of the Bible was dependent upon nonbiblical religion, the description of Israel's and the church's history and faith took a new turn. Resemblances between Babylonian, Egyptian, and Israelite royal enthronement rituals were supposed to prove that Israel believed in the divine kingship of its rulers. Great importance was attributed to cults of dying and rising gods, and by reference to these cults an explanation of Paul's statements about the death and resurrection of Christ was given. Paul was now proved to be a Hellenizer, if not a falsifier of the simple, original Christian faith. The "discovery" of a Gnostic mythical pattern that included the decisive role of a primordial man who descends from, and returns to heaven as a "redeemed redeemer" led to the assumption that the same pattern underlies the Johannine and Pauline statements about Jesus Christ's descent to earth and his ascent into glory. Perhaps too little attention was given to the time factor, for it is by no means certain that the syncretistic belief in such a redeemer, which is found in second-century A.D. Christian Gnostic writings, was widespread before the time of Paul and John. The fact that enlightened Jewish and Greek teachers included practical exhortations for the benefit of old and young, man and wife, slave and free man, in their addresses or writings was considered proof that Paul's admonitions to married people, to parents and children, to masters and lords, were a barely Christianized version of Jewish or Gentile rules of behavior. The fact that almost all the ideas and words found in Jesus' Sermon on the Mount (Mt 5–7) are also found in the Jewish rabbinical tradition persuaded many that the historical Jesus was no more than a rabbi who preached the radical implications of God's law.

It is the merit of such comparative studies that they show that many features of the faith, life, liturgy, and conduct of God's people were shared with its neighbors. When a history of biblical religion is written, it obviously has to demonstrate that this "religion" is full of strange elements and assimilations. The biblical historian understands the phenomenon of religion as a complex expression of a whole people's experience, tradition, and aspirations.

How full the Bible is of seemingly irreconcilable contradictions! Here the sanctuary belongs in the center of Israel's camp; there, far outside the camp. Here a prophetic message is concerned exclusively with the day's moral issues; there, all prophetic emphasis is laid upon an eschatological interference of God. Here prayers reveal the need of a specific individual in dire straits; there, the same prayer occurs in a public liturgical framework. Here the New Testament affirms that all promises are already fulfilled and that the old aeon has passed away; there, it speaks of future events that will bring fulfillment. Here an amazing loyalty is shown to Jerusalem, the Law, Israel; there, a concern with the language, the culture, the cities of Greece and Rome takes its place. Here is the so-called mysticism of Paul and John; and there, the pragmatism of Luke and James. It is certainly impossible to derive from such utterances an impeccable system of truth. But when they are seen against the background of the religious life of Near Eastern communities, the Bible's manifold utterances may begin to make sense.

All the apparently inconsistent features of the life of Israel and the church are now no longer considered contradictions. Instead, they reveal that the Bible is a faithful description of a people that lived, and marched, and rested, and grew. When this people's life and faith are compared with the world of Eastern and Western religions, unique features of the biblical testimony can be brought to light. Great contributions were made to the understanding of Genesis 1 by comparing this chapter with Mesopotamian and Egyptian theogonic and cosmogonic myths. Light fell on the Gospel of Matthew when it was explained as a response to Essene theology. In many cases those thoroughly acquainted with the history of religions are ready to discern and to enjoy the theological position of the biblical writers.

The history of religion school may have had to go through more than one childhood disease; it may have combined phenomena that need not have been related; it may still be blind to others that belong together. But because of its keen interest in religion—rather than in a series of facts that may be unearthed, or a series of ideas that reflect modern man's value judgments—it has made an important contribution to the interpretation of the Bible.

Still, using the methods of the history of religion school, it is impossible to prove why a Bible reader should or must believe in the God of Abraham, the Father of Jesus Christ, rather than in another god. Whenever Christian or Jewish historians of religion attempt to demonstrate the superiority of biblical religion over other religions, they fail to convince people who are not already convinced. If it is hard to describe the qualities which distinguish the biblical tales from those of other religions, how much more difficult it is to give evidence of their higher value!

3) The procedure and results of the *form-critical school* have been sketched above.[176] It may be sufficient to state here that this school presupposes textual, philological, literary, and archaeological studies, as well as the achievements of the comparative religion school, and that it concentrates its efforts on elucidating the cultic life, the liturgical forms, and the traditions of faith in Israel and the church. The facts for which such critics are asking are rarely the actual events that lie behind the affirmations of belief and the

cultic celebrations to which biblical texts bear testimony. Instead, the origin, content, form, and development of creeds, confessions, and liturgies are studied, with a view to discovering how they reflect what is unique in Israel's and the church's faith. There is awareness of the danger of forcing the biblical witness into the shape of a preconceived concept of religion. Faith in Yahweh, faith in Christ the Lord, and faith in bodily resurrection (rather than religious belief in general) now occupy the center of attention.

Since form criticism is primarily a quest for the manifold witness of faith, a certain skepticism prevails concerning the verification of those events to which the confessions of Israel and the church refer. The tools of the historians are applied to the forms rather than the content of testimony and faith. So far, the most promising results have been achieved in Old Testament research. They pertain to a clarification of the origin, meaning, liturgy, and relevance of Israel's festivals; to the roles of prophet and king, priest and scribe; to the content, growth, and interpretation of tradition; and to the place of eschatological and Messianic hopes.

None of the three historical schools just described has succeeded in giving final answers to the question of what actually happened. Each page of the Bible continues to present new puzzles. If one question is answered, others spring up. The meaning of the term historicity is ambiguous; great historical scholars have defined it in different ways. L. v. Ranke and R. G. Collingwood, A. v. Harnack and A. Toynbee are working in different directions. No biblical scholar can avoid making a selection among available methods. It is, for example, highly debatable whether at least three conditions have to be fulfilled when something is to be considered historical. Has it to be continuous with history as everybody experiences it? Has it to be explained by reference to cause and effect? And must it be analogous to other events? With these criteria of continuity, causality, and analogy, a fourth is easily associated. It is assumed that "miracles don't happen." Applied to the Bible, this means that historical criticism must "explain" all miraculous events to which the Bible refers. The original endeavor of historians to ascertain as much as possible may thus turn into the fatal belief that nothing can be true unless scholars can prove it to be true—whether by laboratory, psychological, or other tests.

When the criteria used by philosophers and natural scientists during the nineteenth century, as well as those used by modern psychologists and sociologists, are applied as measuring sticks for establishing what is and what is not historical among the biblical reports,[177] a drastic reduction takes place. The mystery of the events related is then no longer felt, and the Bible's voice is replaced by scholarly decrees. The interpreter has made himself master over the Bible. But the miracles told in the Bible are essential to it. They defy the manipulations of unimaginative historians. A rationalist or pragmatist explanation cannot possibly do them justice.

The attempt to explain away what is miraculous is a direct result of the tendency of historical research to employ standards derived from sources outside the content and the testimony of the Bible. However, the dangers and temptations involved in this procedure by no means demonstrate that all historical interpretation, as such, is devious.

Victims of Progress

The new methods developed during the last two hundred years have two things in common.

First, the application of these methods has not achieved the surprising and moving insights into the intention and content of the Bible that interpreters like Origen, Athanasius, Augustine, and Luther achieved. What they heard from the Bible, and what they were enabled to tell others of Jesus Christ, of resurrection, of grace, and of justification has neither been outmoded nor equaled by any of the achievements of modern scholarly exegesis. It is still an open question whether the actual teaching and preaching that goes on in churches and synagogues has substantially benefited from historical interpretation of the Bible. It is certain that much preaching and teaching is done—and by no means the least effective—which does not rely upon academic exegesis. Often enough, preachers and Sunday-school teachers are criticized for their lack of concern for solid exegesis. But perhaps the fault is not in the laziness or neglect of church workers, but in an internal weakness of critical interpretation which has yet to be overcome.

Second, even where the new methods were successful, they proved incapable of suppressing other procedures of Bible study that followed, more or less timidly, the methods used either by the biblical authors themselves, or by those biblical scholars who remained opposed to the rationalist pragmatism of literary and historical Bible criticism. One of the most influential recent Bible commentaries is Karl Barth's *Epistle to the Romans*.[178] This book, and the approach to interpretation chosen by its author, were, at the time of publication, considered an insult to scholarly academic interpretation. Still, it was this interpretation which caused the voice of Paul to be heard afresh, and which led to a revolution in theology, in preaching, and in the theory and practice of church life. The claims made for critical interpretation cannot be upheld against an interpretation that bears the slightest resemblance to a truly prophetic and apostolic message.

In conclusion, the historical-critical schools have not replaced or overthrown the more traditional ways of interpretation. However, some traditional methods have been so affected by the new methods that they can no longer be enjoyed with undisturbed and genuine pleasure.

Three methods have become discredited, and a fourth should no longer be trusted either:

1 *Atomism*

The formula, "It is written," is well known. It is found in Joshua, Samuel and Kings, and in the Psalms; it is used by rabbis, Jesus, Paul, Satan, early and medieval theologians, Luther, Calvin, Fundamentalists, and many others. The use of this formula cannot be avoided when the speaker or writer wants to make it evident that his argument is based upon a strong and binding biblical voice which he has heard and to which he owes obedience. A well-chosen Bible quotation may give strength to an argument which might otherwise not inspire confidence. There is a well-known statue of Martin Luther, where the hero of the Diet of Worms, and of many another battle, displays the source of his courage and wisdom: the Bible.

But the image of a man who is sure of himself because he can quote the Bible for the stand he takes is not unambiguous. In the second century, Ignatius, the Bishop of Antioch, records the following incident: "I heard some men saying, 'If I find it not in the charters in the Gospel I do not believe.' And when I said to them that it is in the Scripture, they answered me, 'That is exactly the question.' "[179] Ignatius' report reminds us that even the man who says he is willing to submit his faith to the test of Scripture will often reject the selection and interpretation of a specific passage which is made to prove a specific point. When the serpent questioned God's word, or Jeremiah denounced those who quoted the Law to him, when Jesus resisted pharisaical harshness against sinners, and Paul struggled against legalistic Judaizers (Gen 3:1 ff.; Jer 8:8; Jn 8:3–11; Gal 2–5), mere citation of the Bible did not prove that the quoted passages were rightly understood and applied. It was observed before that the history of synagogue and church is full of both the use and abuse of Scripture. Both the believer and the heretic will be able to find proof texts for whatever they want to prove. If truth were as easily available as any individual Bible verse, its discovery would demand no more than a good memory or a card index.

For speaker and listener alike, there is a trap contained in the formula, "It is written," and in the subsequent quotation. A well-known or surprising verse, quoted out of context, may appear irresistible—especially when the authority of the book cited is not contested. The speaker may assume he has proved his point—though he deceives himself. The listener may feel that his objections have been answered—though he has understood neither the speaker nor the quotation.

Now there are passages in the Bible which appear to invite a free use. In the Psalms, words of God are quoted without reference to their origin or specific historical intention. They prove good in every situation. The Book of Proverbs looks like a random collection of sayings, riddles, and illustrations. Some of them originated and circulated among Egyptians and other Gentiles independently of each other. Proverbs makes sense even if quoted in isolation. The Gospels—the Sermon on the Mount (Mt 5–7), or a passage like Mark 2:21–22, not to speak of apocryphal Gospels—show that collections of sayings of Jesus were made and used with little or no reference to the framework in which they may originally have occurred.

But the fact that many oracles, sayings, and parables can stand on their own does not imply that all biblical words possess the same quality. It is only in exceptional cases that a sentence taken out of its narrative or didactic framework still conveys the meaning it had originally. It takes a careful and responsible man to select a quotation in such a way that the meaning of the whole passage is retained. Behind the use of quotations from the Old Testament in the New, there stands extensive study, a clear notion of the historical or literary content, and careful comparison with seemingly or actually contradictory utterances. The Letter to the Hebrews was a case in point. The Cambridge scholar C. H. Dodd[180] has demonstrated that many brief quotations found in the New Testament make sense only when they are understood as substitutes for the citation of whole Old Testament chapters or for even more extensive units. Neither Jewish nor Christian preachers and interpreters of the Bible can boast of having always exhibited the same care. A highly selective and arbitrary use of scriptural quotations is a great temptation for precisely those who trust the Bible's authority.

But this temptation may be faced and resisted by the writing and study of commentaries on parts of the Bible. The middle of the second century A.D. had passed before Heracleon, an adherent of the Gnostic Valentinus, wrote a commentary on John; before the Roman presbyter Hippolytus commented on the Book of Daniel; and before Origen set out to explain the Gospel of Matthew in detail. Before that time, there probably existed extensive Jewish Targums—vernacular (Aramaic) interpretations or paraphrases of Old Testament books. These originated in Babylonia, Jerusalem, or Samaria, and did not receive their final written form until the fifth century A.D. Among the Christians, beginning with Origen, more and more intensive and extensive studies of biblical books were made; commentaries of great length were written and copied throughout the Middle Ages.[181] But the works that bore the heaviest burden of contemporary discussion and influenced future generations the most were often not biblical commentaries but sermons, treatises, and dogmatic studies. A feature often common to them was the selective use of biblical quotations to substantiate convictions or statements. The rebirth of humanistic studies, ushered in by the Renaissance, and the intensive biblical studies in which the Reformers and their successors engaged, did much to weaken the predominance of the selective use of the Bible. Still, both in the Reformers' writings and at the present time, it has not completely disappeared.

This use of the Bible has been nicknamed "atomistic interpretation"; for as nineteenth-century physics considered the atom the smallest indivisible unit, of which all matter was built, so each Bible verse, or each part of it, was considered an indisputable and safe basis on which to build. The newer ways of interpretation, using the methods of critical research, may be less bewitching and more painful for both the preacher or teacher and those to whom the exposition is addressed, but they lead to a better appreciation of details and to the discovery of treasures still hidden. Atomism may still be alive and refuse to acknowledge its defeat, but it is no longer a real choice for the serious Bible student.

II *Church Dictation*

In his encyclical of 1943, *Divine Afflante Spiritu,* Pope Pius XII reminded Catholic scholars that in their studies of the Bible and tradition they had to "find an explanation faithfully consonant with the teaching of the Church." We have already quoted the Tridentine and Vatican decree, *Ecclesiae est judicare.* Understood in its context, this decree means, "It is the Church's privilege and duty to adjudicate the meaning of Scriptures."[182] "The Church," as understood by post-Reformation Rome, hardly resembles that spiritual community of many inspired members which is called *ecclesia* in the New Testament and is described in 1 Corinthians and Ephesians. "The Church," in the Roman sense, is the result of an historical process of development and organization which is identical with the Roman Catholic Church. Inside that organization, certain institutional committees and staff members, including the Bishop of Rome, are charged with watching over the Bible's authority and interpretation. Thus the interpretation of the Bible is subject to the control and direction of ecclesiastical authorities who, like a supreme court, judge and define the Church's faith and how it is to be confessed.

It is not a post-Reformation Roman Catholic specialty to recognize the necessity for control over Bible interpretation. In the second century, the Church of Rome had already developed a baptismal Confession of Faith by which the use and misuse of Holy Scriptures and inspiration in heretical circles was to be checked. An orthodox believer was recognized by his agreement with the established "Faith." Heretics were not helped by claiming that they had received the special inspiration of the Holy Spirit or a secret tradition of Jesus or the apostles. The church's confession, soon to be called the Apostles' Creed, was used against them. If a heretic claimed to follow a particular apostle, or endorse that apostle's writings, he was told to yield to the united voice of "the twelve." The church's confession and its later doctrinal evolutions, expositions, and applications in the liturgy of many dioceses and congregations, in synodal decrees, and in the recognized books of great teachers, was called the Rule of Faith (*regula fidei*). No biblical interpretation could be true unless it agreed with that Rule. In this way a double-headed supreme authority in matters of faith and morals was created. Tradition was established alongside Scripture. Delivered by, and received from the apostles, confessed in divine worship and defended orally and in writing, the Faith was called, by tacit or explicit reference to 1 Timothy 6:20, the *depositum fidei,* or the Tradition of the Church. Tertullian's book, *Of the Prescription of the Heretics* (*ca.* 200), and the tract, *Commonitorium,* by Vincentius of Lerinum (d. *ca.* 445), are classical expressions of the ancient church's way of assuring an interpretation of the Scriptures which respected the established Creed. The Roman Catholic Church, even to the present time,[183] has not moved from the position then taken. The definition of papal infallibility in 1870, and the restrictions placed on those Catholic scholars who were working toward reform by the encyclical, *Humani Generis* (1950), have rather shortened the reins.

The Reformers, however, protested violently against the submission of both the Bible and its interpretation to the control of the organized church. After Luther's exclusion from the Roman Church, hope of submitting the church to the witness and direction of Scripture, confidence that "the Bible is its own interpreter," and respect for the sovereignty of God's word over man-made tradition—in short, the principle *sola Scriptura*—united all who were concerned with a reform of the church.

But the same practices that had been so violently opposed now found a home among the Reformers as well. In the apology of the *Augsburg Confession* (1531), in Flacius Illyricus' *Clavis Scripturae Sacrae* (1567), and in the *Formula of Concord* (1580),[184] the Reformation doctrine of justification by grace and the distinction between Law and Gospel are described as the keys by which the mysteries of the Bible must be opened. Thus doctrinal criteria of interpretation were set up against the institutional claims of Rome. With alacrity and stubbornness Lutheran, Calvinist, Anabaptist, and Episcopalian divines of the two post-Reformation centuries attempted to justify their respective denominational positions by reference to the Bible. If they failed to convince each other, they nevertheless convinced themselves that their inherited faith, doctrine, and church order were true to the Bible. Even today, too many commentaries, dogmatic and ethical works, and especially sermons and Sunday-school materials, are primarily reaffirmations of doctrines and decisions that, in an earlier time, became characteristic of one or another denomination.

The conclusion to be drawn is obvious. The battle cry, *sola Scriptura,* and its initial courage-inspiring and risk-involving power, did not last. If the tradition or dictation of Rome was rejected, another tradition—Lutheran, Calvinist, Episcopalian, or Anabaptist—took its place. S. Werenfels, an eighteenth-century

Protestant theologian, commented bitterly: "The Bible is the book in which everybody seeks and promptly finds his own dogmas."[185]

When the new methods of biblical exegesis were developed, it was feared by some, and hoped by others, that institutionalism, confessionalism, and denominationalism would be shattered. What the Reformation had left unfinished, Protestant historical-critical scholarship set out to complete. Indeed, the best research of the last two centuries (including those Anglican and Roman Catholic contributions which make use of the historical and literary methods) can be understood as an attempt to liberate the church from the bondage of man-made controls and lead it to an immediate encounter with the biblical witness. Bultmann goes even further. He calls his radical application of the new methods "a parallel to the Pauline-Lutheran doctrine of justification apart from works of Law, solely through faith. Or rather, it is the consistent application of this justification doctrine in the realm of epistemology."[186] This astonishing statement asserts that the new methods, like the Reformers' teaching on grace, open the gates of grace and truth to anyone ready to rely on faith alone! The historical and literary critical Bible interpretation is allegedly as certain and exclusive a way to truth as the faith preached by Martin Luther was considered the *conditio sine qua non* of salvation.

If only nothing more than a better hermeneutics were required to make men free! In reality, what has been achieved by the application of the new methods appears to be no more than the exchange of one yoke for another. When modern Bible criticism has had its way, the dictates of ecclesiastical committees, bishops, creeds, and confessions have been withstood, but all too often a new dictatorship of supposedly indisputable scholarly methods and results has been imposed.

The historical-critical exegetes believed they had to follow the methods of the natural sciences. They regarded and treated their texts as physical objects, breaking them into the smallest possible pieces in order to make an "objective analysis" of the subject matter. The various pieces are then conveniently labeled: ritualism or ethical monotheism, casuistry or spiritualism, Judaism or Hellenism, formalism or fanaticism, legalism or evangelism, tradition or interpretation, Kerygma or Didache. The scholars so engaged have a good time carrying out their research. They learn from each other and correct each other.

Students of theology and candidates for higher degrees in countless schools have to prove acquaintance with, and mastery of, the new techniques. Book after book is produced, giving the results of ever more subtle analysis. But who is the conqueror in this sort of research? Is it the interpreter, or his method? It is certainly not the biblical text, or its author, or the purpose for which its words were originally spoken. This method of exegesis lives on the exegete's enjoyment of his own analytical power; the biblical text has become a tool for its demonstration. Lines of development in the history of biblical personages, communities, and ideas were sought and found. The pattern of evolutionary thought and a network of cause and effect relationships were imposed upon the Bible. The living history of the Bible was transformed into a composite that could supposedly be understood by using abstract terms. The act of understanding and explaining was identified not only with the act of discerning but with that of separating, cataloging, and shelving the elements of a text. By the application of new standards and procedures the texts were to yield their secrets and be truly understood. But did the historical-critical scholars understand? Did they learn what might be learned from natural scientists—and from the limits of their analytical procedures?

A natural scientist will approach the objects he wants to study with a working hypothesis; he will follow his research plan and use the instruments that seem best. In many cases he will be rewarded for his research by some sort of answer that corresponds to his quest. He may then speak of laws of nature which he has found or confirmed. But just as the natural scientist would never pretend that he controls the truth, or nature itself, neither should the Bible interpreter presume that by the employment of new methods he can solve or master the mystery of his texts. He will get answers to those questions which he has first fed into the Bible. The answers he hears will be echoes of the questions he has asked. He may still not have asked the decisive question. Further, the natural scientist must destroy the atom or its nucleus in order to probe its mysterious structure and operation; he will destroy living tissue in order to understand its growth or decay. The interpreter of the Bible, too, often takes the liberty of destroying the very thing he hopes to understand. Sometimes, in natural science, destruction may be necessary to promote further research. At other times it may be frivolous or futile because it was dictated by inadequate questions. It may well be that words, sentences, chapters, and books are even more difficult to understand than atoms and cells. It is probable that there is no one method of labeling, distinguishing, or analyzing which is appropriate to the whole Bible. It is certain that the understanding of a text cannot be achieved by killing it. The mystery of understanding cannot be eliminated—least of all the mystery of understanding God's conversation with man.

Modern biblical research is carried on within the framework, or according to the standards of the Western universities. It owes much to this association. But it is not justified by it. If its results are no more than a replacement of ecclesiastical dictates by academic catch phrases—such as "scientific procedure" or "the results of recent scholarship"—what has been gained? The Bible expects interpreters that are free to be responsive to God. Such responsiveness transcends not only the bonds of confessional and denominational affiliation but also the claims of academic institutions. Even within the framework of a university and in the face of the standards and procedures recognized by modern science, it is the right and duty of Bible interpreters to resist the temptation inherent in assimilation.

Modern interpreters had hoped to fight for the freedom of the

Bible and its interpretation. But if their battle for freedom made a victim of the old overlord, the dictating church, then it finally victimized the freedom fighters as well.

III *Allegorical Interpretation*

An allegory is a statement or story which says one thing and means another. It usually bears the outward form of a narrative, but it contains an abstract, general, often timeless principle. Its words cover a subsense, or spiritual truth; its literal or historical interpretation is to be distinguished from its true interpretation. The term "allegorization" may stand for both the writing of an allegorical text by an author who prefers to be understood by initiated persons only, and the allegorical interpretation (also called spiritual or pneumatic exegesis) of such a text by those who feel that they are equipped to discover its true meaning. Sometimes an interpreter considers a text allegorical and devotes himself to allegorical interpretation, though the text's author did not intend to allegorize.

We observed earlier that allegorical writing was as common among the Greeks of the Hellenistic period as it was among early Christian writers. It was also employed by some rabbis and, later, by Moslem scholars. Allegorical interpretation appeared to be a legitimate way of expressing the content and intention of an inspired text. When the belief in inspiration by the gods, the Muses, or the Holy Spirit was coupled with belief in a text's infallibility, then allegorical interpretation was considered the *only* way. It was often by means of such interpretation that an edifying meaning could be derived from certain texts. Inspiration, infallibility, and allegorization were therefore originally inseparable. Philo the Jew affirms that allegorical interpretation was learned from Gentile scholars.[187]

There are many examples of allegory in the Bible itself—the dreams of a butler, a baker, a Pharaoh, and Nebuchadnezzar, as well as Daniel's visions (Gen 40–41; Dan 2; 4; 7 ff.). In their interpretation, not timeless principles but specific future events are announced. The drama of the marriage of Hosea is treated as an allegory. It is God himself from whom, according to these texts, come both the veiling dreams *and* the revealing interpretation, the obscure event *and* its application. Among the parables of Jesus there are many that have not only one point of comparison but seem to be a composite of several metaphors. Thus they have the character of allegories. Sometimes they tell a story which demands, permits, or invites point by point transposition into nonparabolic speech (e.g., Mk 4:1–20; Mt 13:24–30, 36–43; 21:33–40).[188] Paul occasionally treats Old Testament narratives or laws as "allegorically spoken," and explains their meaning to the churches of his time (see Gal 4:21–31; 2 Cor 3:13–4:6; 1 Cor 5:6–8; 10:1–11).

The method of allegorization is not always the same, but one example will illustrate how it may be used. In 1 Corinthians 9:3–14, Paul sets out to defend his right to receive food and clothing from the Corinthians as compensation for his apostolic work. He recalls to the Corinthians the soldier who gets his keep, the vineyard worker who may eat grapes, the shepherd who is permitted to drink the sheep's milk, and the priest who receives a share of the sacrifices. Though Paul will later (in 1 Cor 9:12, 15 ff.) emphatically renounce all right to reward, he brings home his potential claim with an allegory. "Do I say this on human authority? Does not the law say the same? For it is written in the law of Moses, 'You shall not muzzle an ox when it is treading out the grain.' Is it for oxen that God is concerned? Does he not speak entirely for our sake? It was written for our sake. . . . The Lord commanded that those who proclaim the gospel should get their living by the gospel." In the form of a rhetorical question, Paul gives a reason for the allegorical interpretation of Deuteronomy 25:4. Who would assume that God cares for oxen? A reader may be inclined to ask how Paul knows that God does *not* care for such animals and that, therefore, a literal understanding of

Deuteronomy 25:4 is erroneous. In the context of 1 Corinthians 9, Paul gives no answer. He presupposes that the Corinthians agree with him in assuming that both God himself and the writer of Deuteronomy mean men when they speak of oxen. He therefore equates ox and apostle, threshing and evangelizing, not muzzling and giving a reward. By this daring allegorization, Paul intends to show that there exists a divine or legal authority for his claim. However, it does not appear that Paul learned this by exegesis. For he first announces his right, then he illustrates it with "human" parallels derived from the life of a soldier, a hired hand, and a shepherd. Only then does he refer to Scripture. His allegorical interpretation thus confirms something which was announced and illustrated beforehand. The allegorized text is expected to substantiate a claim which was established before the text was consulted, and upon which Paul will finally not insist. There is a certain playfulness in this allegory, and certainly not a stringent juridical deduction. Paul's ultimate concern is with the work of evangelism. This work must not be blocked by the refusal to respect the Apostle for what he is and does. It is not likely that Paul considered the kind of interpretation found in 1 Corinthians 9 basic or exemplary. In Romans 4, and 9 to 11, when the Old Testament is more extensively interpreted, Paul does not allegorize. Again, in Galatians (4:21 ff.), his allegorization illustrates points which he had made earlier on the basis of nonallegorical interpretation.

The reasons for allegorizing which became compelling for the great masters of allegory—Philo of Alexandria, Origen, and Augustine[189]—are manifold. Among the more important are blatant anthropomorphism in statements about God; descriptions of immoral or indecent behavior; obscure affirmations; inconsistent or contradictory information; historically inaccurate or impossible reports; elements of outmoded scientific opinion and of myth. Since the Bible was considered inspired and supposed to be a means to true knowledge and proper service of God, it was thought impossible that it should really contain things of the kind just mentioned. The aim of allegorization was thus to purge the Bible of what appeared to be dirt or clay, and to expose and glorify the clean and solid treasures hidden there. If the Bible, like Paul himself (2 Cor 4:7), contained "treasure in earthen vessels," the task of the spiritual interpreter was to lift the treasure out of its container. The purpose of allegorization, therefore, was to unveil the clarity, the consistency, the spirituality, and the inerrancy of the Bible. Of course, the allegorical interpreters were forced to ask themselves why an infallible, true, and ethical book contained obscure, immoral, and impossible statements. Two answers were found: God has accommodated his revelation and action to the needs and intellectual capacities of different times and different men, and scribes and interpreters have sometimes misunderstood or distorted God's proper intention. The legitimacy of both the question and the answers was recognized whenever allegorical interpretation was taken up as a sacred necessity.

Allegorization was carried out by etymological interpretation of proper names and important words; by treating words, sentences, motifs, events, and laws as tropes or figures of speech, metonyms, instances of synecdoche, etc.; by explaining the historical and psychological setting, or inventing a suitable framework; and by pressing into the service of liturgy and morals such sayings, events, and institutions as sounded neither cultic nor ethical. We repeat, the Gentile philosophers, orators, and literary critics who were contemporaries of Philo, Origen, and Augustine used a similar procedure. In this field, the Gentiles were masters rather than emulators. Perhaps for this reason Augustine[190] considers a humanistic education in the liberal arts and ancient languages a prerequisite for the search for the Bible's spiritual meaning.

Though the foundations of Gentile and Christian allegorization are identical, some of the results vary. Also, Christian interpretation is often different from that of Philo, the rabbinical interpreters, or later Moslem allegorists. In Christian allegorization, many Old Testament passages become explicit predictions of Christ's coming and ministry. Many biblical texts are so interpreted that they disclose psychic processes which supposedly distinguish the operation of Christian faith and of satanic evil in the individual. Ancient texts are shown to contain statements about the structure of the universe which fully agree with the views of natural scientists contemporary to the interpreters. Certain passages are made consistent with philosophical principles. Others are shown to harmonize with the prevailing orthodox doctrines on the Trinity, on Christ's two natures, on atonement, or on the sacraments. The result of allegorical interpretation always agrees with the teaching of that church, of those dogmas, of that liturgy, and of that constitution and discipline which the interpreter considers orthodox: "The destiny of the mystical interpretation and that of orthodoxy are bound together."[191] Many particularities of specific biblical books, events, situations, and laws disappeared under this treatment. The glory of the church was to shine all the brighter.

It is obvious that there is no way to gain new knowledge of God, his will, his deeds, and the obedience required of man through allegorical interpretation. Allegory can confirm nothing but what is known from other sources. A thousand years after Origen, Thomas Aquinas[192] was to establish the rule that nothing should be stated by allegorical interpretation of a given text that was not explicitly and literally said in another place in the Bible. Thus he tied allegorical interpretation to literal exegesis, and he recognized the literal interpretation as the norm. Only the Bible, not an extrabiblical tradition, was to be confirmed by allegorization. But Philo, Origen, and others had tended to use allegory to confirm what they had learned not only from the Bible but also in the synagogue or church, in philosophy classes, from contemporary scientific books, and as the result of personal experience.

From about A.D. 200 on, the Alexandrian Christian theologians and their imitators were eagerly engaged in the search for deeper meanings in the Scriptures. As a result, they incurred the wrath of their Antiochian colleagues, who repudiated allegorical exegesis altogether. But the Alexandrians did not yield. We now have to ask why they clung to spiritual interpretation if no new insights concerning God, truth, faith, morality, the future, the world, or the psyche could be gained from it. Four answers may be given.

First, an allegorical interpreter of the old school is convinced that he adds nothing new to the text with which he deals. He accepts, as allegorical, texts which *are* allegorical (cf. Gal 4:24: "Now this is said in allegorical fashion [this is an allegory]"); he does not *make* them allegories. By his allegorical interpretation he hopes to disclose what God, who inspired the writer, wanted to say through the story, the law, the person, or the institution of which the text speaks.

Secondly, allegorical interpretation aims at revealing the unity of the Bible. By the removal of contradictions and immoral or anthropomorphic statements, the clarity and consistency of the Bible is to be displayed. The labor invested in this display is enormous and appears to know no norm or limit—although Philo, for one, was convinced that it followed certain rules.[193]

Third, the allegorical interpreter has more than purely academic reasons for employing everything he has learned in his work on the Bible. For him, Bible study is not art for art's sake; his interest lies in communication. Philo attempts to explain the rationality of Old Testament law to the educated among the despisers of the Jews. While his arguments draw heavily on philosophy, he attempts to fulfill both an apologetic and a missionary task. The same applies to Barnabas, Justin the Martyr, the school of apologists to which Origen belonged, and Augustine. They hoped to convince Jews, Gentiles, and Christian heretics of the deviousness of their letter-bound misunderstandings of the Bible. They aimed at conveying the book's true meaning. And they felt they were supported in this task by no less a man than the missionary of all missionaries, the apostle Paul. In 2 Corinthians 3, Paul had made the distinction between the killing letter of the Scriptures and the life-giving spirit; in 2 Corinthians 5:16 he had spoken of a better understanding of Christ, no longer regarding him "from a human point of view"; and in several letters he had actually given allegorical interpretations. According to the Gospels, Jesus Christ himself had spoken in allegories, metaphors, and similes, and had given extended interpretations of their hidden meaning.

But it is necessary to add a fourth reason for the devotion with which allegorization was upheld against all attacks: It has the fascination of a game. *Homo ludens* is at work when all available philosophic, scientific, literary, historic, psychological, and aesthetic resources are sifted and mixed until they prove the Bible's infinite value. Among the intentions of many learned and passionate exegetes, one should not overlook the simple desire to play with the potential content of a given text, and to display the expositor's skillfulness. The great allegorizers are true artists who deserve not scorn but admiration.

Allegorical interpretation is sometimes used in such a way that it is almost identical with typological exegesis. The difference[194] lies in the fact that typology affirms the concreteness and historical character of a past word, event, person, or institution, and considers it a precedent. It proceeds to illustrate, by reference to the precedent, how meaningful or superior a new concrete event, person, or order is. Allegory, however, is ashamed of the concrete, and interprets it so that an underlying timeless, spiritual, abstract meaning becomes triumphant. As mentioned earlier, the intention of the Old Testament writers and the earliest Christian historiographers and biographers was typological; the prophets and apostles used as types or precedents both the tradition they received and the example of their own lives. There are probably few sermons delivered in synagogue or church that are not—if they are at all based on the Bible—typological interpretations. Typology appears everywhere in the Bible, and is probably an inescapable necessity for the interpreter. It flourishes wherever history is enjoyed, and whenever men are willing to learn from the past. Allegory may have grown out of typology, and it may still resemble it occasionally, but because of its basically negative attitude to historical events, it is something essentially different. For the allegorist, history is nothing but tinder for the fire of the Spirit.

Whenever reports of God's action in history and his involvement in human events were taken seriously, the excesses of allegorization met with passionate resistance. After the Antiochians had uttered their protest, and after Thomas had announced his opposition to uncontrolled allegorization, Nicolaus of Lyra (d. *ca.* 1350), Luther, Calvin, and others took up the fight against distinguishing among different meanings in the Scriptures, and the concomitant spiritual or allegorical interpretation. Scholastic and Reformation declarations of war against allegorization did not, however, suffice to extirpate the long-established method. Luther's commentary on Genesis (1535–45) and some of his finest sermons, and much later still, A. Jülicher's battle against an allegorical understanding of the parables[195] show that the pleasure or refuge offered by allegory continued to be attractive. Whenever the defense of "orthodox" faith, current moral values, this or that denominational organization or sacramental practice made it desirable, allegorization was not shunned. Theological opponents were ridiculed or condemned for their use of allegorization, but the attacker was prone to disregard his own allegories.

Historical-critical Bible interpretation sometimes provided a remedy. Its exponents asked for the one authentic reading of biblical texts. They developed tools and criteria to help them toward restoration of the original text and its genuine understanding. They were able to demonstrate that there was no primeval orthodoxy in doctrinal, ethical, and disciplinary matters, but that different confessions, constitutions, and concrete decisions have always existed side by side, both in Israel and in the church.[196] They proved how exciting Bible study can be, if only it is liberated from the task of confirming previously held beliefs. Allegorical interpretation suffered a dreadful blow from the newer methods of interpretation. It was called arbitrary, fantastic, a product of wishful thinking. This accusation was no longer reserved for theological opponents alone; wherever allegorization was met, it was decried as an outmoded, impossible, inaccurate procedure. It was hoped that now, finally, interpreters in synagogue and church would submit themselves to careful, humble, study of those things which the Bible really says, that they would listen to the Bible even when it speaks out against sacred concepts, formulae, habits, and institutions.

The expectation that everybody would certainly gain in his search for truth if he accepted the results of scholarly study was not immediately fulfilled. For many decades historical-critical Bible research had proved destructive rather than constructive. The unity of the Bible was lost under a variety of religious myths, histories, ideas, and personalities. Since about 1920, however, critical Bible commentaries and monographs on biblical themes and biblical theology showed an increasing tendency to recuperate the unifying elements in the Bible and to lend support to the needs of actual teaching and preaching, and of ecumenical unity.

The potential value and relevance of critical Bible study is immeasurable. The historical-critical Bible scholars might be considered liberators, who use the Bible for exactly the purpose for which its various books were written, preserved, and gathered together. Unfortunately, their victory is not as splendid as it might be. Because each method has to be tested by the fruits it produces rather than by the claims it makes, we shall expose a fallacy inherent in the historical method by referring to one of its much discussed recent children:

"Demythologizing" is a method of interpretation developed after 1940 by the German New Testament professor, Rudolf Bultmann. It was taken up first by his pupils, and is embraced today by systematic theologians as well. Apparently the formulation and application of a doctrine of demythologization has given new courage to Bible readers. For it has provided them with a key to interpretation that they had never used before, or has entitled them to do, with academic approval, what they had attempted to do only with a bad conscience before.

Demythologizing has its roots in the history of philosophy, theology, and church life. These cannot be discussed here.[197] Some of its foundations, however, are found in the history of scholarly biblical exegesis. Form criticism had demonstrated that the literary forms found in the Bible had to be taken into consideration if the meaning of the biblical themes was to be properly understood. The comparison of ancient Near Eastern and Hellenistic religions with the contents of the Bible had revealed the presence of a considerable amount of mythical material in the holy texts. The ambiguities in biblical reports of certain miraculous events (Israel's march across the Red Sea, or the ascension of Christ to heaven) were taken as an indication that meanings, rather than verifiable historical facts, were of primary importance. The Bible was understood as a witness or confession of faith; many interpreters set out to make the kerygma, or saving message, heard in a manner which would bring listeners face to face with a decision of faith.

On the basis of these presuppositions, demythologizers proceeded to make a distinction between the form and the content of the Bible. All descriptions of God and his actions that speak of God in human terms; all attempts to prove divine interference in history by reference to miracles, sacrifices, and other transrational phenomena; and all reflections of ancient and outmoded scientific views concerning the origin and structure of the universe, belong to the form of the Bible and are called mythical. On the other hand, all that concerns man's understanding of himself, all that affects man's struggle with the issues and events of his existence in time, and finally, all that touches upon his ultimate transcendence of temporality is considered the content of the Bible. The critical Bible interpreters of the nineteenth century were inclined to eliminate or overlook mythical elements in order to concentrate on features that appeared to possess lasting value. But demythologizing is, "not elimination but interpretation." The mythical material in the Bible is now "interpreted" in such a way that it agrees with the Bible's supposed "intention." The mythical form is now revealed to be nothing but a form of existential challenge which can and must be brought up to date. The belief that mythical events happened in history is radically devaluated. "Historical faith" cannot save. But faith in God, as proclaimed in the Bible, is described as an ever-new decision to let go of all earth-bound proofs and to find meaning and direction in the cross alone. The God of faith is always before man. He is identified with the future. His will can only be sought, never possessed. Historical faith is to be equated with works, righteousness; existential faith with the gift of God's grace.

The demythologizing of the Bible appears to make faith in God easier, for man may now believe in God without having to accept the creation stories, the three-decker concept of heaven, earth, and hell, the miracles, the resurrection and the second coming of Jesus Christ, or the fiery tongues of the Spirit. But the intention of the demythologizers is not to make faith easier for man; it is rather to expose man to the encounter with the God who is "totally other."

One element of this program is most puzzling and should not be overlooked. The intention and method of demythologizing resemble certain features of allegorical interpretation so strongly that we must ask whether demythologizing is merely a twentieth-century form of allegorization. Instead of two or more senses of the Bible, scholars now speak of form and content, or form and intent. Instead of an ecclesiastical orthodoxy, there is now a dual standard: the image of the supposedly well-known and easily defined modern man, and the notion of an ultimately unknown God. Instead of the infinite variety of allegorical interpretation, there is today a certain monotony of Heideggerian language and the call to "authentic" self-understanding. On the other hand, both the allegorizers and the demythologizers appear to be ashamed of the concreteness of biblical statements. Both of them reinterpret the specific in such a way that something abstract, general, and timeless becomes apparent. In both cases this abstract truth is in some sort of harmony with current scientific views on the structure of the universe and the operation of the human psyche. And in both cases only a select group of initiates is able to follow on the way from the flesh of the letter to the spirit of the meaning.

The majority of the modern historical-critical interpreters do not possess Bultmann's systematic power and imagination; many of them lack his sense of responsibility for communicating the Bible's ultimate meaning to modern man. They stop short of serious involvement in questions of philosophy, psychology, or actual preaching. In their fight for literal and historical interpretation they have not exposed themselves to the danger of a relapse into allegorization. But those who take greater risks may, even if they fall, make a more important contribution to the progress of interpretation than those who have never fallen because they never dared jump. Three thousand years of exegesis has shown that a contribution to better and deeper understanding of the Bible always involves a great risk.

But what does the Bible itself say about myths? The term myth occurs in those books of the New Testament that may have been written last (see 1 Tim 1:4; 4:7; 2 Tim 4:4; Tit 1:14; 2 Pet 1:16). It is used for a sophisticated sort of Greek or Jewish teaching which easily seduces men and of which Christians have to beware. But however "myth" is defined—as a primitive world view, as an interpretation of symbols or rituals, as a summary expression and ultimate justification of man's daily needs and decisions, or as a religious ideology—neither the Old nor the New Testament purports to promote myths. Even when it appears that mythical elements, motifs, or forms are taken up and used by biblical writers, only fragments of their original content remain recognizable. Three thousand years before a modern school wrote "demythologization" on its flag, the biblical authors were already concerned with the task of demythologizing the gods, the beliefs, the institutions of their environment, and of preventing faith in Yahweh and in Jesus Christ from becoming a mythical notion. Instead of reciting a struggle like Marduk's against the powers of darkness, the Bible tells of God's mighty historical act by which Israel was saved from the terror, darkness, and bloodshed prevailing in Egypt. Instead of yielding to the deification and religious exploitation of sex that characterized certain types of Babylonian and Canaanite worship, Hosea tells the history of his marriage and of God's relationship to Israel. He announces the promise that God will be Israel's bridegroom. The temple prostitutes' sacred occupation is denounced; there is no room for the king's "holy wedding" and its mythical implications for the fertility of the land. Jesus Christ is begotten by the Holy Spirit, not by a male deity who visits earth and has intercourse with a daughter of man. He is not a half-god, but is described as very God and very man. In contrast to the perplexing resuscitations of gods and heroes, the resurrection of Jesus occurs secretly, but those who saw the risen Lord are enumerated. The mythical doctrine of the soul's incarceration in man's fleshly body is replaced by the hope of bodily resurrection—a hope founded, not on a dualistic world view, but on the conviction that God will vindicate his servants.

Among biblical scholars today, it is generally acknowledged that the Bible takes history more seriously than those religious systems that reflect the belief in a cyclical devolvement of events. The festivals mentioned in both the Old and New Testaments celebrate and preserve the memory of unique historical deeds of the Lord God, and there is a strong tendency to fight the ever-threatening and ever-present danger of converting images, sacrifice, prayers, and fasting into tools of magic.

Nevertheless, the Bible contains features that recall a mythological background. These features appear in both the form and the content of the worship of Israel and the church.

The Old Testament gives testimony of a yearly festival cycle which may reflect and oppose the mythological thinking of Canaan. Among prophets, and priestly and historical writers, various opinions existed and different decisions were made regarding the limits of assimilation to forms of Gentile life. Some support the idea that Israel should have a king "like the nations"; some are against it. Judah is ruled by a dynasty that claims to be established by God's grace over all tribes. But prophets belonging to the secessionist Ten Tribes also claimed divine appointment for their kings. In Samaria, the capital of Northern Israel, features of pagan divine kingship were admitted earlier and more readily than in the Southern capital, Jerusalem. The sect of the Rechabites, and with them many prophets, fought the man-made Temple and its sacrificial practices in the name of the simpler forms of worship belonging to the tabernacle and the migrant people of the period of the Exodus. Some New Testament writers have a warm and lasting interest in the Temple; others shed no tears over its destruction. Some are for circumcision of Christians; some against it.

It is probable—though by no means proved—that all ritual is either a source, occasion, or consequence of mythical beliefs. Indeed, the diverse judgments passed by different prophets and apostles express divergent opinions on how far demythologizing has to go. If biblical writers disagree on the extent of necessary demythologization, it is little wonder that their interpreters also make different decisions. Those who presume to pass final judgment on myth and cultus may be true to some part of the Bible, but they will tend to overlook the strange and bewildering attitudes that are also attested in that book and defended in the name of God. There is no sweeping solution to the problem of myth.

The method of demythologizing employed by R. Bultmann and his followers not only suffers from a preconceived idea of faith but also pays too little attention to the problem of myth and worship as stated in the Bible itself. For both of these reasons it is still too close to allegorization. The victory of historical-critical Bible research is therefore neither convincing nor complete. Perhaps biblical scholarship is not yet as critical of itself as it is of certain elements in the Bible. If it were, it might be spared the bewildering experience of being hurt by its own weapons while victimizing other methods.

IV *Hermeneutics*

Hermeneutics is related to the actual interpretation of biblical texts as the *ars amandi* is related to making love. It is the systematic attempt to test, to refine, and to define the art of understanding. To compare it with the ways and mysteries of Eros is neither novel nor devious. For in the Bible (especially in Hosea) understanding and love of God are identified; in Plato, knowledge and the love of ideas; and in Augustine, apprehension of truth and *caritas*. Passion, if not jealousy, appear to belong to both. There is a definite analogy between the theory and practice of interpretation, on the one hand, and the study and performance of sexual love, on the other.

A perfect mastery of the *ars amandi* does not make anyone a true and successful lover. And there have always been great lovers who never laid their hands on a book teaching them how to love. It is the bystander, the cynic, the failure, on the one hand, and the historian and doctor, on the other, who engage in finding out the methods used. They compare and evaluate the ways of love, and ultimately produce a "methodology." Similarly, the greatest ability and pleasure in discussing the problems and needs of another man do not guarantee that in a given confrontation the student will be ready to understand the neighbor before him. The history of the Jews and of the church is full of men who were faithful and inspiring Bible interpreters, and who never had time, or sufficient reason, to give an exact account of their procedures. And even if they had done so, they would have been the first to break their own rules. It was the privilege of later generations to extract hermeneutic principles from their exegetic, dogmatic, and homiletical works. The comparison of different hermeneutics and the elaboration of a method has proved to be a task which is secondary to the task of actual exegesis.

In the Talmud seven, or thirteen, or as many as thirty-two modes of interpretation (*middoth*) are distinguished.[198] Origen spoke of three senses of the Bible to which three types of men and three potential states of each individual correspond; namely, the fleshly, the psychic, and the spiritual.[199] Following the lead given by John Cassian, a contemporary of Augustine, medieval theological schools, with the exception of the Victorine scholars of Paris, accepted a fourfold interpretation of the Scriptures: The letter reported the events; the allegory told what was to be believed; the moral sense contained what was to be done; and the anagogical sense gave instruction in what to hope for. Actual interpretations, however, rarely involved an enumeration of four senses in which a given scriptural passage could be understood. In many cases a distinction of two meanings, the literal and the spiritual, was made in practice. Books on the Reformers' hermeneutics[200] describe their postulates for biblical interpretation: The reader should look for the testimony to Jesus Christ; the Bible should be interpreted by the Bible, according to the Spirit's guidance, not atomically but always in context, without taking refuge in allegorization, and in respectful consultation with, but not in slavish dependence on the fathers. Still, the reader of the Reformers' commentaries and sermons does not receive the impression that the quality of their exegesis is solely or primarily due to their obeying certain rules. Other factors contributed to both the exemplary and the less exciting achievements of their interpretation.

But most recent German New Testament scholarship[201] shows an inclination to concentrate on the problem of hermeneutics itself. The true understanding of a text involves man's understanding of himself, his historicity, and his existence. The language of the Bible and its meaning are not at the interpreter's disposal. He is exposed to the "language event" of which the Bible is a testimony. Promises have been made regarding the new hermeneutics' forthcoming contribution to the study of the historical Jesus, of Paul, of the essence of faith. But the commentaries, monographs, sermons, or other works that would substantiate the claims made, have not yet appeared in print.

It is surprising that after more than two hundred years of experimentation with the various methods of newer criticism, a uniform hermeneutics should be constructed of fragments borrowed mainly from Heidegger's philosophy (either in its earlier or its later stages). For the strongest opponent of careful interpretation is the belief in an infallible method of interpretation and in criteria foreign to the Bible. The new hermeneutics manifests features that may one day form a complete philosophical system. But an honest, historical, and critical Bible interpretation will never constitute such a system. The belief that one hermeneutic system might serve as an "Open sesame" to all chambers of exegetical mysteries is preposterous and superstitious.

Whenever exegesis attempts to be free from prejudice, it will also be free from uniformity, from a belief in its own finality, and from the assumption that all but one mode of interpretation is necessarily misleading and wrong. A truly historical and critical exegesis is always in the process of being formed, informed, and reformed by the problems which continually arise from the texts with which it deals. Each text it seeks to understand will shape its interpretation. Each text calls for a form of interpretation appropriate to itself. Just as there is no key to understanding each living person, so there is no one method for the whole Bible. Each of the Testaments and each of its parts, each author and each of his works, each chapter, each verse, and each word is a member of a body. These members fulfill different functions and have to be understood in different ways. In each case obedience to rules may be important at the beginning. But real understanding of any biblical text will remain a miracle that cannot be forced to happen.

It is the burden of freedom—the freedom given by God, documented by the Bible, and required of the Bible reader—that it is inseparable from responsibility. No one can force a man to be free. The best laws cannot preserve his freedom. A free man will be recognized when he takes the responsibility of the free. He will be willing to bear its risks, and unable to enjoy its benefits unless others share in it. If he builds new prisons to protect it, he may be the first to disappear behind their walls.

Before we proceed to describe the ways in which the Bible interpreter enjoys the freedom given to man, we have to enumerate those problems of interpretation that most urgently need a responsible, scholarly solution.

Unsolved Problems

Whether he is an occasional reader or a professional expositor of the Bible, every student becomes aware of a number of specific questions that cry out for answers. They are too many to be enumerated and too manifold to be classified easily, but three general problems that concern the understanding of almost every page of the Bible should be mentioned.

1 *The Sense and Senses of the Bible*

It is easy to become exasperated by the allegorization of some interpreters, and to call their results fantastic and absurd. But it is extremely difficult to know when a biblical author may have had more than one meaning of a word, a sentence, or a story in mind. No one will deny that if Jesus intended a given parable to be an allegory, then it should be interpreted allegorically. But how do we know whether Jesus, or a prophet, an apostle, or a biblical author, wished to be understood allegorically—and in which cases, and to what extent? Even if the special problem of allegory is set aside, biblical metaphors offer basically the same problem.

Three examples should make the problem a little clearer. First, when God is called Father (as in Mt 6:9; Jn 20:17; Rom 8:15; Lk 11:11–13; Eph 3:14–15), or when a story such as that of the prodigal son is told (Lk 15), it becomes apparent that language is anagogic or analogical. It points or directs to truth, but does not define it. In the New Testament, God is not said to be a father after the image of earthly fathers, though the word "father" is used for both. Is he, then, called "Father" in order to tell us that he is like, or that he is unlike an earthly father? What is the "sense" of the name "Father"? Are there many senses to be distinguished? God is Father of Jesus Christ, and yet even this fatherhood implies both similarities to, and differences from earthly fatherhood. The question of what is meant has to be asked afresh in the interpretation of each passage that treats of God the Father. The name "Father," as it is applied to God, is only understood when its multiple meanings are unfolded. He is Father of Jesus Christ; he is our Father in heaven; he is good, as an earthly father is good; he is the Father of all men; and he is all these things at the same time.

The problem might also be illustrated by reference to the language used by John to describe Jesus' ascent. When, in the Fourth Gospel, it is said that Jesus "goes up," or "is exalted," these statements may concern Jesus' journey to a city or a mountain; it may mean his hanging on the erected cross and his dreadful death; it may finally describe his ascension into heaven after the resurrection (Jn 7:8; 3:13–14; 20:17). Each time the author used such a phrase, he may have thought of all these meanings; his intention was probably that his readers should do the same. In this case the interpreter must speak of three senses of the Johannine verbs that describe the going up of Jesus.

Finally, the parables of Jesus may have gone through a number of changes in wording, accentuation, and setting. Between the time when Jesus spoke and the time when Mark or John wrote, a major role was played by the hazards of oral tradition. To illustrate this, the parable of the sowing of the wheat may be mentioned.

Apparently it is a theme with variations. Perhaps the first stage was strictly Christological and eschatological: as the grain is sown and "dies" before it bears fruit, so Jesus must die before he rises in power (Jn 12:23–24). The second version may have been concerned with the crisis connected with the Kingdom of God: As a farmer has to bear damage and disappointment because much of what he sows seems wasted and lost, and as he enjoys all the more the surprising multiplication of the seed that has been sown on good ground, so the Kingdom of God is defeated, lost, hopelessly and aimlessly squandered; it suffers a dreadful crisis, and yet it bears abundant fruit! Only the disciples are told of this "mystery" (Mk 4:1–12). The third stage is reached when the parable is pedagogically and psychologically interpreted, when the mode of understanding is allegorical. In Mark 4:13–20, the seed is equated with the preaching of the Gospel; to the different successes of the seed correspond different types of men and different modes of receiving the Gospel. The parable is thus a promise that the Gospel will be heard, and an exhortation to heed it.

If we could be certain that only the first stage is authentic, i.e., that the version of the parable found in the Fourth Gospel is closest to the words Jesus spoke before his death; if we were sure that the second was added shortly after the resurrection, when the risen Christ or the Spirit (through inspired members of the congregation) added interpretations to words spoken earlier by Jesus (as indicated in Jn 2:22; 14:26; Lk 24:25 ff.; Acts 1:3); finally, if it were ascertained that the third stage of the parable's development (Mk 4:13–20) is a homiletic addition, then the task of interpretation would be easier. Instead of three senses hidden among one another, the interpreter would find three successive meanings; instead of the mystical coexistence of three senses, he would find a time sequence of meanings. The last, the allegorical interpretation of the parable, might no longer appear to be the highest, or "spiritual" interpretation. But Jesus' own intention would then have to be considered basic, and the first or second among the three senses would be considered more authentic than the third.

But the Gospels assert that all three versions and meanings were given by Jesus himself. How is the interpreter to know which of the three versions is Jesus' own? None of the scholarly reconstructions of allegedly authentic words of Jesus is free from the historical, philosophical, or theological prejudices of the respective reconstructors. Jesus himself may have spoken, or John, or Mark, not to mention Matthew and Luke, may intentionally have written in such a manner that different hearers and readers were free to understand their words differently and to draw different conclusions. We have said before that the words of the Bible call for the thought and decision of free men. The parables, in particular, continue to evoke new insights and to stimulate new interest and application.

These examples may suffice to show how complex is the problem of finding the authentic sense or deciding among many possible interpretations of a given biblical word or passage.

A solution to this problem has recently been suggested by French and Belgian Catholic scholars who developed the theory of a *sensus plenior* of Holy Scriptures. The *sensus plenior* is that "additional deeper meaning, intended by God, but not clearly intended by the human author, which is seen to exist in the words of a biblical text (or a group of texts, or even a whole book) when they are studied in the light of further revelation or development in the understanding of revelation."[202] The reasoning of the promoters of the *sensus plenior* may be illustrated by an example: When God inspired the first Isaiah to write, "A young woman shall conceive and bear a son, and shall call his name Immanuel" (Is 7:14), God knew that the mother of that child would be a virgin. Isaiah, however, did not realize this, and the word he chose for "young mother" did not convey the meaning, "virgin." However, when the same text was translated into Greek several centuries later, the translators rendered the Hebrew word "young mother" by the Greek "virgin." It is not known for what reason this was done, but it may be surmised that, either special enlightenment granted by God, or the decadence of the house of David, or the miraculous deeds of God experienced since Isaiah's time made them conclude that the future king would be of supernatural origin. At any rate, the Greek Bible now contained the term virgin in Isaiah 7:14. Finally, after Jesus had been born of a virgin, Matthew and his interpreters were fully justified in studying their Greek Bible, in finding the reference to the miraculous birth of a child to a virgin in Isaiah 7:14, and in concluding that Isaiah himself had prophesied Jesus' birth *ex Maria virgine* (Mt 1:18–23). When God made the Virgin Mary the mother of Jesus, he revealed what he originally had in mind when he made Isaiah write of a "young mother." In his reading of Isaiah 7:14, Matthew discovered the authentic, the final, the "fuller" sense of the words written by the prophet. Matthew did not impose a foreign meaning upon the text; he was given to realize its true meaning.

This interpretation differs from that of the allegorists in that Isaiah is no longer forcibly pressed into the service of the church's beliefs concerning Jesus' birth. It is admitted that Isaiah may not have foreseen Mary's virginity. The Old Testament prophet is permitted to have his own say. Only God knew the ultimate meaning of his revelation to Isaiah, and God waited for centuries before he revealed it to chosen men through the miraculous event of Jesus Christ's incarnation.

The search for the "fuller sense" requires something more of the exegete than lofty flights of imagination and the application of the methods of the liberal arts. He has to live as one of God's people and keep himself ready not only for manifestations of God but for the way in which God himself, through his deeds, contributes to the understanding of the Scriptures. As was shown in Chapter VII, the author of Hebrews lived, thought, and worked as such a member of God's people. Many issues concerning the understanding of parables may one day be brought to a solution through the *sensus plenior* theory. It is wise to live in the conviction that God alone can solve the mysteries of his revelation.

Interpretation, however, is still a problem and will perhaps remain problematic as long as God's people are pilgrims on earth. Whenever an interpreter believes he has arrived at the fuller sense of the Bible, he believes he has moved closer to God himself. But the more his interpretation respects the inscrutable depths of revelation and abstains from proclaiming pat solutions, the more convincing it will be.

II *The Intention of the Author*

What is the meaning for which the interpreter has to ask in his study of a Bible text? He may ask, for instance, what sense a biblical book, or passage, or word made to its first readers; how it was understood by the church fathers and their heretical antagonists; what it conveys to philosophers and natural scientists of the past and present; and finally, how it affects himself. It is instructive and profitable to ask and to answer such questions. But the sense which a text has made, or has failed to make, to some groups and persons, including the interpreter himself, need not be the criterion of its meaning. Neither the antiquity of an interpretation, nor its support by a majority of Jews or Christians, nor its enforcement by church authorities, nor the subjective fervor with which an individual may utter it and suffer for it are sufficient to prove it true. Where shall the interpreter turn in his search for a text's true sense or senses?

He will certainly turn to God and pray for light. Without prayer to God the Father, Son, and Spirit no biblical interpretation can succeed. But prayer does not release a Bible student from the privilege and duty of doing honest work according to the most rigid standards.

It has often been said that the interpreter has to ask primarily for the intention of the author. This is the quest to be pursued in the interpretation of every text, be it a law, a lyric poem, an editorial, an encyclical of Rome, a Communist manifesto, or the books of the Bible. A thorough quest for the author's intention will include a loving study of his environment, his resources, his life, his vocabulary, and many other things. When his specific concerns are understood and explained, when his words are heard as he wanted them to be heard, then some of the essential preconditions of interpretation are fulfilled. A sincere biblical interpretation will therefore be recognized, above all, by the humble submission of the Bible student to the direction which the prophets and apostles wanted to give.

But at least three problems remain, even when this rule is observed. First, the intention of a speaker may be different from the meaning his words possess. According to John 11:50–52, a Jewish high priest in Jerusalem made the statement, "It is expedient for you that one man should die for the people, and that the whole nation should not perish." This high priest was obviously a shrewd opportunist and spoke as such. The intention of his words was political. But in flagrant contradiction to this intention, the Evangelist calls this statement a prophecy: "Being high priest that year he prophesied that Jesus should die for the nation" (Jn 11:51). That the Roman Pontius Pilate's remark, "*Ecce homo,*" received a similar relevance in the context of the Fourth Gospel was shown in Chapter I. In Daniel 12:8 it is stated that on a given occasion the prophet hears but does not understand the things shown or said to him. The Second Letter of Peter (1:21) mentions that the prophets were "swept away [moved] by the Holy Spirit," and John of Patmos attests a similar experience (Rev 1:19; 4:2).

It is not only possible but probable that prophets and apostles, Old and New Testament writers, sometimes wrote down traditions received, words heard in God-given dreams or visions, and announcements and directions whose ultimate meaning and relevance they did not or could not know. On many occasions revelation included what must be called an ecstatic experience (e.g.,

Ezek 1 ff.; 2 Cor 12). When the Spirit himself speaks in and through a man, this man may be far from clear about his own intention. Therefore it cannot be stipulated that there be a clear "intention of the author" in or behind each biblical text, and that this intention be the sole criterion of the text's meaning. Of course, the greater part of the Bible may have been written after careful reflection, and it may express what the authors intended to say. But there are many passages, too, that are beyond the scope of what a man may have planned or hoped to say.

Second, a law may be better than the lawgiver, and a sermon better than the preacher. Paul may never have thought of the emancipation of women, the liberation of slaves, civil rights and political democracy, racial integration, or an organization serving world peace. Since he was a child of his time, his vision could not focus upon, nor his intention contain what nineteen hundred years after his death appears to be the necessary and true application of his message. "The author's intention" is therefore too narrow a concept to serve as the only criterion for determining what his writings actually mean. A man's words have a history in the speaker or writer before they are pronounced or put on paper. And the same words, once they are uttered or written down, have a life and history of their own. True understanding of the meaning of those words can only be found when not only their formation but also their life after the author's death is studied. It often happens that many features of the words' later history run contrary to the intention of their author. But it also happens that unexpected and unintended dimensions of the original words become apparent.

Third, modern research has made it seem probable that comparatively few biblical texts are due to only one author. Preachers and teachers, congregations and priests, unknown individuals and long-lived traditions frequently stand behind those who wrote the biblical books. Even formulations of non-Israelite authors were sometimes incorporated into Israel's or the church's testimony. If this is true, who then is the author of a given text? Whose intention determines a given utterance's meaning? Is it God's intention that inspired the prophets and apostles, the congregations or individuals? Is it that of the prophets or apostles who dictated or wrote? Is it that of the redactors who arranged sayings that were recognized as inspired? Is it the scribe's, who copied or edited an earlier document? The manifold intentions of so many authors may find expression in a single passage that it is no longer advisable to ask for "the author" and his "intention"!

The problem of what human criterion the interpreter of the Bible has ultimately to respect in his search for understanding therefore remains open. The quest for the author's intention is indispensable, but for the reasons just enumerated, it does not exhaust the interpreter's responsibility.

This brings us to another unsolved problem.

III *Fact and History*

As there is no myth without its cultic re-enactment, there is no history of events, persons, or facts without a historiographer who records, or people who remember. The very term, "history," is derived from the Greek word *historeo,* to inquire, to examine, to tell, to record. Events to which meaning is attributed, and which are therefore told and retold, constitute history. What is called history is, therefore, a series of events that are interpreted and told. Because of this inseparable interrelationship of event and evaluating narrative, it should not be held that facts alone are history. They can make history only when they are noticed; they require interpretation and an echo. Neither should it be supposed that the telling and remembering of a tale are alone sufficient to prove that it is history. If fantasies, errors, and lies occasionally make history, they live by the misuse of man's ability to evaluate, to narrate, and to remember. Only when man is given to discover the relevance and special meaning of certain occurrences; when he dares single them out from among the enormous mass of things that deserve to be forgotten; when he retains them for himself and presents them to others in such a way that he lives in awareness of them and makes others realize their value—only then does he live "in history." The consciousness of past and present history, and the responsibility of a voluntary response appear to be a privilege and a burden at the same time—a privilege and burden that distinguish man from animals, plants, and inanimate creatures.

The Bible is written by men who live in history. They bear witness to a special history whose distinction lies in features such as the following:

1) The history to which the Bible gives testimony is the history of God and his chosen people. This history includes the "ways of the Gentiles," but it is not defined by their concepts and experiences alone. It is a history in which man is not alone with himself. God approaches man—first a few servants, then a great people, and thus the whole world. The history narrated in the Bible is the history of God's struggle for man. By attesting to this history, prophets and apostles contribute to making it. As servants of God they make their hearers and readers aware of what concerns all.

2) This history consists of deeds and events that, from the very beginning, are not dependent on their discovery by men, their selection by men, their interpretation by men. For God himself, through his voice from heaven, through prophets and apostles, and finally through Jesus Christ, reveals which future, present, or past events are important. He selects the events that are to be remembered. And he determines what importance they possess. The making, breaking, and renewal of the covenant between God and man is the focus. Who else but God can properly interpret God and his deeds? The same God who creates the events also decides their meaning. He who makes history also decides what form selection, evaluation, and narration are to take. The history of an individual, a nation, an idea, a culture, or a religion is made and written by men who may be more or less bound—by tradition or inclination—to select, appreciate, retell, or forget certain elements of the past. In each case the handling of events is subject to revision by those

who come later. And the latecomer has an indisputable right to test and readjust the connections between fact and meaning which were made earlier. But the same privilege is not used by the writers of the history of God and man. Though they present different judgments on the character and meaning of past events, each one of them feels bound to express nothing but God's selection and interpretation. The history to which they refer is not composed of naked facts; it consists of the meaning which God has given his mighty deeds. Unless the Bible interpreter pretends to know God's will better than the prophets and apostles whose testimony is recorded in the Bible he cannot separate the facts to which the Bible refers and the interpretation given to them in the Bible. Biblical history cannot be divided into a factual core and an evaluating shell, and it is impossible to work for the elaboration of one without retaining the other. For biblical history is an inseparable whole. It consists of the deeds of God, explained and remembered in God's name.

3) This history is not over. Though in given places and at given times, deeds were performed and events occurred that possess uniqueness, individuality, and temporality, they also possess a quality that gives them lasting importance. This quality is not inherent in man or in man's memory. It comes from God, who is faithful to himself. He is present in all that he does. In his deeds, he shows who he truly is. His deeds are neither a lie nor an act that will be followed by another role. God's mighty deeds of the past show his eternal concern for man, which remains from age to age and from day to day. By them he manifests his love. God has provided that his former deeds be attested and remembered for one reason only: By striking examples of his might and his love, he gives assurance that he will complete his will in the future as well. God's history with man is evidence that he will not reduce to nothing his work of creation, redemption, and revelation. The history of his covenant with man continues.

Jesus Christ, the union of true God and true man, is the essence of this history. He is God's way to Jews and to Gentiles, and their way to him. He is the content and the form of the love of God, the revelation of all that is hidden, the unification of all that appears diverse. He is the same yesterday, today, and tomorrow.

So much concerning the specific character of the history recorded in the Bible.

The problem of how this marvelous history of God with man is related to modern academic historical research is as yet unsolved. Will man be able to verify the facts that are narrated? Since he is a partner in this history and is the beneficiary of its relevance and interpretation, man appears to have not only a right but a sacred duty to measure and to test its verity and meaning with the best tools that are at his disposal. For if this history were simply beyond man's reach, how could any *man* acknowledge that he is involved? On the other hand, if this history could be completely explained by man, where would the mystery of God's interference in history be? The narratives of the resurrection of Jesus Christ provide an example. Since the New Testament's message and the foundation of the Christians' faith hinge on Jesus Christ's resurrection, many would like to make certain that it is a factual event in history and that it possesses the verifiable qualities of other events. And yet it is also argued that since this event is God's own immediate and incomprehensible revelation, and an all-comprehending interference of God himself in human affairs, wonder, awe, and fear are the only appropriate reactions to it.

A way out of this dilemma has not yet been found.[203] The distinction between a history that is verifiable by historic research (in German, *Historie*) and a history that is recognized as true because it has proved effective and self-imposing (in German, *Geschichte,* with the emphasis on the root, *geschehen*) has not solved, but restated the problem. All history, not only God's history with men, contains essential elements that lie beyond rational explication and verification. Therefore, nothing specific is said of God's history when it is relegated to the realm of *Geschichte* and withdrawn from the area of historical scientific scrutiny. On the other hand, God's history with man, as it is told and interpreted in the Bible, has in some cases left verifiable traces. If this were denied, God's successful revelation to man would be negated. Avoiding the problem or taking refuge in general philosophical, existentialist, or psychological observations concerning man's historicity has not produced satisfactory results.[204]

It may well be that the questions posed are still inappropriate to the subject matter. Perhaps one day it will be recognized that the very quest for facts behind the biblical testimony—for the life of the historical Jesus, or for Paul's psychic development—was undertaken in the wrong way. It is the burden of free research that it is at times led to admit defeat, and that more careful and less prejudiced research must be started all over again.

The review of the last two hundred years of scholarly Bible study appears to have led to both encouraging and depressing results. But it should be remembered that we started out with a reference to children who, while enjoying the freedom to play, are noisy—and occasionally destructive. They get hurt and hurt each other. They are still children. Their play is a necessity and a pleasure. Embittered criticism of the Bible scholars is more likely to be displeasing to the Father than all the errors to which the interpreters are so obviously inclined.

In the next and final chapter, some conclusions will be presented concerning the fundamentals of biblical interpretation, its basic task, and its actual fulfillment.

CHAPTER IX

THE ENJOYMENT OF FREEDOM

The Spirit and Bible Study

Whether a man rejoices in reading the Bible, and whether he and others profit from his Bible study, depends on his relationship to the Holy Spirit. When he knows and attests that Spirit's peculiar quality and mode of operation, then he will appreciate the Bible. But when the Spirit has never touched him, the Bible will remain a boring, self-contradicting, abstruse book.

Now the Holy Spirit is concerned to know God and to make him known (1 Cor 2:10–16). The Spirit is free, and he makes free (Jn 3:6–8; Cor 3:17; Gal 5). In the act of creation he gives life to things that were not; in the act of illumination he gives light to the blind; where he is poured out, love and peace and joy rule instead of hatred, enmity, and sadness. In the choice of men upon whom the Spirit falls, no special selectiveness can be discerned. But he is particularly involved in the ministry of Christ. Through the Spirit, prophets prophesied his suffering and glory. Through a unique interference of the Spirit, the Virgin Mary became his mother; the Spirit is with Jesus and is to remain with him; the Spirit will explain the words of Jesus to the disciples. It is in the name of Jesus that he makes men address and trust God the Father in their prayer. Wisdom and courage for the public confession of Jesus Christ are given by him to the followers of Jesus. Weak men are filled with strength. Old men are reborn. He inspires words of witness. He brings God's word to man, and makes man respond with words of private prayer and public profession. He is at all times a rich Spirit who enjoys being lavishly distributed (Jn 3:34), "poured out," so as to drench, or "baptize" those to whom he is given (1 Cor 12:13).

It is this Spirit who has prevailed upon Old and New Testament men of God to give oral and written testimony of their knowledge of God, of election, of redemption, resurrection, revelation, communion, prayer, confession. Other spirits prefer other topics and are recognized by their preferences and achievements. This Spirit has, with his breath, called the Bible into being. And he uses it still. For this reason the Scriptures were called *theopneust,* inspired and inspiring.

At no point in our discussion of the content, authority, and interpretation of the Bible could any conclusion but this be drawn: A doctrine of the Bible and its interpretation must necessarily be built exclusively upon the operation of the Spirit. At no point in the long history of the church has this been completely forgotten.

When the second-century Christian apologists formulated their concept of inspiration or dictation; when the Alexandrians asked for the inspired texts' spiritual meaning and called for perfect, spiritual Christians to discern that meaning; when medieval scholars hoped to ascend from the lower to the higher and highest sense of the Bible and of each of its atomized sayings; when the Reformers attempted to live up to the challenges of *sola Scriptura,* of literal interpretation, and of the internal testimony of the Spirit, and when they heard, from the Scriptures, a message that had not been preached clearly for a long time; when finally, long after the Reformation, nineteenth-century theologians urged a reformation according to the Spirit, many ways of understanding the testimony of the Spirit became apparent. Although they often contradict and exclude each other, all agree that reliance upon Scripture and dependence upon the Spirit's testimony are inseparable. For whenever emphasis is placed upon Scripture alone, different kinds of bibliolatry invariably arise. Among them, legalism, liturgical and magical abuses, and dogmatic or historical rationalism have been mentioned. The principle, *sola Scriptura,* is rightly understood only when it is received as a counsel to submit oneself to both the Word and the Spirit of God. On the other hand, when the emphasis is solely on the Spirit's testimony, scandalous excesses, such as those of the extravagant left wing of the Reformation, or the no less harmful insulation of man from God the Father and the Son of God toward which nineteenth-century literal theology tended, were the inevitable consequence. The Reformers' reference to the inner testimony of the Spirit has to be understood not as a *passe partout,* or master key, to wild subjectivism, but as a correlate and indispensable complement to the external operation of the same Spirit in and through the testimony of the Scriptures.

It appears that Calvin[205] neither sought nor found a final reply to the question whether the inspired word or the internal testimony of the Spirit to the Scriptures' words possessed ultimate authority. Since God administers his word to men through the Spirit, since he alone gives man the Spirit to discern God's word, the word and the Spirit are subtly joined. The Word of God and the hearing of living words, the encounter of inspired prophets and apostles of the past with inspired readers and interpreters of the Bible, the dialogue and communion of spirited predecessors or archetypes with their successors or imitators—this conversation is the life, the heartbeat, the government of the church. Promise and hope, commandment and obedience, challenge and response stand side by side. God, from whom the first call goes out, also creates the response to his call. Through the Spirit he equips men to speak in his name. Through the same Spirit he enables many to recognize him and to respond in prayer and profession. Only through the Spirit can the Bible be recognized as Word of God.

Therefore no one can speak of the "absolute" authority of the Bible without disregarding the indispensable and continuing work of the Spirit; the Bible and its authority are always relative to the Spirit. And no one can claim to possess the Spirit and to honor God's authority except when he thankfully recognizes his lasting indebtedness to the Bible's testimony to God, to Jesus Christ's obedience, and to the promised inspiration of a great people. Gratitude for the gift of the Bible is the root of all reference to the authority which God has manifested and is manifesting wherever the Bible is heard and obeyed. If the Spirit's work was over and done with, the Bible would be a book of dead and deadening letters, and its interpretation would be an empty pastime.

The Bible reader and interpreter who recognizes and enjoys the Spirit's specific mode of manifestation and operation will do four things:

1) He will give up the attempt to separate the Word of God from the word of man. He will not try to become a master who can determine where and when God is or is not speaking. God quotes man and man quotes God! Through Jesus Christ the highest word was brought down to earth and said in a human voice; the most desperate human cries were placed in the mouth of the Son of God. The Bible's center lies not in the separation of what is God's from what is man's, but in the covenant community of God and man in which God's righteousness, truth, and faithfulness find a response in man's walk on the path of rightness, faith, and obedience. The Bible reader may therefore expect to find the voice and word of God everywhere in the Bible. And he

will not be shocked when he hears man's voice everywhere as well. He will accept the fact that there is no "authentic" word of God or Jesus in the Bible except in its rendition by witnesses. He will therefore desist both from the claim that he possesses or can reconstruct God's word without human additions, and from the belief that he hears nothing but human words. Instead, he will enjoy the manifold opportunity offered in the Bible, to hear and meet God even in unexpected quarters.

2) Belief in a mechanical inspiration of letters and lines will be abandoned, as well as any legalistic use of the Bible. Knowing that the Bible's own statement about the inspired, or inspiring, Scriptures (2 Tim 3:16) is abundantly interpreted as the inspiration of persons—of prophets, apostles, and disciples of the biblical message—he will deem it a waste of time to accumulate reasons for an inscripturation of the Spirit, of truth, or of authority. Instead, he will ask for the gift and guidance of the Spirit whenever he studies the Bible, and he will examine whether his own interpretational remarks are of a legalistic, apodictic, or tyrannical sort, or whether they give evidence of the presence of that Spirit by which "God's love has been poured into our hearts" (Rom 5:5).

3) The Bible student will no longer pretend that he knows the whole Bible. He will live thankfully with that insight and understanding granted him, and he will recognize the right of others to enrich or to criticize him on the basis of their insight and understanding. He will not pretend to master the whole biblical canon. But he will be open to the witness of neglected parts of the canon that may be brought to his attention through fellow Bible students. He will consider the collection and canonization of the Bible's sixty-six books an act of interpretation which is as commendable and fallible as any other careful interpretation made by the church or by individuals. He will respect the collection of those

books that were accepted or received by the canonizing fathers. But he will respect the present extension and limits of the Bible as he honors his father and mother; and according to Jesus Christ's teaching, cases may occur in which, for Jesus Christ's sake, he may have to "hate" or "leave" them (Lk 14:26; Mk 10:29). As a child of God is thankful for the gift of brotherly advice and for assistance in trust and obedience, so a Bible reader and interpreter will also be thankful and respectful in regard to his brothers' and sisters' multiform obedience and trust in their understanding of the Bible. From the manifold biblical witness and its many interpretations he will learn to be an ecumenical, brotherly, humble Christian.

4) The reader and expositor of the Bible will consider the effects his interpretation produces among other men as the criterion of the appropriateness of his exegesis. When his fellow men perceive "evidence of Spirit and power"; when they are led to believe in the God of Abraham, and the father of Jesus Christ in whom prophets and apostles believed; when they are moved to participate in the worship God's people offer to God in their daily lives and festival assemblies—then the Bible student may justly assume that his understanding, exposition, and application of biblical texts has been true to the biblical witness. An interpretation which fails to render a service to fellow men cannot be right and appropriate. The sign and reward of good interpretation is the praise of God in the hearts and lives of the interpreter's fellow men. Those who are privileged to see the slightest ray of the light to which the Old and New Testaments point have every reason to dance with joy!

We repeat, the living Spirit is the precondition and standard of all spirited interpretation of the inspired prophets' and apostles' books. We shall now describe in outline the nature of actual interpretation.

Interpretation in Action

What sort of interpretation appears most appropriate to the specific character and content of the Bible? In three propositions we will draw together the positive results of all former observations and considerations.

1 *Exegesis is the Enjoyment of a Given Text's Energy*

It was shown above that the biblical texts are to be understood not primarily as a composite of letters, written or printed with ink on paper, but as the voice of an address or a dialogue. Its words wish to live and to hit their mark. "Human words are like arrows, deriving their meaning from the goal at which they are directed and from the purpose which they serve."[206] The interpreter who looks at a given text is like a man who hears and sees an arrow flying through the air. He did not shoot the arrow, and it was, perhaps, not aimed at him. But it was sent to reach a goal. If the observer is alert, if he has watched other arrows, if he is an archer in his own right, then the flying arrow will excite him. He will be moved to action. He will cry out, "Watch that arrow!" To raise that cry and, if need be, to extend and support it so that nobody will miss hearing it—this is exegesis.

It is obvious that the observer cannot change the speed of the arrow. But he has become aware of its energy. If he knows who sent the arrow, at whom it is aimed and for what purpose, he will wish it Godspeed. May the biblical message of good news arrive! May the biblical prayers for righteousness be heard! The exegete does not invent or create Gospel and prayer. But he will enjoy and point out their energy and relevance. This is the only appropriate exegesis.

But the history of interpretation has met with many catastrophes. In Switzerland, on Sunday afternoons, young farmers like to play a game called *hornussen*. In this game, a ball is shot from a small inclined ramp into the air by a member of one team. The members of the opposing team are suitably deployed over the field in front of the ramp. They are all equipped with square wooden boards to which a handle is affixed. When the ball is in the air a cry goes up, and the wooden boards are thrown up to meet and stop the ball high in the air and make it drop down.

Many exegetes have behaved like such players. They have snatched the arrows out of the air, not for Sunday sport but for the honor of scientific method, for the sake of truth as they understood it. There is no need to mention again the deadly analytical tests to which the catch was submitted. Though they were shot with great energy, the biblical words did not reach their goal. For preachers and teachers it proved extremely difficult, if not impossible, to feel encouraged by this unkind, though in its own way successful treatment of the Bible.

There are reasons to consider the development of form-criticism as an attempt not to continue with the destructive analysis of the texts. Form critics have rightly emphasized that the content of the Bible is preaching, teaching, confession, and prayer. The intention of the biblical words to present the challenge of the good news and the response of faith is no longer brushed aside. Especially among Old Testament scholars in Germany and the United States, the joy in the discovery of the biblical texts' inherent energy and actuality is playing an increasingly important role. Roman Catholic theological schools in Rome, Belgium, France, Germany, and Washington have also become centers of exegetical studies. While learning from the mistakes made by Protestant pioneers, Catholic scholars are now producing remarkable work, especially in the field of the New Testament and its hermeneutics.

In sum, wherever a Bible interpretation joyfully and bravely follows the flight of the biblical arrows, it is worthy of free men, and makes many rejoice in the charter of liberty. This joy manifests an important fact. The interpreter can never be a master over his text; instead, he has to participate as a secondary witness in the events recorded by the text. The word that bears testimony to God is living because God lives and the Spirit makes it heard. The Holy Spirit's power to create, to inspire, and to resuscitate can be neither denied nor taken over by the interpreter. The true exegete will but point out and enjoy the ways of the Spirit.

II *Exegesis Is Participation in the History of God with Man*

That the interpreter need not and cannot himself give energy or actuality to the text was stated in the last section. But the task of interpretation has to be limited still more strictly. It might appear that the interpreter has to shape the text in such a way that it becomes acceptable to modern man, or that he has to bring the present generation and its specific problems, questions, and needs to the text. In this case the interpreter would be charged with preparing God's word for human consumption, or transforming man into a being that may understand God's word. He would have to create a new encounter and a new history between God and man.

This is certainly not the purpose of exegesis. For interpretation is exposition, and it is no more than the verb "expose" indicates. Interpretation must not be an *im*position upon the text, or an *ap*position of something strange. Rather, it is an act of unpacking, unfolding, displaying, the manifold contents and the one or several senses of the text.

What, then, does the exegete find in the text? What does he "expose" for the benefit of his contemporaries or future generations? He discovers that the biblical texts are already the result of interpretation! For, in order to address their contemporaries or give future generations something to remember, the biblical authors have given form to a tradition. They themselves interpreted what they had received, heard, or seen. Their very words *are* interpretations. The scribes who copied the words of the prophets and apostles have shown how much or how little they understood. The very transmission of the letter of the text was an act of interpretation. In turn, the synagogue and church, which canonized the Holy Writings and recommended that the faithful and unbelievers alike respect and heed them, have performed an important act of interpretation. Above all, the very content of the Bible, the story of God's interference in man's life, shows plainly that God has, in his way, interpreted man's need. The Bible attests to God's interpretation of man! The Bible interpreter who takes the texts for what they are need not ask what interpretation he can add. For he is invited to discover how God has already interpreted the human condition, how church and synagogue have respected that interpretation, how scribes and copyists have handled the manuscripts, and how prophets and apostles have dealt with the revelation and tradition they received. All these interpretations are contained in each text!

The step which a modern reader of the Bible takes when he sets out to understand, interpret, and apply the contents of this book is not, therefore, a step which has never been taken before. To engage in interpretation means to participate in the history of interpretation. The exegete takes part in a dialogue that takes place before, around, and above him. He perceives the amazement and confusion reflected in the Bible. All that has moved God's heart and called him to action; all that moved the biblical authors to speak and write; all that happened because of their words; all the events that accompanied the copying and gathering of the biblical books; all the excitement and disappointment connected with their translation into other languages; all the wisdom and all the arbitrariness shown in the selection of certain passages for liturgical or private use—all may become the subject matter of today's interpretation.

Real interpretation begins neither with eighteenth-century nor with twentieth-century hermeneutics; neither with Dr. Astruc nor with the philologist K. Lachmann, nor with the idealist J. Wellhausen, nor with the existentialist R. Bultmann. The problem and the miracle of understanding and interpretation are simultaneous with the history of the covenant between God and man. Understanding and interpretation occur only in the course of active participation in the biblical dialogue. To live as a Bible student means to recognize and show that each man lives in that history and participates in it.

Truly historic interpretation is that in which the Bible student discovers and makes known that his own story and that of his contemporaries is changed and directed by the living God as much as was the history of the patriarchs, of David, or of Jesus Christ and his disciples. Unless a Bible student learns to see and enjoy the fact that he himself and all those to whom he speaks are already involved in the history of God with man, he has not understood and explained the Bible. For the Bible relates a history in which no one is a bystander or onlooker. It tells of God's history with all men, including modern man.

We have defined this history earlier as God's struggle for man. The exegete is untrue to his text when he resents or resists that history. He is true to the Bible when he enjoys being a part of that history. He is a historian of this history, inasmuch as he lets it determine his own history. Objectivity in regard to this history can be found only by way of the most complete and passionate subjective involvement. The Bible treats of your history and mine, of your life and my life!

For this reason, the interpreter cannot start from the assumption that the Bible and modern man have nothing to do with each other and must, at great cost, be brought together. When he follows the Bible he will recognize and say publicly that God has already made a covenant with all men, even with the problem children of his household. His interpretation will presuppose rather than deny the fact that man is not master in this house, but one of the problem children. Long before he started to study and to interpret, he was made a partner of God's covenant and a participant in the dialogue characteristic of its history.

The consequence of this participation has to be spelled out still more clearly.

III *Exegesis Is the Response of a Free Man*

It was observed that exegesis does not add essential elements to the text. And yet it has to be admitted that each exposition does add something. When the interpreter uses more words than his texts, a different terminology, and new illustrations, what exactly is he adding? Only one thing can be appropriate to that God who calls for a free man's trust and obedience; only one action is appropriate to that mediator, Jesus Christ, who is the full word of God to man and the sum of man's word to God, and only one deed corresponds to that Spirit who likes to manifest himself in many tongues and many-sided dialogue: By his interpretation the exegete gives an *answer* to what he has heard. He responds to a challenge. He will hesitate and reflect, but finally he has to yield to the power exerted over him. For he finds himself so involved that he cannot remain where he was and who he was. He may be enamored of his own ideas, but ultimately he responds by being moved.

It has sometimes been considered a weakness of professional exegetes like Origen, Augustine, Luther, and Bengel that they did not, and apparently could not write a systematic theology. Too often they had to contradict themselves when new insights came to them. But they gave, and they expected a living response to the living word.

Exegesis cannot, therefore, be compared to an echo resounding from a canyon wall; it is not the reflection of a ray by a mirror, neither is it the mere spelling back of words heard or prescribed. It is acceptance of the punishment due to sin. It is awakening to new life after the call to awaken has been heard and the life-giving Spirit has been received. It is the overflow of the thankful heart which praises God and urges others to join that praise in word and deed. We have said before, however, that exegesis is an enormous risk. What else could it be when the Bible is not a code of Law, or casuistry, but a collection of types or precedents that force the reader to seize and enjoy freedom, and to make his own responsible decisions?

This observation leads to a grave conclusion. Exegesis faithful to the intention and character of the biblical witness involves the obligation and privilege of taking a stand on contemporary issues. Today, Bible interpretation is not true unless it leads to decisions regarding world peace, atomic war, integration, anti-Semitism, slum housing, and the suppression of freedom. A slavish exegete will feel excused when he can say that the Bible does not explicitly tell him to do this or that. But a responsible citizen of a free state will not wait for laws before he takes a stand for the freedom he enjoys and others lack. The Bible was written for the commonwealth, redeemed and freed by God. It is rightly understood and applied when its readers enjoy the privileges granted by God. They will respond by repenting for the sins they have committed, by taking a stand for the righteousness, truth, and peace guaranteed by God's rule over all men, and by the voluntary suffering of loneliness, mockery, and beating which may be the reward of their public witness.

The understanding, explication, and application of the Bible is, for this reason, a most necessary, daring, and costly enterprise. The Bible cannot make man free; God does this through his Son and Spirit. But the Bible attests man's freedom. Thus it presupposes that man has been freed and it calls him to the awareness, the enjoyment, and the responsibility of freedom. It is a wonderful book. No interpretation, however subtle, can change the living voice of its marvelous contents.

Courage to Wonder

Not every reader of the Bible will be inclined or equipped to become an expert interpreter. But no reader of the Bible can lose by becoming, in one way or another, a student of the Bible. Ultimately, in the conversation with God, no man is an expert; there are only brothers who seek to understand.

All who look into the Bible discover that this book of God's love and labor calls for love and labor on man's side. There are many mechanical or technical things that may be done to open ways toward understanding. Languages can be learned; grammars, dictionaries, and books on the prebiblical, biblical, and post-biblical meanings of words may be consulted; the history of nations, cultures, and ideas may be studied and reflected upon; the context of a given Bible passage and biblical topic and parallel or contradictory treatments of similar topics call for study. An intensive Bible reader will ask for the most trustworthy, perhaps the oldest form and the best possible translation of the text. He will compare different versions. He will seek to form as clear a picture as possible of the historical setting. He will ask which oral and literary traditions may have contributed to the written words' present form. He will try to find out the purpose for which the message and exhortation were used. He will reflect upon the many things that other interpreters have heard from the text and said about it in commentaries, sermons, official church documents, books of worship, and personal prayers. Since earlier interpretations influenced, and were reflected in the history of Israel, the synagogue, the church, and the world, church history and almost the whole of world history will become a living commentary on the text.

Thus the Bible student's interest will be extremely narrow and infinitely broad at the same time—narrow, because he will never understand the whole Bible but has to concentrate on a single passage or question at a time; broad, because the Bible is a book for people living in the world, not in caves or clouds. The Bible student will attempt to listen carefully to what is said both in God's name and, at times, in protest against God. He cannot limit himself to asking, "What is said to me, and what does it mean for me?" For, though he cannot exclude himself from those addressed by the biblical voices, he will realize that much greater problems than his own are involved. He will attempt to become open to the biblical dialogue, and he will not refrain from applying to himself what is said to other times.

But neither the application of the techniques of interpretation, nor the discovery of the world's and the interpreter's spiritual involvement in the dialogue of the Bible guarantee that real comprehension and understanding will take place. True understanding, like love, is a miracle. The Bible was certainly not written only for experts and believers. "They shall all know me, from the least of them to the greatest, says the Lord; for I will forgive their iniquity. . . . The earth shall be full of the knowledge of the Lord as the waters cover the sea" (Jer 31:34; Is 11:9).

In order to benefit from Bible study, the reader does not need to lose himself in the work of analyzing or labeling the text, or to sit back and wait for the miracle of understanding to happen. He may set out on the path of understanding when he discovers and acknowledges three things.

First, there is no reason for a modern Bible reader to think that because he is a modern man he will never be able to understand. Of course, modern man has created, and has to face many problems that did not exist for earlier generations. Todays's natural science and technology are post-Copernican and post-Paracelsian! Psychology, sociology, historiography, and the humanities have made discoveries from which all the peoples of the world may one day benefit. On the other hand, two world wars and the possible annihilation of mankind by atomic weapons have created an atmosphere of sinister futility which has overcome the optimism and belief in progress held by earlier generations. Despite all these changes, there is no reason for that narcissistic self-pity which hides beneath so-called existentialism. Instead of pitying himself, as a victim of modern enlightenment and disillusionment, and instead of considering the laws of human logic, of causality, of evolution, or of complementarity as supreme, the Bible reader can still try simply and humbly to listen to what the Bible says. It speaks about God and man. It relates how man is understood, known, and loved by God. It calls every man to worship God. It gives a direction and hope to life which no science or philosophy can supply. It takes time, the individual, his sin, and his death seriously. But it does more than that: It attests that God is present and that, to sinners, a "new and living way" (Heb 10:19) is open. The Bible contains a glorious message of liberation according to which no man need feel sorry for himself.

Second, the Bible reader may be a sophisticated or a primitive person, but in no circumstance whatsoever should he approach the Bible in the belief that his awareness or knowledge of God is in any way adequate. Whether he is a distinguished orthodox teacher or a militant atheist, he has more to learn. The Bible is not a collection of texts proving that this or that theory or practice is right. It is a book of mysteries beyond man's comprehension. To each generation and each reader it gives new instructions and tells a story that leads to repentance and hope. Because it treats not only of God's dealings with man but also of man's inadequate responses to God; because it speaks of promises, and of the beginnings of true faith and obedience, it makes the reader wonder.

It strikes him now with awe, now with terror, now with enthusiasm. It makes him think and decide anew.

But above all, it makes him wonder. There are those who appear to have stopped wondering at anything. They believe that with reason and new techniques, they have solved, or are about to solve all problems. Such people are not only poor and frustrated Bible readers; they are also poor specimens of man. A man who will not allow himself to wonder, to admit something greater than himself, to be overcome and inspired by new insights and prospects, prevents himself from learning, and thereby shuts himself off from one of the great privileges and joys of humanity. If, on the other hand, the reader of the Bible does not stop wondering, asking, knocking at seemingly barred doors, then he will not feel ashamed to pray to the God of whom the Bible tells. His search for understanding will then be most adequate when his Bible study is accompanied by prayer, when it becomes a way of praying. Bible study is a form of prayer to God and of intercession for men.

Third, the Bible reader needs to be warned of his isolationism and egotism. He may be inclined to presume that he is, or that he has a very special problem whose solution neither God, nor a prophet or apostle, nor a congregation of faithful men has ever faced. He may be tempted to consider his questions so unique and so important that no one, in heaven or on earth, can help to solve them. He may measure the value and validity of the Bible with one measuring stick only: How does it help me to find a gracious God? What meaning does it give to my life? No one can be prevented from asking these questions. Every man is, at least to God and to himself, a very special problem and of specific concern. But it is neither wise nor natural for man to detach himself from the rest of humanity, or to try to withdraw from God, his creator and redeemer. Awareness of the difficulties present in the Bible does not begin with this or that Bible reader; in their bewilderment, prophets and apostles, as well as many generations of Bible readers and expositors, are brothers and sisters of the modern reader. The Bible reader is a member of a great living community. He belongs to the family of those who are troubled enough to need God and his love. Certainly he is a very special child who deserves very special treatment. But he is still a child, a brother, a sister, or a nephew of many others who are all of his kin.

Why does the Bible reader use dictionaries and commentaries when he seeks a better understanding of the Bible? Not because paper explains paper, or letter elucidates letter, but because books are the voices of fellow men. A library is a conference of old and young, wise and less wise. If he works at the Bible, the student already has a small library in his hand. As many books as constitute the Bible, so many voices, and more, are heard conversing in it! The Bible student will enjoy the fact that this conversation is continued in commentaries and other aids to Bible interpretation, and he will listen in many directions. The special problem he believed he had discovered has, perhaps, long ago been carried toward a solution. The same applies to the reader's quest for personal salvation or individual experience of the gracious God's presence and help. It has already been taken up and answered! If only the student would forget for a while his own toothache and devote himself to the way in which God has treated and will heal the great and deadly disease of a great people! As soon as he becomes really engaged in discovering, enjoying, and witnessing the help God provides to others, he will find himself cared for too. He need not feel left out, because God has not left him out of his covenant! But if he puts his own happiness before God's love of the world, he may never understand what happens in the Bible.

No man can be forced to read and enjoy the Bible. Neither is there a way to prove that this book is the only and eternal standard of faith and life for all. Among Jews and Christians alike, there is but one way to speak of the Bible. They may call each other, and the world, to *listen* to what it has to say! For they know that they have found these voices and words to be living; nowhere else do they hear what they hear in this book.

There is no need for a higher doctrine of the Bible. But a more appropriate use of the Bible is necessary for all men. And this can spring only from an increasing enjoyment of the freedom to which prophets and apostles bear testimony.

NOTES

1 By "the Bible" is meant the collection of thirty-nine Israelite books written somewhere between the years 1000 and 150 B.C. and twenty-seven Christian books whose origin lies, probably, between A.D. 50 and 100.

The first group of books consists of the "Law" (or Pentateuch), the "Prophets," and the "Writings." The "Law" appears to have been given its present form and to have received recognition as canonical by 600 B.C., or at the latest by 400 B.C. Subsequently, prophetic writings, to which historiographic works also belong, were collected and edited. Jewish synods held in and near Jamnia (Palestine) around A.D. 90 completed the Jewish collection of Holy books with the addition of the Psalms, Proverbs, Job, and other "Writings." The recognition of books as holy is usually called "canonization." The result of the canonization of a given number of books is the "canon."

The complete Jewish canon is called the "Old Testament" by Christians. In the first decades after Jesus Christ's death and resurrection, the Christians' canon consisted exclusively of Old Testament books. Some Christians even treated as canonical writings and appendices to writings about whose canonicity the leaders of the Synagogue were unable to agree.

The second, much smaller, group of biblical books was written by

Christians of Jewish origin. These twenty-seven books were subdivided into the Gospel (i.e., the four Gospels) and the Apostle (i.e., the Acts of the Apostles, the letters bearing names of Apostles, and the Book of Revelation). Some of the apostolic Letters were received for liturgical reading and churchly instruction before the four Gospels were written or commonly considered canonical. By about A.D. 200, the outlines of a collection of the twenty-seven "New Testament" books were discernible in the composition of catalogues or lists of books "received" by all congregations. Between A.D. 367 and *ca.* 400, a formal canonization of all twenty-seven New Testament books took place in the Western churches.

The inclusion of the Old Testament books in the Christian canon met with considerable opposition in the second century and later. In the Councils of Florence (1442) and Trent (1546), the Roman Catholic Church included in its Old Testament the so-called Apocrypha, i.e., those Israelite writings whose canonical rank and use remained in dispute among the Jews.

In the following, the terms the "Bible," the "Scriptures," the "Holy Writings," are used as synonyms for the collection of sixty-six books which at the time of the Reformation was reaffirmed as "the Canon."

2 Augustine *De doctrina Christiana* I, 35–40; cf. G. Strauss, *Schriftgebrauch, Schriftauslegung und Schriftbeweis bei Augustin* (Tübingen, 1959), pp. 29–41.

3 Except in the later chapters of the previously named work, III 24 ff.

4 Different translations of this verse appear justified. E.g., "The Lord is our God, the Lord is one"; or, "The Lord is our God, the Lord alone."

5 *Christianity Among the Religions of the World* (New York, 1957).

6 Scholars give many reasons for this prohibition. The oneness of God distinguishes him from those gods who could be collected into a pantheon; the spirituality of God and of his presence defies his participation in matter, or his reproduction and representation by it; the majesty and invisibility of God exclude his exposition to fabrication and handling by man, and his profanation by being exposed to the stares of the multitude; the revelation of God is by words that are to be heeded, rather than by things to be grasped; the ever-new and ever-obedient remembrance of God's mighty historical acts is opposed to a fixation of God's essence in timeless symbols of natural or spiritual powers; the freedom of God to appear, to be present, to be a helper, contradicts magic means by which a deity's presence is enforced and exploited; the destiny of man, through obedience and faith, to be God's representative servant in the realm of nature, and to be God's witness to fellow men, stands against the captivation or control which forms or institutions of worship tend to exercise over mankind. However, this is not the place to discuss the strength or weakness of such rationalizations. For further discussion, see G. v. Rad, "Aspekte alttestamentlichen Weltverständnisses," *Evang. Theol.*, 24 (1964), 57–73, especially 59 ff.

7 A. Jeremias, *Der Alte Testament im Lichte des Alten Orientes*, 4th ed. (Leipzig, 1940), pp. 9 f. A report on the present discussion concerning the meaning of man's creation in God's

image is given by J. J. Stamm, "Die Imago-Lehre," in Antwort, *Festschrift für K. Barth* (Zürich, 1956), pp. 84–98.

8 Cf. R. Bultmann, *Theology of the New Testament,* I (New York, 1951), par. 17.

9 As R. Bultmann, *op. cit.,* I, pars. 16 ff.; II (1955), pars. 41 ff., would have it in his interpretation of Pauline and Johannine literature.

10 Concerning concepts like sacrifice, reconciliation, atonement, justification, see M. Barth, *Was Christ's Death a Sacrifice?* (Edinburgh, 1961) and *Right and Wrong and Resurrection* (New York, 1964). It appears that all attempts to understand and explain biblical intimations regarding these mysterious events are far from attaining final or generally acceptable solutions. The apostle Paul's teaching, especially, is so full of surprising features that it is still true that "Nobody has ever understood Paul, and those who pretended they did, as the second-century Gnostic, Marcion, have misunderstood him." Cf. Fr. Overbeck, *Christentum und Kultur* (Basle, 1919), pp. 54, 218 f.

11 Dorothy Sayers calls it "The greatest drama ever staged."

12 E.g., Thomas Wolfe, *Look Homeward Angel;* J.-P. Sartre, *No Exit;* Albert Camus, *The Fall.*

13 "Peter said . . . 'Women are not worthy of the Life.' Jesus said, '. . . I will make her [i.e., Mary] male that she too may become a living spirit, resembling you males.' " *The Gospel According to Thomas,* ed. A. Guillaumont *et al.* (New York, 1959), log. 114.

14 On this point, the otherwise excellent booklet of C. H. Dodd, *The Apostolic Preaching and Its Development* (London, 1936), is misleading.

15 Calvin, in his French preface to the *Institutes,* editions of 1541–51, uses similar metaphorical language; for him a book like the *Institutes* is destined to help find the way toward the Bible, which in turn contains "perfect doctrine." See Joannis Calvini, *Opera Selecta,* ed. P. Barth and W. Niesel, III (München, 1928), 7.

16 This is beautifully pointed out in R. Morgenthaler, "Die lukanische Geschichtsschreibung als Zeugnis," *Abh. z. Th. A. T. u. N. T.,* 14 (Zürich, 1948).

17 As it was posed and answered—at least to his own satisfaction—by the rationalist G. E. Lessing.

18 R. Bultmann's article, "Gnosis," in G. Kittel's *Theologisches Wörterbuch zum Neuen Testament* (Stuttgart, 1932), I, 688 ff. (Eng. trans. in *Bible Keywords,* London, 1949, and in *Theological Dictionary,* I, Grand Rapids, 1964, pp. 689 ff.), and Th. Bowman, *Das Hebräische Denken im Vergleich mit dem Griechischen,* 2nd ed. (Göttingen, 1954; Eng. trans.: London, 1960) are typical examples.

19 See, e.g., E. Brunner, *Offenbarung und Vernunft* (Zürich, 1941), p. 192 (Eng. trans.: *Revelation and Reason,* Philadelphia, 1946); F. Gogarten, *Entmythologisierung und Kirche* (Stuttgart, 1953), pp. 17, 43 ff. (Eng. trans.: *Demythologizing and History,* New York, 1955); R. Bultmann, *The Presence of Eternity* (New York, 1957), pp. 120, 133.

20 A similar idea is found in Gnostic documents of the second century A.D., and in Neoplatonic writings. Gnosis is ascribed to revelation; it exists in the reception of a self-eradiation or emanation of true being. See H. Jonas, *Gnosis und spätantiker Geist,* II (Göttingen, 1954).

21 These days a so-called "new hermeneutics" is being developed by post-Bultmannian German scholars on the basis of the later works of the philosopher M. Heidegger. The new school of thought made its first serious appearance in the United States in *The Later Heidegger and Theology* (New York, 1963), edited by J. M. Robinson and J. B. Cobb. By its reference to the *Sprachereignis,* this new hermeneutics intends to do justice both to the true being or the event which causes itself to be spoken of and therefore "exists historically," and to the word which generally, and as the word of God, expresses being in action and manifestation. The Hebrew word *dabar,* which indeed has a full meaning transcending the alternative "word or event" is drawn into the discussion in order to give additional weight to utterances of the late Heidegger. Cf. note 201.

22 A. Nygren, *Agape and Eros* (New York, 1932; London, 1953).

23 There exists a narrow, historical sense of the term "biblicism." It may denote a churchly theological movement and a hermeneutical method that originated in Württemberg, Germany, during the eighteenth century and is represented by men like J. A. Bengel, F. C. Oetinger, J. C. K. Hofmann, G. Menken, and M. Kähler. This movement was born of late Protestant rationalism. Its goal was to prove the Bible, as a whole and in each of its parts, a codex of divine doctrine, a corpus of moral prescription, and a compendium of supernatural, saving history (*Heilsgeschichte*). The Bible reader was specifically warned not to submit to older or more recent dogmatic formulations of an orthodox character, or to the dictates of modern culture or science. It is sometimes held that this historical biblicism thrives upon its opposition to culture; some critics tend to identify it with bibliolatry. However, in the following we shall use the term in a wider sense, i.e., as designating all attempts, with or without contact with modern scientific and anthropological arguments, to prove the Bible's supreme authority.

24 The following elements of Jewish doctrine are selected from the first-century B.C. book of Jubilees, the philosopher Philo of Alexandria, and the Talmud; for references, see G. F. Moore, *Judaism,* I (Cambridge, 1954), 235 ff.; A. Wolfson, *Philo,* II (Cambridge, 1948), 36 ff.; Strack-Billerbeck, *Kommentar zum Neuen Testament,* IV (München, 1928), 435 ff.; III (1926), 554 ff.; G. Vermes, *Scripture and Tradition in Judaism* (Leiden, 1961). It is impossible, in this context, to describe and distinguish the different medieval and modern shades of Jewish doctrine as represented by mystic, rationalist, liberal, conservative, and orthodox Jewish scholars and schools.

25 This material is collected and discussed by O. Betz, *Offenbarung und Schriftforschung der Qumransekte* (Tübingen, 1960).

26 E.g., in Irenaeus (d. *ca.* A.D. 200), *Adv. haer.* IV 12:3.

27 *Ibid.,* IV 33:8.

28 Officially at the Council of Trent (1546) and the Vatican Council (1870); see H. Denzinger and B. Umberg, *Enchiridion Symbolorum,* 18th–20th ed. (Freiburg, 1932), §§783 and 1787. Earlier material treating the same topic is discussed by G. Tavard, *Holy Writ and Holy Church* (New York, 1959).

29 E.g., K. Rahner, *Über die Schrift-*

inspiration (Freiburg, 1958), pp. 7, 43, 80 (Eng. trans.: *Inspiration of the Bible,* New York, 1961); and G. Tavard, *op. cit.* Books like J. R. Geiselmann, *Die Heilige Schrift und die Tradition* (Freiburg, 1962), and Y. Congar, *La tradition et les traditions* (Paris, 1960), have contributed to the start of the dramatic exchange which took place at the Second Vatican Council in the fall of 1962 and which ended at that time in the replacement of the ominous schema title, "About the Two Sources of Revelation," by the new title, "About Revelation." Cf. note 183.

30 E.g., H. Denzinger, *Ench. Symb.* (1932), Index syst. s.v. *Revelatio* I f. The latest edition of Denzinger (1963) contains a new index which no longer suggests two different sources of revelation. The following references to Denzinger use the numbers given in the earlier editions.

31 Irenaeus, *op. cit.,* II 28:2.

32 *In Dan.* 4:6; *ca.* A.D. 200.

33 *Adv. haer. Pan.* 70:7; *ca.* 375.

34 *Ep.* 28:3.

35 Leo XIII, *Providentissimus Deus* (1893), Denzinger, *op. cit.,* §§ 1950, 1951; cf. Pius X, *Lamentabili* (1907), Denzinger, § 2011.

36 Philo *De spec. leg.* IV 49; Justin Mart. *Apol.* I 36:1; *Dial.* 115:1–4; Ps.–Justin *Cohort ad Graec.* 8; Theophilus of Antioch 2:9; Athenagoras *Leg.* 9; Epiphanius *Adv. haer.* 48:4, etc.

37 For references, see R. P. C. Hanson, *Allegory and Event* (London, 1959), pp. 195 f.

38 E.g., in *De praescriptione haer.* 38; *ca.* A.D. 200.

39 *Conc. Tridentinum* (1546): *Conc. Vaticanum* (1870); Denzinger, *op. cit.,* §§ 786, 1788, 1793.

40 *Conc. Vaticanum* (1870), Denzinger § 1839.

41 See the discussion of reasons for this claim in L. Berkhof, *Introductory Volume to Systematic Theology,* revised ed. (Grand Rapids, 1932); L. Boettner, *The Inspiration and Canonicity of the Bible* (Grand Rapids, 1957); B. B. Warfield, *The Inspiration and Authority of the Bible* (Philadelphia, 1948); J. I. Packer, *Fundamentalism and the Word of God* (London, 1958); B. Ramm, *Special Revelation and the Word of God* (Grand Rapids, 1961). Among the studies critical of Fundamentalism, see G. Herbert, *The Authority of the Old Testament* (London, 1947); J. K. S. Reid, *The Authority of the Scriptures* (London, 1957); R. C. Johnson, *Authority in Protestant Theology* (Philadelphia, 1959).

42 Warfield, *op. cit.,* pp. 83 ff., 152 ff., 203.

43 Packer, *op cit.,* pp. 78 ff. D. M. Beegle, *The Inspiration of the Bible* (Philadelphia, 1963), a teacher at a conservative school, has announced a sharp protest against this view. He believes in inspiration, but he has collected examples of all sorts showing that there are contradictions and factual errors contained in the Bible. It is his opinion, however, that these elements do not pertain to the things decisive for faith. The conservative weekly, *Christianity Today,* has devoted almost a complete issue (April 26, 1963) to expressing its anger and resentment against this encroachment of liberal thought.

44 Warfield, *op. cit.,* pp. 100 f., 111 f., 139, 148, 183, 337 ff., 391 ff.; Packer, *op cit.,* pp. 54, 67.

45 Warfield, *op. cit.,* p. 139.

46 For references, see R. M. Grant, *Letter and Spirit* (London, 1957), pp. 5 ff., 32 ff., 85 ff. Allegory and allegorical interpretation will be more fully discussed in Chapter VIII; see pp. 263–277.

47 Packer, *op. cit.*, pp. 91–93; C. van Til, in Warfield, *op. cit.*, pp. 3–70.

48 Eusebius *Hist. eccl.* III 24.

49 An illustrative collection of relevant Catholic utterances is found in Joh. Gerhard's *Loci Theologici* (1610), II, 37.

50 J. Calvin, *Institutes,* I 7:4 f.; M. Luther, *Weimar Ausgabe,* X 1:2, pp. 335, 18, 609, 653, 47, 183; H. Heppe, *Dogmatik der ev. ref. Kirche,* ed. Bizer (Neukirchen, 1935), pp. 21 ff., G. Schmidt, *Dogmatik der ev. Luth. Kirche* (Gütersloh, 1893), pp. 271 ff.

51 See especially A. Sabatier, *Religions d'authorité et religion d'esprit* (Paris, 1904); cf. R. C. Johnson, *Authority in Protestant Theology* (Philadelphia, 1959), pp. 63–88.

52 C. H. Dodd, *The Authority of the Bible* (1929); (New York, Harper Torchbooks 73, 1958), pp. 296 ff.

53 *Der Christliche Glaube* (1821).

54 *Fragments* (1844); *Postscript* (1846). For references see R. C. Johnson, *Authority in Protestant Theology,* pp. 89–100.

55 This is, e.g., the opinion of A. G. Herbert, *The Authority of the Old Testament* (London, 1947), pp. 23 ff.; L. S. Thornton, *Revelation and the Modern World* (London, 1950), pp. 29–95; J. Baillie, *The Idea of Revelation* (New York, 1956).

56 Foremost in his *Confessions* and in *De Civitate Dei.*

57 A careful description of Augustine's hermeneutics and its philosophical foundations is given by G. Strauss, *Schriftgebrauch, Schriftauslegung und Schriftbeweis bei Augustin.*

58 E.g., W. F. Zuurdeeg, *An Analytical Philosophy of Religion* (New York/Nashville, 1958).

59 In *De vera religione; De utilitate credendi;* cf. G. Strauss, *op. cit.*, pp. 1 ff.

60 H. Wh. Robinson, *The Christian Experience of the Holy Spirit* (London, 1928; 8th ed., 1944), p. 96.

61 C. H. Dodd, *op. cit.*, pp. 18, 25, 33 ff.

62 Again, by C. H. Dodd, *op. cit.*, pp. 19 ff., 134

63 *Ibid.*, p. 285.

64 K. Rahner, *Über die Schriftinspiration,* pp. 43, 56, etc.; G. Tavard, *Holy Writ and Holy Church,* pp. 66, 246, etc.

65 J. G. v. Herder first drew attention to this in 1782 in his *Vom Geist der Ebräischen Poesie.*

66 See Judg 9:7–15; 14:14, 18; 2 Sam 12:1–4; Prov 23:29–35. Innumerable other examples might be given of the combination and interpenetration of poetic and prosaic elements.

67 See Lk 1:68–79; 2:29–32; Phil 2:6–11; 1 Cor 15:3–4; 1 Tim 3:16; Rom 4:25; Col 1:15 ff.; 1 Pet 3:18, 22; Jn 1:1–5, 9–18; 1 Jn 1:1–4; Heb 1:5–13; Rev 1:5–6; 5:9–10, 12–13.

68 Cf. G. van der Leeuw, *Phänomenologie der Religion,* 2nd ed. (Tübingen, 1956), pp. 494–509 (Eng. trans.: *Religion in Essence and Manifestation,* London, 1938, and New York, Harper Torchbooks 100–101).

69 In an especially moving way by the above-mentioned C. F. D. Schleiermacher and A. Sabatier.

70 The materials and reflections presented in this section have been previously published in a slightly dif-

ferent form, under the title, M. Barth, "Vom Geheimnis der Bibel," in the series, *Theologische Existenz, Neue Folge*, No. 100 (München, 1962).

71 In an "all-out global war" and in "head-on collision," as C. van Til suggests. See B. B. Warfield, *The Inspiration and Authority of the Bible*, pp. 23 ff., 39.

72 For which J. Knox, *Criticism and Faith* (New York, 1952), may serve as an example.

73 *Institutio Rel. Chr.* I 7:4.

74 In Chapter Two, "The Knowledge of Truth," II.

75 In *Adv. haer.* IV 10:1.

76 See H. U. v. Balthasar, *Origenes* (Salzburg, 1938; 2nd ed., n.d.), especially pp. 121 ff., 210 ff., 247 ff.; H. de Lubac, *Histoire et Esprit* (Paris, 1950), pp. 336–373, especially pp. 363 ff.; J. Daniélou, *Origène* (Paris, 1948), pp. 144 ff., 238 ff.; R. P. C. Hanson, *Allegory and Event* (London, 1959), pp. 193 ff.

77 *Fragm. in Matt.*, Migne P. G. 17, 289 A.B.; *Hom. in Is.* I 5; *Hom. in Jer.* XI 1; XXXIX; *Philocalia* XV; *Hom. in Lev.* I 1.

78 *Op. cit.*, p. 121.

79 *Op. cit.*, pp. 337, 340, 364.

80 *Op. cit.*, p. 194.

81 In the *Fragm. in Matt.*

82 *Hom. in Jer.* IX 1.

83 *Philocalia* XV.

84 *C. Celsum* VI 68; VII 39; *Comm. in Joh.* II 3.

85 In *De migr. Abr.* 93; *De conf. ling.* 190; *De vita contempl.* 78.

86 *Op. cit.*, p. 261; cf. pp. 258–264; 74 ff.

87 *Op. cit.*, pp. 283, 329.

88 *Op. cit.*, p. 373, note 159.

89 *Op. cit.*, pp. 189, 297, etc.

90 *C. Celsum* III 41.

91 *Op. cit.*, pp. 30, 38.

92 *Op. cit.*, pp. 344 ff.

93 *Capitula theol. et oecon.*, cent. 2, c. 60 (Migne P. G. 90, 1149 ff.).

94 In *Luc.* I 6, 33 (Migne P. L. 15, 1677).

95 In *Ps* 103:4 (Migne P. L. 37, 1378).

96 *W. A.*, X 1:1, p. 576.

97 *Formula Concordiae* (1580), Epitome, Proem; Westminster *Conf.* (1647), I 5; H. Schmidt, *Dogmatik der ev. Luth. Kirche*, pp. 11, 21 f.

98 *Der christliche Glaube* (1821; Eng. trans.: *The Christian Faith*, 3rd ed., Edinburgh, 1956), p. 600.

99 *Offenbarung und Vernunft* (Zürich, 1941; Eng. trans.: *Revelation and Reason*, London, 1947), pp. 12, 276.

100 I 1 (München, 1932; Eng. trans.: Edinburgh, 1936), pp. 124 f.

101 *Op. cit.*, I 2 (Zollikon-Zürich, 1938, pp. 540, 555; Eng. trans.: Edinburgh, 1956, pp. 487, 501).

102 *Revelation and the Modern World*, p. 130.

103 *Über die Schriftinspiration*, p. 22.

104 In the *Bulletin of the Department of the World Presbyterian Alliance*, 2 (1961), 8.

105 *Op. cit.*, pp. 248 ff.

106 *Op. cit.*, I 2, p. 555 (Eng. trans., p. 500).

107 *Op. cit.*, pp. 554 ff., 570 (Eng. trans., pp. 500, 513). Cf. K. Runia, *Karl Barth's Doctrine of Holy Scriptures* (Grand Rapids, 1962).

108 *The Inspiration and Authority of the Bible*, p. 162.

109 *The Authority of the Scriptures*, p. 68.

110 *Calvin's Doctrine of Word and Sacrament* (Edinburgh, 1953), pp. 22 f., 114, 167 f.

111 *Corp. Ref., Calvini Opera* 36, p. 158.

112 Books like J. Pelikan's *Luther the Expositor* (St. Louis, 1959), or

W. Niesel, *Die Theologie Calvins* (München, 1938; Eng trans.: *The Theology of Calvin,* Philadelphia, 1956), contain no evidence to the contrary.

113 E.g., *W. A.,* XLIX, 208:17 ff.

114 As expressed in his *Church Dogmatics,* I 1 and 2.

115 While the doctrine of God presented in *Church Dogmatics,* II 1, indicates what reasons made him change, the doctrine of reconciliation unfolded in Volume IV 1 and 2 presents the new understanding.

116 *Op. cit.,* p. 132; cf. J. K. S. Reid, *op. cit.,* p. 184.

117 In his review of Reid's book in *Scot. Journ. of Theol.,* XI (1958), 90–91.

118 B. B. Warfield, *The Inspiration and Authority of the Bible,* p. 162; J. I. Packer, *op. cit.,* pp. 82–83; Pius XII, *Div. Affl. Spir.* (1943).

119 See, e.g., Sirach 24:23; Wisdom of Solomon 4:12; Strack-Billerbeck, *Kommentar zum Neuen Testament,* II (München, 1924), pp. 353 ff.; IV (1928), p. 126; H. Ringgren, *Word and Wisdom* (Lund, 1947); C. Rylaarsdam, *Revelation in Jewish Wisdom Literature* (Chicago, 1946); G. v. Rad, *Theologie des Alten Testamentes,* I (München, 1957), pp. 415–451, especially p. 439 (Eng. trans.: New York, 1961); O. Cullmann, *Christology* (Philadelphia, 1959), pp. 249 ff.

120 G. Ebeling, in his essay, "Wort Gottes und Hermeneutik," in *Zeits. f. Theol. u. Kirche,* 56 (1959), 224–251 (Eng. trans.: *Word and Faith,* London, 1963; pp. 205–332), has summed up what Luther writes in, e.g., *W.A.,* X 1:1, pp. 625–628; X 1:2, p. 48; V, p. 537; XII, p. 259; *Schmalk. Art.,* Vom Evangelio, in *Bek. Schr. der ev. Luth. Kirche,* I (Berlin, 1930), p. 449. In his own way, and for his own reasons, Plato (in *Phaedros,* §§ 274 ff.; *Ep.* VII, §§ 341 ff.) spoke up against the writing of, and trust in books. See note 149. Unlike the Egyptians, classical Greek writers did not use canonization formulae (as found in Rev 22:18–22), or insist on respect for the written word.

121 G. van der Leeuw, *Phänomenologie der Religion* (Tübingen, 1956), p. 499.

122 Quoted in J. Leipoldt and S. Morenz, *Heilige Schriften* (Leipzig, 1953), from Plutarch, *Isis and Osiris.* The Corpus Hermeticum is accessible in the edition by A. D. Nock and A. J. Festugière (Paris, 1938); a part of it, including Chapter XIII, which is a most relevant source for the reconstruction of a Hermetic doctrine of the word, is extensively discussed by R. Reitzenstein, *Poimandres* (Leipzig, 1904); cf. *Die hellenistichen Mysterienreligionen,* 3rd ed. (Leipzig, 1927). C. H. Dodd, *The Fourth Gospel* (Cambridge, 1954), attempts to show that the Fourth Gospel is thoroughly influenced by this literature.

123 Among the historians of religion, M. Eliade has specific merit for describing ultimate concerns of myth, sanctuaries, and rituals.

124 *The Authority of Scripture,* p. 132.

125 See notes 28 and 29.

126 B. M. Vellas, *E Agia Graphe en te Orthodoxe Ekklesia* (Athens, 1958).

127 *Religions d'authorité et religion d'esprit* (1904).

128 *Revelation and the Modern World* (1950).

129 *Journals.*

130 H. Vogel comes nearest to a full elaboration in *Gott in Christ* (Berlin, 1951), pp. 99–156.

131 *Kirchliche Dogmatik* (München, 1932), I 1, p. 178; II 1, pp. 254 ff. (Eng. trans., I 1, p. 195; II 1, pp. 225 ff.).

132 E.g., in his book *K. Barth* (Köln, 1951, pp. 175 ff.; Eng. trans. to be published by Holt, Rinehart and Winston, New York).

133 E.g., in *Theol. Lit. Ztg.*, 78 (1953), 17 ff.; 85 (1960), 225 ff.

134 In *Scot. Journ. of Theol.*, 12 (1959), 1 ff.

135 B. B. Warfield, *The Inspiration and Authority of the Bible*, p. 146. To mention but one example, in Gal 3:8, 22, Paul speaks of Scripture where he might speak of God himself.

136 According to Abodah Zarah 14b–18b. Quoted in J. Leipoldt and S. Morenz, *Heilige Schriften*, p. 143.

137 *De principiis* IV 2; *Hom. in Lev.* V 1.

138 The last may be the most appropriate theory concerning the ambivalent meaning of the Greek word *theopneustos*, for its sense appears to be active as well as passive. See J. A. Bengel's interpretation of 2 Tim 3 in his *Gnomon* (1742).

139 K. Stendahl's essay, "The Apocalypse of John and the Epistles of Paul in the Muratorian Fragment," in *Current Issues in New Testament Interpretation*, essays in honor of O. A. Piper, edited by W. Klassen and G. F. Snyder (New York, 1962), pp. 239–245, contains documentation showing that in the early church, canonization by no means implied the belief in cessation of inspiration after the death of the last apostle.

140 *Kirchliche Dogmatik*, I 1, p. 115 (Eng. trans.: I 1, p. 126).

141 The following material was published under the title "The Old Testament in Hebrews," in *Current Issues in New Testament Interpretation.* Special acknowledgment is due to the commentaries on Hebrews by J. Calvin, M. Luther, M. Riggenbach, B. F. Westcott, H. Windisch, O. Michel, W. Manson, and C. Spicq; to monographs and essays on the use of the Old Testament in the New Testament, in Paul or Hebrews, by P. Padva, F. Büchsel, J. v. de Ploeg, J. Bonsirven, E. Ellis, J. Daniélou, G. B. Caird, and F. C. Synge.

142 Eusebius *Hist. eccl.* VI 26.

143 See Y. Yadin in *Scripta Hierosolymitanae*, IV, 36–55; C. Spicq in *Rev. de Qumran*, 1 (1958–59), 365–390; H. Kosmala, *Hebräer, Essener, Christen*, 1 (Leiden, 1959).

144 Scholars who have counted the occurrences give different figures. An explicit quotation may conflate two Old Testament texts (as, perhaps inadvertently, in 1:6) and be counted either as one or as two references. The hunt for allusions is still an unfinished task; the more work is applied and the smaller the unit sought for, the greater the resulting number will be.

145 The author appears to use a Greek, rather than Hebrew or Aramaic text of the Old Testament. It is not yet known what version of the Greek Old Testament he was reading, or how free he felt, consciously or unconsciously, to make changes. His quotations and allusions agree, in part, with that Septuagint version (made in Alexandria after 300 B.C.) which is preserved in the fourth-century Codex Vaticanus; sometimes he appears to quote from a manuscript whose readings were identical with those of the fifth-century Alex-

andrinus; and he sometimes quotes a text which agrees with no known Septuagint edition. The attempt to uncover a Hebrew text preceding the medieval, or "Masoretic" Hebrew texts used among Christians and Jews today has been given a new impetus by material found since 1947 in the Qumran caves, and it now seems possible that the Greek version used by the author may occasionally be nearer the oldest Hebrew texts than a *Biblia Hebraica* based upon the medieval Masoretic revision.

146 See especially B. B. Warfield, *The Inspiration and Authority of the Bible,* pp. 317 ff.; B. F. Westcott, *Epistle to the Hebrews,* 2nd ed. (London, 1892), pp. 67–70, 469–495; J. Bonsirven, *Exégèse rabbinique et exégèse paulinienne* (Paris, 1939), pp. 29–32, 339–345; B. Metzger, "The Formulas Introducing Quotations," *J. B. L.*, 70 (1951), 297–307; E. E. Ellis, *Paul's Use of the Old Testament* (Edinburgh, 1957), pp. 48 f.

147 The authority of the Bath Qol (cf. Mk 1:11; 9:7; Jn 12:28–30) was not accepted without reservations by rabbinical interpreters of the Bible. See Strack-Billerbeck, *Kommentar zum Neuen Testament,* I, 125–134; G. F. Moore, *Judaism,* I (Oxford, 1954), pp. 421 f.

148 Cf. Josh 24:26; 1 Sam 10:25; Deut 17:18; 31:9; 2 Kings 22:8; Jer 31:33; Neh 9:38. Consequently, reference to what is written may have the intention of pointing out the valid law; see, e.g., 1 Chron 15:15; 2 Chron 30:5, 18; Mk 10:5, and the emphasis on "writing" in Acts 15:23 ff., Gal 1:20; 6:11; 1 Jn 2:12–14 f. More material is presented by G. Schrenk in Kittel's *Theol. Wörterbuch,* I (Stuttgart, 1932), pp. 742–773, especially pp. 746 f. (Eng. trans.: Grand Rapids, 1964).

149 Among the reasons Plato offers in *Epist.* VII 344 (cf. *Phaedros,* pp. 274 ff.) for decrying the writing of books, the following may be quoted here: "Every serious man in dealing with really serious subjects carefully avoids writing, lest thereby he may possibly cast them as a prey to the envy and stupidity of the public. . . . A man's written compositions—whether they be laws of a legislator or anything else in any other form—these are not his most serious works, if it be that the writer himself is serious." To write down "something about the highest and first truths of Nature" is "to expose them to unseemly and degrading treatment" (quoted from the Loeb Classical Library *Plato,* London: Cambridge, 1952, VI, 541). G. van der Leeuw makes the following, somewhat sweeping observation: "*Das Schreiben ist eigentlich ein Zauber*" (*Phänomenologie,* p. 494).

150 For Jews faithful to the Talmud, there could never exist the slightest doubt that both the written and the oral Torah are living; for one and the same Torah proved alive in the ongoing interpretation. But for Christians faced with Jesus' "antitheses" to the interpretation of the Law by contemporary Jewish scholars (Mt 5:21–48; 23) and with Paul's discriminating statements about Moses' ministry, the problem was much more actual. Marcion solved it by eliminating the Old Testament and some parts of the later New Testament. Orthodox teachers did not honor all biblical books equally; they showed a preference for this or that part of the Old or New Testament. Many took refuge in allegorical interpretation in order

to overcome obstacles presented by the biblical text (see Chapter VIII). Luther taught that Jesus Christ, the New Testament, and each spiritual preacher made a living voice of the written words of the Old Testament (*W. A.*, V, p. 537; X 1:1, pp. 625 ff.). Calvin was convinced that the Bible receives full authority among the faithful only when they recognize that "it has flown from heaven, as if there God's own voices were heard" (*Institutes*, I 7:1). Similarly, B. B. Warfield states (*op. cit.*, p. 124; cf. pp. 148, 316) that the Bible contains "a Word of God in which God speaks directly to each of our souls." Until the studies of men like K. Rahner and G. Tavard (see note 29), the more or less official Roman Catholic position was different. K. Adam (*Das Wesen des Catholizismus*, 4th ed., Düsseldorf, 1927, p. 162; Eng. trans.: *The Spirit of Catholicism*, London, 1929, p. 53) speaks of the contrast between the vitality of oral tradition and the dead word of the Scriptures. J. K. S. Reid (*The Authority of the Scriptures*, p. 114) quotes from a Catholic book on the Bible which explicitly puts a living, teaching authority above every book of divine Scripture and claims that "the church is superior to the Bible in the sense that she is . . . [and] possesses the living voice of Christ." The Papal encyclical, *Humani Generis* (1950), reaffirms the Trentine and Vatican statements according to which only the living, teaching ministry of the Church can verify scriptural interpretation.

151 M. Albertz, *Die Botschaft des Neuen Testamentes* (Zollikon-Zürich, I 2, 1952), p. 417, speaks of *innertrinitarisches Wechselgespräch;* cf. C. Spicq, *L'epitre aux Hebreux*, I (Paris, 1952), p. 337.

152 Concerning the identification of the living word of God with Jesus Christ (Jn 1:1; 1 Jn 1:1), see H. Clavier, "O logos to theou," in *New Testament Essays* in memory of T. W. Manson (Manchester, 1959), pp. 81–93.

153 For a discussion of the different modes of exegesis, see L. Michel, *Paulus und seine Bibel* (Gütersloh, 1929); G. F. Moore, *Judaism* I, 239 f.; J. Bonsirven, *Exégèse . . .* ; K. Stendahl, *The School of St. Matthew* (Uppsala, 1954); E. E. Ellis, *Paul's Use of the Old Testament* (1957); F. L. Cross, *The Ancient Library of Qumran* (Garden City, 1958). A Dead Sea Script called *4Q Testimonia* has been published by J. M. Allegro in *Journal of Biblical Literature* 75 (1956), 182–187. Cf. also F. C. Synge, *Hebrews and the Scriptures* (London, 1959), pp. 17, 53 ff.

154 These types of interpretation will be discussed in Chapter VIII.

155 R. M. Grant, *The Letter and Spirit* (London, 1957; especially Appendix II, pp. 120–142) has collected information about the meanings of "type," "hypodeigma," "parabole," and many other hermeneutical technical *termini* that are employed in the Jewish, Greek, and early Christian environment of Hebrews. The careful reader of Heb 8:5; 9:24; 1 Cor 10:6–11; Rom 5:14, and 1 Pet 3:21 becomes aware that in each of these passages, *typos* (*v. antitypos*) has a different meaning. In 1 Cor 10, the Old Testament event is a warning example of what may happen to the Christians. In Rom 5:14, Adam is called an inferior antitype of Christ. In the complicated and ambiguous

beginning of 1 Pet 3:21, salvation through baptism is either an antitype of the salvation of eight souls from the flood; or, together with the salvation from the flood, it is an antitype of Christ's death, descent, and resurrection; or it is (and this is least likely) a visible type of an invisible reality. For a discussion, see B. O. Reicke, *Disobedient Spirits and Christian Baptism* (Uppsala, 1946), pp. 143 ff. In Heb 8:5, "type" means archetype; the antitype mentioned in 9:24 corresponds to it. According to Heb 8–9, both type and antitype are present and operative in Israel's history and worship. In view of this complex use of the term type, it is not advisable simply to amalgamate the New Testament passages that speak of type and antitype, and to conclude that there exists one common form or method of "typological" interpretation. Cf. J. Daniélou, *Sacramentum Futuri* (Paris, 1950; Eng. trans.: *From Shadow to Reality,* Westminster, Md., 1960); and G. W. H. Lampe and K. J. Woolcombe, "Essays on Typology," *Stud. in Bibl. Theol.,* No. 22 (London, 1957).

156 See C. K. Barrett, "The Eschatology of the Epistle to the Hebrews," in *The Background of the New Testament and its Eschatology,* W. D. Davies and D. Daube, eds., in honor of C. H. Dodd (Cambridge, 1956), pp. 363–393.

157 As B. F. Westcott, *The Epistle to the Hebrews* (London, 1903), suggests.

158 Deut 18:15, 18; Hos 2:11–20; Amos 9:11, 13; Is 1:21–26; 11:6–8; 52:11–12; 65:17–21; Ezek 16:54–63; 40 ff. G. v. Rad, "Typologische Auslegung des Alten Testamentes," in *Ev. Theol.,* 12 (1952–53), 17 ff., (Eng. trans. in *Essays in Old Testament Hermeneutics,* Richmond, 1963), speaks (p. 31) of an unlimited number of Old Testament types. Cf. G. Fohrer's essay on *Entsprechungsmotive* in *Theol. Lit. Ztg.,* 85 (1960), 415 ff.

159 While there exists a bold book relating the whole of the Gospel of John and each of its parts to the Scriptures read during synagogue services at the various festival periods of the Jewish liturgical year (A. Guilding, *The Fourth Gospel and Jewish Worship,* Oxford, 1960), a corresponding work on Hebrews has not come to my attention.

160 In commenting on 1 Tim 3:16, J. Jeremias (in *Das Neue Testament Deutsch,* 5th ed., Göttingen, 1949, IX, 21) has spoken of the "enthronement hymn" found in Heb 1:5 ff. Since H. Mowinckel's *Psalmen-Studien* II (Christiania, 1922; Eng. trans.: *The Psalms in Israel's Worship,* II, Oxford, 1962; cf. *He That Cometh,* New York/Nashville, 1956), and J. Pedersen's *Israel,* I–IV (London, 1946–47), books edited or written by the following scholars have each in their own way thrown light on the idea of the so-called divine kingship and on a corresponding New Year festival of ancient Eastern nations: S. H. Hooke (*Myth and Ritual,* London, 1933; *The Labyrinth,* London, 1935; *Myth, Ritual and Kingship,* Oxford, 1958), I. Engnell (*Studies in Divine Kingship,* Uppsala, 1943), H. Frankfort (*Kingship and the Gods,* Chicago, 1948), A. Bentzen (*King and Messiah,* London, 1955). Cf. also A. Weiser, "Die Psalmen I," in *Das Alte Testament Deutsch* 14 (Göttingen, 1950), pp. 17 ff., 35 ff. (Eng. trans.: *The Psalms,* Philadelphia, 1962). Elements or traces of a divine origin of Israel's kings and of

a yearly or heptannual celebration of God's kingship and the earthly king's enthronement have been found in Ps 2; 110; 1 Chron 29:23.

In the wake of the work done by the so-called Scandinavian School, more or less daring connections and identifications of Israelite covenant, king, and tabernacle festivals were discovered or construed by H. Riesenfeld, *Jesus tranfiguré* (Copenhagen, 1947), especially pp. 56 ff.; H. J. Kraus, *Die Königsherschaft Gottes im Alten Testament* (Tübingen, 1951), especially pp. 117 ff.; *Gottesdienst in Israel* (München, 1954); cf. J. Daniélou, "Le Symbolism eschatologique de la Fête de Tabernacles," in *Irenikon*, 31 (1958), 19–40. The conclusions drawn by these authors are far from identical or harmonious, as Mowinckel's criticism of Riesenfeld (in *He That Cometh*, pp. 341 ff., 467 f.) and H. J. Kraus' "explicit refutation" of the "really shocking" Scandinavian Old Testament interpretation may illustrate (*Königsherschaft*, pp. 145 f.; *Gottesdienst*, pp. 97 ff.). Cf. M. Noth, *Gott, König, Volk im Alten Testament*, reprinted in *Gesammelte Studien* (München, 1957), pp. 188 ff. (Eng. trans.: Philadelphia, 1961).

The information on the King's role at the Tabernacle Festival given by Strack-Billerbeck (*Kommentar*, II, 34, 709; IV, 146 ff., 155) and G. F. Moore (*Judaism*, II, 43 ff.) is still untainted by this discussion.

161 By observing (and building upon) common features of Ps 2; 8:5–7; 22; 34; 80:17; 110:1; Jer 53; Dan 7, etc., A. Bentzen, "Messias, Moses redivivus, Menschensohn," *Abh. Th. A. T. N. T.*, 17 (Zürich, 1948; Eng. trans.: *King and Messiah*, London, 1955), and C. H. Dodd, *According to the Scriptures* (New York, 1953); cf. H. Riesenfeld, "The Mythological Background of New Testament Christology," in Davies and Daube, *The Background of the New Testament*, pp. 81–95, reach the daring conclusion that the Man, the Son of Man, the suffering Servant, the Messiah and Son of God may be different titles for one and the same figure. If we follow Bentzen, the figure of Moses (*redivivus*), the King, and the Son of Man were somehow derived from, or conflated into the image of an *Ur-Mensch*. If this view is correct, the combination of references to the Son in Heb 1, to the Man and Servant in Heb 2, and to Moses in Heb 3:1–6, no longer seems so strange.

162 F. C. Synge, *Hebrews and the Scriptures* (1959), pp. 17, 53 ff., takes up suggestions made previously in other contexts by F. C. Burkitt, J. R. Harris, and C. H. Dodd.

163 The first volume of a planned standard work, *The Bible as Read and Preached in the Old Synagogue*, has been published by J. Mann (Cincinnati, 1940). Only if a similarly thorough work on the use of the Old Testament in the Herodian Temple, and especially on the annual and septannual Tabernacle Festivals were available, could a less tentative word be said on the nature and meaning of the quotations in Heb 1 ff.

164 As an example of haughty contempt we mention R. Bultmann (see his essay, "Weissagung und Erfüllung," in *Glauben und Verstehen*, II, Tübingen, 1952, pp. 166 f.). H. Windisch, *Der Hebrärbrief*, 2nd ed. (Tübingen, 1931), speaks of a midrash. Rather haughty forgiveness is granted "our author" in A. C. Purdy's commentary on Hebrews in *Interpre-*

ter's Bible, II (New York/Nashville, 1955).

165 The Scandinavian scholar H. Ringgren writes, in *The Messiah in the Old Testament* (London, 1956), p. 24, "The Christian theological interpretation of the so-called messianic texts in the Old Testament is to a certain extent justified. Applying the view of the Epistle to the Hebrews we might regard Old Testament Kingship as a prefiguration or a shadow of that which was to come. But this does not mean that the original historical meaning of these passages is contested; it is not even called in question, but stands out clearer and sharper. . . . These passages are placed in their proper context in the history of revelation." Ringgren goes as far as to say, "God could make use of non-Israelite ideas of a divine king. . . . The belief in Christ the Messiah is rooted ultimately in the ancient Oriental ideas of the divine king." Such statements may overshoot the mark. But they illustrate that the modern form-critical and traditio-historical method of Bible interpretation has opened a way to a less haughty and condemning evaluation of the Old Testament references made in Hebrews.

166 The prophetic protests against the static, stony temple, and the idealization of the movable tent-sanctuary; the rejection of sacrifices, and the call for obedience rendered from the heart are taken up by both Stephen and the author of Hebrews. To use examples, Amos 5:25 and Ps 40:7–8 both speak out against the misuse of sacrifices. Amos 5:25 is quoted by Stephen in Acts 7:42; Ps 40:7 f. appears in Heb 10:5 f. Concerning theological resemblances between Hebrews and Stephen, see W. Manson, *The Epistle of the Hebrews* (London, 1949), especially pp. 25 ff.; H. J. Schoeps, *Theologie und Geschichte des Judenchristentums* (Tübingen, 1949), pp. 233 ff.; C. P. M. Jones, "The Epistle to the Hebrews and the Lucan Writings," in *Studies in the Gospels*, ed. D. E. Nineham (Oxford, 1957), pp. 113 ff., especially pp. 122–125; C. Spicq, in *Revue de Qumran*, I (1958–59), 365–390.

167 It is surprising that allusions to the Passover festival are missing from Hebrews—except in 11:28. For Paul (1 Cor 5:7) and the passion stories of the four canonical Gospels (see also Jn 1:29, 36; 1 Pet 1:19) explain the meaning of Jesus' death by reference to the Passover. It is equally surprising that the rite of circumcision is never mentioned in Hebrews; the Jerusalem church, Paul, and the churches Paul addressed were obviously very much concerned with its true and its falsified character (Rom 2:25–29; 4:9–12; Gal 2:3; 5:2–6; Phil 3:3; Eph 2:11; Acts 5:24; 15:1; 16:3; 21:21). New Moons, Purim and other occasions of festival celebration are equally ignored in this letter. Each and every established form of cultus is not considered a fitting frame of reference.

168 Reference was made in Chapter IV, p. 130, to the methods and results of the form-critical and traditio-historical schools. In the first section of Chapter VIII, more will be said about these schools of interpretation.

169 See, e.g., the literature mentioned in note 153.

170 As examples and material for study we mention the dialectical relation of John's Gospel to the Synoptic Gospels of Matthew, Mark, and Luke; the relationship between Mat-

thew, Luke, and Mark; the tension between Paul and some of the self-appointed delegates from Jerusalem; the contradictions between the Pauline Epistles and the Acts of the Apostles; the alleged contradiction between Paul and James; and finally, the judgment found in 2 Pet 3:15–16, according to which the letters of the beloved brother Paul are "hard to understand" and easily twisted by the unstable "to their own destruction."

171 R. E. Brown, *The Sensus Plenior of Sacred Scriptures* (Baltimore, 1955), p. 55.

172 Attempts to give comprehensive descriptions of the successes and defeats of the interpreters of this period are made by H. J. Kraus, *Geschichte der historisch-kritischen Erforschung des Alten Testamentes* (Neukirchen, 1956); W. G. Kümmel, *Das Neue Testament, Geschichte der Erforschung seiner Probleme* (München, 1958). Among shorter treatments of the same topic are R. M. Grant, *The Bible in the Church* (New York, 1948); E. G. H. Kraeling, *The Old Testament Since the Reformation* (London, 1955); A. M. Hunter, *Interpreting the New Testament* (London, 1951); G. E. Wright and R. H. Fuller, *The Book of the Acts of God* (New York, 1957); E. C. Colwell, *The Study of the Bible* (Chicago, 1937); St. Neill, *The Interpretation of the New Testament* (London, 1964). A good popular presentation is given by B. W. Anderson, *Rediscovering the Bible* (New York, 1951). The necessity, methods, and achievements of studies in the New Testament texts have recently been competently described by B. M. Metzger, *The Text of the New Testament* (Oxford, 1964). A new summary of the history of English Bible translation is given by F. C. Grant, *Translating the Bible* (New York, 1961). These books contain bibliographical references to earlier works on the same topics.

173 As, for example, H. C. Thiessen states in *Introduction to the New Testament* (Grand Rapids, 1952), pp. 92, 128, etc.

174 In *The Letter of Aristeas,* which describes, in legendary form, how the Law was translated into Greek, fears are expressed that by translation a secularization might take place which could (as demonstrated by pagan tales) incur the wrath of the deity (3:13–14). In the Corpus Hermeticum IV 1–2, the translation of Egyptian words into Greek is called "the greatest distortion and obscurantism." It is remarkable that the Hebrew Holy writings were translated into Greek, and that despite the predominance of Greek among the earliest Western Christian writers, in Africa, Italy, and Gaul, Latin translations of the Bible and Latin theological tracts were edited as early as the second century A.D. Syriac and Egyptian versions are of an equally early date. This fact shows that a belief in the impossibility or inappropriateness of translation did not prevail among Jews and Christians. They were willing to share what they possessed with people of other tongues (cf. Acts 2, the miracle of Pentecost!). They recognized that they were witnesses to all nations and that the testimony contained in their Holy Writings had to become available even to Gentiles. Philo (*De vita Mose* II 37) writes that the Bible interpreters were *inspired!* It is his conviction that God himself equipped

the translators with the power and wisdom to do their work.

175 Innocentius X, *Error de duplici capite Ecclesiae* (Denzinger, §1647), *Enchiridion Symbolorum* (§1091; cf. §2147a).

176 See Chapter IV, pp. 130 ff.

177 R. Hooykes, *The Principle of Uniformity in Geology, Biology and Theology,* 2nd ed. (Leiden, 1963), promises a direct treatment of the problem at hand. The book came to my attention too late to be consulted.

178 First ed., 1918; 2nd ed., 1921. Eng. trans., E. Hoskyns (London, 1933).

179 Ignatius *Philad.* VIII 2, quoted from K. Lake's translation in the Loeb edition of *The Apostolic Fathers,* I (London: Cambridge, 1952), p. 247. It is not known to whom Ignatius refers. The meaning of the first statement would be clear if, either after the word, "charters," or after the two words, "charters" and "Gospel," a comma were inserted. The Greek wording, however, does not permit a decision between these alternatives. It is not evident, therefore, whether Ignatius' opponents identified the so-called "charters" with the Gospel and intended to obey the *New* Testament witness only, or whether they meant by charters some Old Testament or other religious books, and were willing to trust the Gospel only inasmuch as its contents could also be found in these books.

180 Especially in his book, *According to the Scriptures* (New York, 1953).

181 The commentaries of the scholastic scholars have been rediscovered and found worthy of editing only in recent decades. For a description of medieval hermeneutics, see B. Smalley, *The Bible in the Middle Ages* (Oxford, 1927); C. Spicq, *Esquisse d'une histoire de l'exégèse au moyen age* (Paris, 1944); H. de Lubac, *Exégèse mediévale; les quatre sens de l'Écriture* (Paris, 1959).

182 In the encyclical, *Providentissimus Deus* (1859), the same proposition is reaffirmed. See Denzinger, §§786, 1788, 1942.

183 During the second session of Vatican II, in the fall of 1963, the issue of Scripture and Tradition was not officially brought before the assembly. Oral reports indicate that the Schema, *De Revelatione,* will be dropped from the agenda of the Council because it is believed in the highest quarters that the time is not yet ripe for a new decision on this delicate matter. A careful and moving account of the victory of the conservative Curial forces over the earlier majority of "progressives" among the Catholic bishops is contained in M. Serafian's *The Pilgrim* (New York, 1964). If his interpretation should prove correct, the *aggiornamento* envisaged by Pope John XXIII is no longer in the foreground of Pope Paul VI's intentions.

184 *Epitome* V, 1–8.

185 *Hic liber est in quo sua quaerit dogmata quisque, invenit et pariter dogmata quisque sua.*

186 "Zum Problem der Entmythologisierung," in *Kerygma und Mythos,* II, ed. H. W. Bartsch (Hamburg, 1952), p. 207.

187 "We must turn to the way of allegory which is so dear to natural philosophers" (*De post. Cain* 7).

188 A new period of research in the parables was opened by J. Jülicher, *Die Gleichnisreden Jesu* (Tübingen, 1910); the most important commentaries on the parables today are C. H. Dodd, *The Parables of the Kingdom* (London, 1935); J. Jeremias, *Die*

Gleichnisse Jesu (Zürich, 1947; Eng. trans.: *The Parables of Jesus,* 3rd ed., London, 1955). These three authors agree in denouncing an allegorical interpretation.

189 Apart from the writings of these men, the following main sources of information regarding their hermeneutics should be mentioned: H. A. Wolfson, *Philo,* I (Cambridge, Mass., 1948), pp. 115–138, 158–160; R. P. C. Hanson, *Allegory and Event* (London, 1959); G. Strauss, *Schriftgebrauch . . . bei Augustin.*

190 In *De doctr. Christ.* II 16 ff.

191 H. de Lubac, quoting Cardinal J. H. Newman in *Histoire et Esprit,* pp. 65 f.

192 *Summa Theol.* I Q. 1, art. 10.

193 In *De Spec. leg.* I 287, he speaks of the "canons of allegory."

194 To follow R. P. C. Hanson's definition, *op. cit.,* p. 7.

195 See note 188.

196 Any "History of Israel," or of its religion, or of the Old Testament, and any history of the New Testament, of the early church, or of one of its special features such as its attitude and confession toward the state or slavery, will illustrate this. The multiplicity of forms of early Christianity is the special concern of such works as W. Bauer, *Rechtgläubigkeit und Ketzerei in ältesten Christentum* (Tübingen, 1934); S. L. Greenslade, *Schism in the Early Church* (New York, 1953); J. Knox, *The Early Church and the Great Future Church* (New York, 1955).

197 The collected essays of R. Bultmann (*Glauben und Verstehen* I–III, 2nd ed., Tübingen, 1954 and following years) are available in English editions. Especially important for the issue here discussed is the collection, *Existence and Faith,* ed. S. Ogden (New York: Living Age Books). A competent brief account of the philosophical background of demythologization is found in I. Henderson, "Myth in the New Testament," *Stud. in Bibl. Theol.* No. 7 (London, 1952). Essays both favorable to, and critical of demythologization have been collected and edited in Germany by H. W. Bartsch, under the title *Kerygma und Mythos* (Hamburg, 1948). An English translation of selections from these volumes was made by R. Fuller (London, 1954 and 1962). Among American books, S. Ogden's *Christ Without Myth* (New York, 1961) contains the most positive evaluation of this method of interpretation. R. Fuller, *The New Testament in Current Study* (New York, 1962), tells the story of the movement.

198 See H. L. Strack, *Einleitung in Talmud und Midrash* (München, 1930), pp. 96 ff.; J. Bonsirven, *Exégèse rabbinique . . .* (Paris, 1938); G. F. Moore, *Judaism,* I (Cambridge, 1954), pp. 248 f.

199 In *Lev.* V 1.

200 E.g., G. Ebeling, *Evangelische Evangelienauslegung* (München, 1942); J. Pelikan, *Luther the Expositor* (St. Louis, 1959); R. Wallace, *Calvin's Doctrine of Word and Sacrament* (Edinburgh, 1953).

201 As presented by men like R. Bultmann, F. Gogarten, E. Fuchs, G. Ebeling, H. Braun. Recent volumes of the *Zeitschrift für Theologie und Kirche* contain the decisive essays of these men. A preliminary report on this movement and its characteristics is given by A. Wilder in *Issues in New Testament Interpretation,* ed. W. Klassen and G. F. Snyder (New York, 1962), pp. 38 ff. For a more detailed recent critical account, see

R. E. Brown, "After Bultmann, What?" in *Cath. Bibl. Quart.*, 26 (1964), 1–30. Important contributions from an exegetical rather than philosophical point of view were made by S. Zimmerli, *Gottes Offenbarung* (Münich, 1963), pp. 120 ff., 277 ff. The curious mixture of philosophical and exegetical arguments found in, e.g., J. M. Robinson, "The Historicality of Biblical Language," in *The Old Testament and Christian Faith,* ed. B. W. Anderson (New York, 1963), pp. 124–158, is not yet convincing. Also, it cannot yet be predicted what results contact between this new hermeneutical movement and the Oxford school of language analysis may yield. P. v. Buren, *The Secular Meaning of the Gospel* (New York, 1963), appears to be overly optimistic.

202 R. E. Brown, *Sensus Plenior* (Baltimore, 1955), p. 92. The same author gives an instructive report on the last ten years' discussion of the *sensus plenior* in *Cath. Bibl. Quart.*, 25 (1963), 262–285.

203 M. Kähler, *Der Sogenannte historische Jesus* . . . (1892; reprinted, München, 1953), and E. Hoskyns and F. N. Davey, *The Fourth Gospel* (London, 1940; 5th ed., 1954), pp. 17–135, are among the most searching, moving, and frustrating attempts to solve this problem. Recent careful studies on the Resurrection, such as H. Grass, *Ostergeschehen und Osterberichte* (Göttingen, 1956) and G. Koch, *Die Auferstehung Jesu Christi* (Tübingen, 1959), have sought to disentangle what is historical and what is an accretion. They agree on one point: it appears essential to the Resurrection that its center cannot be touched or proven by historical-critical research. If the means to prove it do not yet exist, then neither have the tools that would be necessary to disprove its historicity been forged. Perhaps they will never be.

204 See, e.g., J. M. Robinson, *A New Quest for the Historical Jesus* (London, 1959), and the previously mentioned S. Ogden, *Christ Without Myth.*

205 See, e.g., *Institutio Rel. Chr.*, I 7:4–5; 9:2–3.

206 J. McIntyre, in his essay, "Analogy," in *Scot. Journ. of Theol.*, 12 (1959), 2.

INDEX

Books of the Bible

General Index